Construction
Management
JumpStart

Construction Management JumpStart™

Barbara J. Jackson, Ph.D., DBIA

Wiley Publishing, Inc.

Associate Publisher: Joel Fugazzotto
Acquisitions Editor: Elizabeth Peterson
Developmental Editors: Brianne Agatep, Maureen Adams
Production Editor: Mae Lum
Technical Editor: Paul A. Weber
Copyeditor: Suzanne Goraj
Compositor: Kate Kaminski, Happenstance Type-O-Rama
Graphic Illustrator: Jeffrey Wilson, Happenstance Type-O-Rama
Proofreader: Nancy Riddiough
Indexer: Nancy Guenther
Book Designer: Judy Fung
Cover Designer: Richard Miller, Calyx Design
Cover Photograph: Digital Vision

10 9

To Jim Rodger, for dedicating 26 years of his life to quality construction management education and for always putting the students first....

Acknowledgments

No great accomplishment ever happens in a vacuum. There are always a lot of people behind the scenes who deserve much of the credit for any good thing that makes it to the light of day. I believe this book is one of those good things, and it would never have happened without the hard work and dedication of several people.

I want to start by thanking Sybex Publishing for launching the JumpStart series. I believe that it serves a unique purpose by introducing the public to a number of career paths that they may otherwise never encounter. I am especially grateful to Elizabeth Peterson for discovering my web page and making the phone call asking if I would be interested in writing this book. I want to acknowledge her for recognizing construction management as the untapped career opportunity that it is. Elizabeth, by initiating this book on construction management, you have provided a great service to the construction industry and the clients it serves. Thank you.

I also want to thank the many other talented members of the Sybex team who helped put this book together. I'll start by thanking my developmental editors, Brianne Agatep and Maureen Adams, for walking me through the writing process and taking care of all of my formatting errors. Next I want to give a special thanks to Suzanne Goraj, who cleaned up all of my grammatical gaffes and helped my message ring loud and clear. And to Mae Lum, the production editor, a special thank-you for keeping everything on track while I traveled around the country teaching seminars and doing consulting work for the construction and design-build industry.

Of course, I would be remiss without thanking the rest of the Sybex team responsible for tying up the loose ends and putting the whole thing together: compositor Kate Kaminski of Happenstance Type-O-Rama, illustrator Jeff Wilson of Happenstance Type-O-Rama, proofreader Nancy Riddiough, and indexer Nancy Guenther.

In addition to the fine folks at Sybex, there are a number of other supporters who must be mentioned. Let me start by acknowledging several authors, most of them good friends and fellow faculty, who have written really good texts used as general references in the writing of this book.

- *Managing the Construction Process: Estimating, Scheduling, and Project Control* by Frederick E. Gould (2002)

- *Construction Jobsite Management* by William R. Mincks and Hal Johnston (2004)

- *Management of Construction Projects: A Constructor's Perspective* by John E. Schaufelberger and Len Holm (2002)

- *Construction Management Fundamentals* by Clifford J. Schexnayder and Richard E. Mayo (2004)

I extend a very special thank-you to my dear friend, colleague, and technical editor, Paul Weber, for his diligent review of every word in the manuscript for technical accuracy and application. Paul, I greatly appreciate your support and assistance in helping me achieve this goal. And as always, your abilities to communicate graphically were put to good use in several instances throughout the book.

To my department head, Allan Hauck, colleagues, and students at Cal Poly State University, thank you for putting up with my mental absences while I was focused on the completion of this book and for encouraging me every step of the way.

And finally, as always and forever, I thank my husband Wayne for his continued support, love, and understanding year after year while I continue to pursue the passions of my heart.

Contents

Introduction

Congratulations! You are about to embark on an adventure. This book is about the processes, the people, and the practices that we call construction management—a term, and a profession, that may be unfamiliar to many people. Construction, as most individuals understand it, is an activity or a series of activities that involves some craftsmen, building materials, tools, and equipment. But you will learn that there is a great deal more to it than that. If you think that construction is all about brawn and not much about brains, then you probably haven't been paying very close attention to what has been going on in the built environment in the past several decades. Buildings today can be very complicated and the building process has become extremely demanding. It takes savvy professional talent to orchestrate all of the means and methods needed to accomplish the building challenge.

This book's focus is not on construction per se. Its focus is on the construction process and those individuals who manage that process. Construction management involves the organization, coordination, and strategic effort applied to the construction activities and the numerous resources needed to achieve the building objective. Construction management combines both the art and science of building technology along with essential principles of business, management, computer technology, and leadership.

Construction management as a profession is a relatively new concept, which may explain why you have not heard of it before. Up until the 1960s, the management tasks associated with large construction projects were typically handled by civil engineers. But in 1965, faculty from nine universities gathered in Florida to form the Associated Schools of Construction. What started as a movement to upgrade the status of construction education at universities evolved into a standardized construction management curriculum leading to an exciting new career choice, and one for which there was increasing demand. Men and women who love the idea of transforming a lifeless set of plans and specifications into something real—a single family home, a high-rise office building, a biotech facility, a super highway, or a magnificent suspension bridge—had found an educational program that provided both the academic course work and practical management tools needed to plan, organize, and coordinate the increasingly complex construction process.

If you are one of the many individuals who desire the intellectual challenges of architecture, engineering, technology, and business, yet long to be outside in the thick of things, getting your hands dirty, ultimately producing a tangible result—something of lasting value—then construction management might just be the ticket for you.

The purpose of this book is to give you a jumpstart on understanding what construction management is all about. After reading this book, you will have a good sense of what the job of a construction manager entails and what is needed to be good at it. You will learn about the diverse tasks associated with planning, organizing, and managing a construction project to a successful end. You will also discover the many opportunities available for individuals interested in pursuing a career in CM.

You can continue to explore these opportunities by reading other books about construction management, taking construction management classes, and by networking with practitioners in the industry. And for those of you who want to take your interests and careers in construction to the next level, you can consider pursuing professional certification through either the American Institute of Constructors (AIC) or the Construction Management Association of America (CMAA). Both of these organizations and their certification programs are introduced in Chapter 1.

And after you've read this book, the next time you see some construction, I hope that, besides being fascinated by the activity, you will also be impressed by the ingenuity, creativity, and heart of the people who can achieve such feats. It's also my goal to give you a new appreciation for the men and women who built this nation in the past and who continue to contribute to the built environment in a significant way. Enjoy!

Who Should Read This Book

If you have picked up this book, I suspect that you have already experienced construction at some level and are curious about what construction management is. You may currently be working in construction on the building side as a craftsman or laborer, and want to know how you can move over to the management side. Or you may be a construction management student wanting a glimpse into the day-to-day challenges faced by the construction professional. On the other hand, you may currently have nothing to do with construction other than having a longtime interest in the building process. Some of you may have had a home built or a room added on, and are simply interested in learning what the fuss was all about.

I hope that architects and engineers will pick up this book to get a better understanding of the contractor side of the equation. Some designers, tired of sitting behind a desk all day, may even contemplate giving CM a try just for the heck of it. I suspect that there will be more than a few real estate agents, mortgage brokers, and interior designers who will use this book to become better informed regarding the construction process, integrating the new knowledge into the services they provide their clients. Then, of course, there are those of you who are already working in construction management but have been looking for a resource that will help explain what it is you do for a living!

No matter what your reason for buying this book, I feel confident that it will be money well spent. For those of you who have little or no experience with construction, I venture to guess that some day you will, and when you do, your knowledge and understanding of construction management will become quite valuable.

As for those of you who already have experience in construction, I have tried to write a comprehensive overview of the construction management process from the constructor's perspective. I'm sure you will relate to the Real World Scenarios presented throughout the text and enjoy the human aspects conveyed in the pages of this book. They are intended to drive home the challenges associated with construction and express the contribution that construction professionals make to the built environment. This book will assist you in communicating to clients, colleagues, and the public at large the significant role that the construction manager plays in the overall success of a construction project.

What This Book Covers

This book walks you through the construction management process—explaining how you take a project from a set of two-dimensional paper drawings to a three-dimensional wood, steel, or concrete building, bridge, or highway. Along the way, you will learn about the seven functions of construction management and how each of them contributes to the successful delivery of the construction project. Here's an overview of what this book covers:

Chapter 1   This chapter introduces you to the construction industry and the opportunities that it offers. Here you will learn about the different industry sectors and the roles of the various participants in the construction process.

Chapters 2–5   These chapters explain in greater detail what construction management is and how construction work is obtained in the first place. You will also learn about the construction contract and about each of the stages leading from design to post-construction.

Chapter 6   Figuring out what a project is going to cost is one of the first steps to getting a construction contract. This chapter deals with the estimating function of construction management. Here you will learn about the different types of estimates and how you price construction work.

Chapter 7   In this chapter, you will learn all about the conditions of the contract and what it takes to manage them. Contract administration is all about handling the red tape, business details, and paperwork of the construction project.

Chapter 8   Once the contract is signed and everything is a go regarding the project, you are ready to start construction. This chapter deals with organizing the job site and coordinating all of the manpower, materials, and equipment needed to get the work done.

Chapter 9   This chapter stresses the importance of good project planning and identifies the various tools used to schedule all of the activities associated with moving the project from startup to completion.

Chapter 10   The only way to know if your project has met its goals for cost, time, and quality is to monitor and track individual components of performance. This chapter gets into the details of project control and explains how to get a job back on track if it should start to go off course.

Chapter 11   Finally, you will learn the importance of quality control and safety management throughout the construction process. No project can succeed without well-established quality and safety plans.

Making the Most of This Book

At the beginning of each chapter of Construction Management JumpStart, you'll find a list of the topics that I cover within the chapter.

infrastructure
The basic roadways, bridges, tunnels, and utilities that support a community or society.

To help you absorb new material easily, I've highlighted new terms, such as *infrastructure*, in italics and defined them in the page margins.

In addition, several special elements highlight important information.

NOTE

Notes provide extra information and references to related information.

At the end of each chapter, you can test your knowledge of the chapter's relevant topics by answering the review questions. You'll find the answers to the review questions in Appendix A.

You'll also find a list of Terms to Know at the end of each chapter to help you review the new terms introduced in the chapter. These terms are compiled in the Glossary at the end of the book.

Chapter 1

The Construction Industry

The construction industry is vast and varied. Just take a look around—from homes to highways to hospitals—and you see the results of this industry. Starting with the need for shelter, we first built primitive huts and houses. Then we constructed buildings for assembly and churches in which to worship. As our needs expanded, so did our building capabilities. We eventually built political capitals, bustling with business and commerce. Though the means and the methods have changed over the centuries, the construction industry is still about building communities that serve people.

Construction is big business totaling over $3.4 trillion annually worldwide, and there is no slowdown in sight. The industry employs about seven million people directly (plumbers, carpenters, welders, and so on) and hundreds of thousands more indirectly. It gives rise to the steel industry, the lumber industry, the carpet industry, the furniture industry, the paint industry, the concrete industry, the paving industry, and so on. It goes even further than that if you consider the trucking, manufacturing, and mining industries. Architects, engineers, draftspersons, building inspectors, code officials, and other professionals would not have jobs if it weren't for construction. As construction projects become more and more complex, the challenges associated with the management of these projects become more complex. The need for qualified construction managers is tremendous and opportunities abound for those interested in the work.

Let's take a closer look at the construction industry and the position it has in our economy and our lives.

Scope of the Industry

Let's first make sure that you understand what construction is really all about. I have found that most people, including many who are already engaged in construction, do not understand the significance of the industry. So let's start by considering the scope and the magnitude of construction and take a look at its impact on our society and our economy.

It's Just Construction

In my experience, the average observer of construction regards the process as rather insignificant and inconsequential—nothing special, nothing unique, not an industry of any major importance—mostly filled with noninfluential blue collar macho types. After all, when compared to medicine, or law, or even architecture, the common notion is—*it's just construction*. It is why our great buildings and structures are typically identified only with the designer, and not with who built them. The contractor is incidental. Let me give you a few recent examples to drive home my point.

The distinctive architectural designs of Frank Gehry are known all over the world. One of his newest creations, the Walt Disney Concert Hall in Los Angeles, is "the most challenging of all Frank's buildings...an enormously complicated structure because of the curved shapes and intricate joinery," according to Terry Bell, project architect for Gehry Partners, LLP, quoted on the Walt Disney Concert Hall website. The website mentions that "extraordinary state-of-the-art construction techniques" were needed for the Concert Hall—"[o]ne of the most technically advanced structures in the world, [with] its lack of right angles and the overall sculptural quality." At any one time as many as 550 construction workers were on site to transform the concrete and steel into one of the most acoustically sophisticated concert halls in the world. However, you would be hard-pressed to find one mention of the building contractor of this magnificent construction feat in the popular press or on the Concert Hall's website. Not one single mention! This incredible construction challenge was accomplished by the M.A. Mortenson Company.

Let's consider another example. In 2002, the third-largest cathedral in the world and the first cathedral to be built in the United States in over a quarter of a century was constructed in downtown Los Angeles. Designed by the world-renowned Spanish architect Professor Jose Rafael Moneo, the Cathedral of Our Lady of the Angels stands eleven stories tall and weighs a whopping 151 million pounds. The Cathedral rests on 198 *base isolators* so that it will float up to 27 inches in any direction during an 8-point magnitude earthquake. It has been stated that the design is so geometrically complex that none of the concrete forms could vary by more than 1/16th of an inch. Having visited the Cathedral several times during its construction and been witness to the extraordinary efforts

base isolators

Large shock absorbers made of alternating layers of rubber and steel attached to a building's foundation to allow movement of the structure without causing damage.

made by the construction team to ensure the quality of the design along with the requirements for the budget and schedule, I was very disappointed, again, not to find one mention of the contractor, Morley Builders, on the Cathedral's website.

Consider any of our architectural jewels: the Sears Tower in Chicago, the Space Needle in Seattle, the Transamerica Pyramid in San Francisco, and the Empire State Building in New York. With a little research, you would find that each of these buildings is easily identified with their designers. However, it would be a real challenge for you to discover that Morse Diesel International Inc. was the builder of the Sears Tower, that Howard S. Wright Construction built the Space Needle, that the general contractor for the Transamerica Pyramid was Dinwiddie Construction (now Hatheway-Dinwiddie), and finally that Starrett Brothers & Eken Inc. was the builder of the Empire State Building.

To me, not recognizing and acknowledging the contractor along with the designers of these buildings is a grave injustice—but, unfortunately, indicative of how our society views the construction industry. Apparently, to some people it is not very important. Well, let me explain why it is *very* important. Drawing a pretty picture on paper or calculating a complex engineering formula does not make a building real—construction does, and that takes tremendous creativity, ingenuity, tenacity, skill, blood, sweat, and tears. So remember, no matter how outstanding the design, it is not architecture until somebody builds it! "Just" construction? I don't think so!

Construction's Contribution

Our society does not take the contributions of the construction industry very seriously. But it should, because without these contributions, this world would be a very bleak place. When you walk out of your office, home, or classroom today, just take a good look at the world around you. I want you to notice the houses, the churches, the hospitals, the shopping malls, the theaters, the baseball stadiums, the bridges, the streets, and even the cars driving around. None of these would exist without construction. There would be no cars, or any other manufactured products, because there would be no manufacturing plants—no Nike shoes, no McDonald's restaurants, no Gap stores. There would be no commerce, no transportation, no manufacturing. Progress and construction go hand in hand—we can't have one without the other. Our society, our economy, and our culture are all dependent upon the construction industry. So the next time you hear someone complaining about construction workers stirring up dust at the intersection or delaying their trip to work in the morning, I hope that you will take the time to point out what our world would be like without construction.

When a building is notably impressive, people ask—who designed that wonderful building? But when a building design is particularly unimpressive, people ask—who built that eyesore? Why aren't people as curious about who builds the great structures as they are about who designed them?

NOTE

Construction Statistics

Let's put it all in perspective. Construction is one of the nation's largest industries, accounting for approximately nine percent of the gross national product. It is larger than the automobile and steel industries put together. Housing starts (which are identified by building permits issued) are one of the major economic indicators reflecting the overall health and direction of our economy.

According to the U.S. Department of Commerce, the year 2003 ended with approximately $922 billion worth of construction (all private and public sectors) put in place for the year. The U.S. Department of Labor estimates that there are at least 700,000 construction companies employing just under seven million people in the United States. Construction offers more opportunities than most other industries for individuals who want to own and run their own businesses, and statistically an additional 1.6 million individuals do just that.

Construction impacts the quality of life for every human being and plays a major role in all of society, and has for a very long time. Anyone who is involved in construction—from the grading laborer to the electrician to the estimator to the construction manager to the construction company executive—needs to understand that what they do makes a *big* difference in the world.

Construction has been around a very, very long time. Construction means, methods, and motivations have changed over the past 12,000 years or so and the trek has been absolutely fascinating. Let's continue this adventure by taking a look at some of the factors that have influenced this very significant industry.

A Historical Perspective

The purpose of spending some time on the history of the construction industry is to further reveal the impact of construction on society. As you read this brief history, imagine the creativity, ingenuity, and tenacity that these early constructors must have possessed in order to achieve such extraordinary building achievements. What started as a craft motivated by necessity (shelter from the elements) gradually turned into building science motivated by curiosity, intrigue, and genius. The building challenges of today are just as complex as in the past, and even more sophisticated, inspiring the same attributes exhibited by the early master builders. Let's take a brief walk through time and visit some of the world's greatest construction accomplishments.

Ancient Times

Although agriculture is probably recognized as the oldest industry in history, construction is most likely a close second. The construction industry can trace its roots back to at least the Stone Age, as early as 12,000 B.C. Using materials readily available—mud, wood, and stone—early man began constructing simple structures for protection from the rain, cold, heat, and snow. During this same period, the development of bronze and iron allowed man to make stronger tools that significantly expanded the possibilities in building construction, allowing builders to develop their skills.

As construction skills and tool development increased, real expertise in the building trades began to emerge. Simple shelter grew into planned settlements, villages, and cities. Soon, the need for common gathering places became a part of the building challenge, and this period saw the start of public building for special events, religious ceremonies, manufacturing, and commerce. Small villages became large cities, and large cities grew into great civilizations, and at the heart of it all was construction.

Egypt and the Pyramids

Many of these early civilizations were building with one of the first manufactured building materials, dried mud bricks. However, the Egyptians began to use stone as their primary building material. Although the process of moving these very large masses of rock was difficult, to say the least, the ingenuity of these ancient builders conquered these challenges, resulting in some of the most facinating building projects in all of history—the great pyramids.

At this time, there was really no distinction between architecture, engineering, or construction. All three disciplines were embodied in one person—the master builder. The master builder concept would survive for many years, until the complexity of structures and construction techniques warranted a separation of disciplines.

It was during the building of the pyramids that the first known building code was recorded, dating back to approximately 1792–1750 B.C. These written rules and responsibilities were among the laws carved into stone tablets, collectively known as the Code of Hammurabi. The building code dictated acceptable workmanship standards for the master builder. Failure to meet these standards brought stiff penalties, in some cases including death.

Greek Influence

During the pyramid-building era, the Egyptians used large numbers of unskilled workers to construct their massive undertakings. However, the Greek master builders, who were building many beautiful temples made of marble and limestone (such as the Parthenon in Athens), started to organize and utilize small groups of skilled stonemasons. This idea of congregating workmen around a particular craft represents the beginning of the building trades concept, in which a particular building skill is honed to a level of expertise associated with a master craftsman. Although much of the work was still performed by an unskilled workforce, the use of skilled artisans allowed for a finer detail and design to be applied to the architecture. This is clearly a turning point in construction history.

The Roman Empire

The Roman Empire represents one of the most influential periods of time for architecture, engineering, and building science. During the Roman Empire, significant strides were made in construction techniques. An early form of concrete, a staple in every present-day building project, was invented by the Romans. This early version consisted of a pasty, hydrated lime and pozzolan ash mixture made from rock. In addition to utilizing concrete in the foundations of their structures, the Romans began adding domes and arches to their buildings, achieving engineering and construction feats that were astounding. During this time, some of the world's most impressive structures were built, including the Colosseum and the Pantheon. The first glass was also incorporated in the first century A.D. and decorated many Roman structures. Road construction was another highlight of the Roman Empire, and many of these ancient pathways are still carrying travelers today.

Around 40 B.C., a Roman writer, engineer, and architect named Marcus Vitruvius Pollio wrote the first design and construction handbook. His writings included topics on building materials, construction processes, building styles, road and bridge design, water-heating techniques, acoustics, and other building physics. With Vitruvius' writings, the concept of master builder or architect took on even greater distinction. The master builder was responsible for both the design and the supervision of the construction. Surprisingly, Vitruvius' work was recognized as the authority on building and design for centuries.

The Middle Ages

With the downfall of the Roman Empire came a real decline in building activity and technology. Then around 900 A.D., the powerful Roman Catholic Church revitalized stone construction as they intensely pursued church- and cathedral-building throughout Europe. Even during this somewhat stagnant period, great building efforts were taking place. Glorious Gothic cathedrals highlighted the European landscape and many other impressive structures were being designed and built all over the world.

Craft training and education became a major focus and craft guilds were organized, even forming special brotherhoods around specific trades. Building construction became a major industry in and of itself. The two most important building trades were carpenters and stonemasons. Three distinct stages of ability were recognized—master, journeyman, and apprentice. These three stages of organized labor are still widely recognized today among the trade unions.

The Renaissance

Toward the end of the Middle Ages, a renewed interest in architecture, building, and science took place, continuing the transformation and evolution of construction and building design. It was during this time that the concept of the master builder began to be questioned as the most efficient way to build. Leone Battista Alberti, considered by some to be the precursor to the modern-day architect, argued that he could create drawings and models as a way to direct master craftsmen without actually being involved in the building process. Alberti was a theoretical architect rather than a practical hands-on architect-builder. He furnished plans of his buildings but never participated in the actual construction. This was the first application of a new philosophy that would eventually separate design and construction as distinct functions. Interestingly, there is a real push today to return to the master builder concept—but with the recognition that the modern master builder is a collaborative team.

The Industrial Revolution

The Industrial Revolution had a major influence on all of society. The construction industry was no exception. As construction became recognized as separate and unique from design, more theoretical concepts involving physics, mathematics, chemistry, and thermodynamics were being applied, and building science as a discipline began to emerge. The various building professions took on increasingly defined roles—the art of architecture, the science of engineering, and the craft of building became even more distinct. As architecture moved further away from the building process, the engineering disciplines took on a greater role for overall technical coordination, while general contractors were left to assemble, organize, and manage the labor force, equipment, and materials on a project. Cast iron and wrought iron became the building materials of choice. These materials were being used to build bridges, railways, great exhibition halls, and various other buildings. New machinery and equipment such as steam shovels, steam hammers, and pile drivers were being invented to support building. The transformation of construction into a modern industry began during this period of time.

Age of the Skyscraper

During the late 1800s, the production of steel and electricity really took center stage as factors that would influence the construction industry in a big way. It was a time of immense growth in building technology. Steel framing replaced iron framing and allowed for high-rise building. Portland cement and reinforced concrete were invented. Glass was now being mass-produced and was used to clad many of these new building frames. The dream of constructing tall buildings reaching to the sky became a reality when E.G. Otis invented the first passenger elevator. Building skyscrapers was seen as a way to conserve land as the pace of growth in American cities became a concern. Technological advancements in building science continued, electric power became commonplace in all structures, and advancements in heating and cooling systems made life easier for people in all climates of the world.

Construction started showing up as big business during this time. Although most building was still being performed by small and medium-sized companies, much larger organizations were forming and the globalization of the construction industry had begun. Opportunities for extensive projects in housing, industry, transportation, and city development were popping up all over the world. The construction industry developed into a major economic sector.

The 20th Century

infrastructure
The basic roadways, bridges, tunnels, and utilities that support a community or society.

Although only a few advances in materials or technologies took place during the 20th century, new challenges were being imposed upon the construction industry. After World War II, there was a construction boom in the United States and around the world. The demand for housing, industry, and *infrastructure* was enormous. Time, cost, and quality became critical concerns for those needing new facilities. The construction industry responded. Mechanized tools, panelized construction, and prefabrication inspired a whole new way to view the building process. New techniques emerged to help regulate and standardize building materials and methods. Building codes, standards, and *specifications* were established to help regulate and control the quality of materials and methods. Over time, as more residential, commercial, and industrial development started to spring up, new issues, such as the environment, energy conservation, sustainability, safety, and workforce diversity started to add to the complexity of the building process in a way that had never been seen before.

specifications
The written instructions from an architect or engineer accompanying the project plans pertaining to the quality of materials and workmanship required for the project.

The industry began to recognize that the correlation between sound management techniques and successful building practices was very important to the success of a project. The ability to measure and monitor progress and economic effectiveness of the construction process became more important as projects became increasingly complex. Although the discipline of engineering had been tapped to provide the management function for years, a new distinction was being drawn.

As early as 1935, a new educational program that focused specifically on construction was popping up at a few universities across the country. These early programs eventually evolved into what is now recognized as construction management. The idea was to merge management principles, methodologies, and techniques with the art, science, and craft of building and create a unique educational experience. In addition to teaching building science, the program introduced estimating, scheduling, project controls, and project administration techniques.

In 1965, representatives from nine universities met in Florida to form the Associated Schools of Construction (ASC). This organization's distinct mission was to promote construction management as a legitimate and unique area of study at the university. The organization's goal was to establish a four-year degree program that clearly identified construction management as a recognized discipline among allied disciplines such as engineering and architecture.

Today, there are approximately 94 four-year colleges and universities listed with ASC offering construction management curricula. The programs are typically identified as Construction Management, Construction Engineering, Engineering Technology, Building Science, or Construction Science, and are often affiliated with colleges or schools of Engineering, Architecture, or Technology. The educational opportunities available today are discussed in greater detail later in this chapter.

Age of Technology

New technologies are impacting every aspect of our lives. The construction industry is no exception. There are computer applications across all aspects of the construction management function: programs for estimating, scheduling, project administration, building design, cost accounting, project controls, and information transfer. Computers are available on every job site and Palm Pilots make schedule or purchase order changes available in an instant. But the technology doesn't stop there. Advanced technologies such as Global Positioning Systems (GPS), computer-aided earth-moving systems, smart structures, robotics, four-dimensional visualization, and virtual reality are already being utilized in the construction industry. According to the January 2004 issue of *Construction Executive* magazine, engineers at Pennsylvania State University are using new software with an immersive projection screen that allows construction managers to enter and interact with the contents of a full-scale nuclear power plant room that exists only in cyberspace. The virtual mock-up is real enough to enable welders to determine whether there is enough room to work.

The technological opportunities in construction methods, materials, and management are endless. In the future, we can look forward to the use of nano-technology, metallic polymers, and micro-electromechanical systems that will allow for embedded intelligence in building materials and produce products such as interactive, "talking" doors, windows, walls, and even kitchen countertops.

Advanced technologies are not limited to computer applications. Today, a much greater emphasis is being placed on the environment and the relationship between our buildings and the communities in which they are constructed. In recent years, a voluntary, market-driven building-rating system called the LEED (Leadership on Energy and Environmental Design) program has been making its way into segments of the construction industry. This program, which evaluates environmental performance from a "whole building" perspective over a building's life cycle, is becoming another level of expertise and certification for construction managers.

The contributions of the construction industry relative to the changing needs and demands of our society are becoming more apparent. Construction management, probably more than any other discipline, holds the promise to help close the gap between design and end user satisfaction by offering constructability reviews, value engineering, and life cycle cost analysis.

NOTE   If you want to learn more about the history of construction, look for Gyula Sebestyén's book, *Construction: Craft to Industry* (Spon Press, 1998). It is a fascinating read and takes a very comprehensive look at the many factors that influenced the growth of the construction industry from the collapse of the Roman Empire to planning for the global frontiers of the future.

Industry Sectors

The facility needs of a society are vast and varied. People need places to live, worship, work, receive medical care, shop, be educated, exercise, vacation, and generally engage life. From a facilities standpoint, all of these needs taken together are often referred to as the built environment. Although many other industries assist in creating the built environment, construction ultimately delivers it.

Each of these different facility needs is manifested as a different market or sector of the construction industry. There are four basic sectors of the industry:

♦ Residential building

♦ Commercial building

♦ Heavy/highway construction

♦ Industrial construction

Each sector is characterized by different means, methods, and materials of construction. The types of equipment, the type of structural framework, the manufacturers, suppliers, and specialty contractors, and even the sources of funding vary with each sector. For example, structural steel frames, steel erection, and steel fabrication are all common components of the commercial sector, but not residential. On the other hand, wood frame structures, rough carpentry, and lumber are common components of the residential sector of the industry, but not commercial.

Each sector requires specific expertise and familiarity in order to optimize the construction operations and management efforts. Therefore, the majority of builders focus their attention on only one sector or market of the industry. Furthermore, each sector has a particular "personality" or character. Everyone interested in pursuing a career in construction management will ultimately have to choose which sector they are most attracted to. So let's take a closer look at each of these sectors.

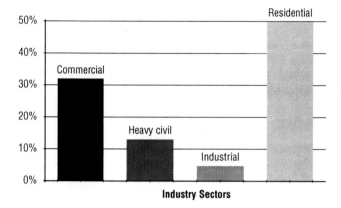

Residential Construction

Residential construction addresses the housing needs of a society. This sector represents the largest of all the construction sectors. Housing construction takes many forms: individual homes, apartments, condominiums, townhouses, and prefabricated units such as modular and manufactured homes.

Individual homes are classified as single-family dwellings. Apartments, condominiums, and townhouses are all referred to as multi-family dwellings.

NOTE

Residential construction is typically funded by private individuals or developers for their own use or for sale. Builders of individual homes generally fall within one of three categories: they are *custom builders* constructing one-of-a-kind homes for specific customers on specific lots, they are single-family *small-volume builders* who build 25 or fewer homes a year, or they are single-family *production builders* who build more than 25 homes a year.

Although custom and small-volume builders account for approximately 70 to 80 percent of all residential builders, they produce only about 20 percent of the homes. On the other hand, production builders construct almost 80 percent of the homes in the United States.

Although some custom homes may be designed by an architect, many house plans are available from catalogs and plan books. In some cases, the contractor may provide the design for the customer. Engineering services are rarely required and construction techniques are relatively simple. The project duration for a typical single-family home is in the three- to six-month range. Even high-end custom homes can be built in one year or less. Large production builders focus their efforts by creating communities of 50 to 400 houses in one location. These large projects will build out over several years.

NOTE   Production builders used to be called "tract" builders. Tract builders gained a reputation in the 1940s, 1950s, and 1960s for producing "cookie cutter" homes—homes that all looked alike. Today's production builders offer numerous custom options and upgrades while still utilizing standard designs and floor plans.

Means and Methods

Residential construction is relatively low-tech in terms of the means and methods needed to produce its product. Hammers, nails, drills, and saws still make up the primary tools and equipment needed to perform the construction tasks, although the hammers are now pneumatic nailing guns. Many contractors joke that any two guys with a pick-up truck, a cell phone, and a dog can start a residential construction company. This exaggeration is not far from the truth. The residential construction market is relatively easy to get into; however, because so many of the companies are very small, they are also at a high risk for failure. One bad job can put the contractor out of business in a hurry. However, the large production builders are big business, generating annual revenues and profits surpassing those of many large commercial construction companies. They are engaged in every aspect of home building, from land acquisition to financing, and are often publicly owned and traded on the stock market.

Primary Materials

Residential construction is often referred to as wood frame construction or light framing. The building materials utilized in this sector are typically wood products such as lumber and plywood. Over the past 25 to 30 years, attempts have been made to replace traditional wood framing with light gauge steel framing in an effort to conserve natural resources. The use of light gauge steel is still quite limited in residential framing; however, great strides have been made in better utilizing every piece of a harvested tree: the branches, the wood chips, and even the sawdust. Numerous engineered wood products have emerged, such as roof and floor trusses, laminated beams, oriented strand board, and wood I-beams. These products are now commonplace.

Exterior finishes for residential buildings are usually limited to siding, brick, or stucco. Single-family dwellings are most often designed with pitched roofs utilizing various types of shingles or tiles made of asphalt, clay, concrete, or slate. Interior finishes typically include sheetrock walls and ceilings, with paint or wall coverings, and carpet, tile, or sheet vinyl floors.

Characteristics

Whether the residential construction firm is a small "Mom and Pop" operation or a huge publicly owned enterprise, there are certain characteristics of this market that anyone contemplating a career in building should understand. Home building is personal. Your client is usually an individual family with individual personalities. This is probably not the sector for you if you are not a people person. Home buyers are spending their personal funds on these projects and usually it is the single largest amount of money that they have ever spent.

As a construction manager, you will be directly involved with the owner on a regular basis. You will get to experience the full range of emotions and temperaments associated with the home-buying public. There is a great deal of personal service and hand-holding that will be required of you. Many construction professionals delight in this aspect of the business, anxious to address every detail and concern that an owner might have regarding the building process, while others cringe at the thought of having to deal with someone at such an intimate level.

Residential construction companies come in all sizes. Some limit their service area to a local market, others might expand operations regionally or nationally, and a few are even building overseas in Europe and South America. Of all the construction industry sectors, the residential sector probably requires the broadest scope of knowledge. Construction is only one facet of the home building business. An understanding of sales, marketing, financing, land development, entitlement, purchasing, construction operations, customer service, and warranty are all needed to participate in this sector of the industry.

Commercial Construction

This sector of the industry primarily addresses the needs of commerce, trade, and government and makes up about a third of the total construction market. This is the category that includes banks, schools, office buildings, hotels, shopping malls, baseball stadiums, theaters, universities, hospitals, courthouses, government buildings, and other facilities where people gather. These projects may range in size from a small medical office to large high-rise office buildings to state-of-the-art biotechnology facilities. The building costs are significantly higher than with residential construction and the project duration is much longer. It is not uncommon for a commercial project to last three years or more.

Funding for these types of building projects may be private, public, or combined in a special private-public partnership. Commercial construction companies are usually categorized by their dollar volume per year. For example, a company that does less than $10 million per year might be classified as a small commercial contractor whereas a large commercial contractor completes over $250 million of work annually. Of course, everything is relative to a given market. What might be considered a large company in Nebraska could easily be classified as a small company in California.

Commercial projects are very wide-ranging in scope and it's difficult to develop expertise in all areas. For example, hospitals and clean rooms, which have very specialized systems, require contractors who possess the special knowledge needed to successfully perform the construction. Therefore it is not unusual for a commercial contractor to focus their attention on only a few building types.

Commercial projects are typically designed by architects. The building systems can be complex and various specialty engineers are engaged to support the architect with the electrical, mechanical, and structural design. Additional consultants may also be brought in for unique requirements of the project. For example, a sound and acoustics engineer is a likely participant on a concert hall project, but would not be called in for a retail facility.

Means and Methods

cofferdam
A temporary watertight enclosure erected to prevent water from seeping into an area, allowing construction to take place in the water-free space.

Commercial construction tends to be far more technically complex than residential construction. Special construction processes are utilized in the building of commercial buildings and specially trained technicians are required. The use of concrete casting beds, *cofferdams*, and *slip forms* are common techniques in commercial construction but would never be utilized in residential construction. Although plumbers, electricians, and painters are some of the trades required in both the commercial and the residential sectors, ironworkers, pipefitters, and glaziers are more likely to be exclusive to the commercial (and industrial) sectors. The equipment needs in commercial construction are much more extensive as well. Cranes are a common sight on most commercial projects, as well as pile drivers, welding machines, and concrete pumps.

slip form
Concrete forms that rise up the wall as construction progresses.

As a construction manager involved in commercial building, you will be required to work with numerous specialty contractors and union workers employed in various trades. The labor management aspect of commercial construction can be complex and requires special knowledge of labor laws and collective bargaining.

Primary Materials

curtain wall
An exterior cladding system that is supported entirely by the frame of the building, rather than being self-supporting or load-bearing.

Just take a look at any downtown city area and you will see a variety of combinations of the three basic building materials associated with commercial building: steel, concrete, and glass. These three materials compose the primary materials utilized in commercial construction. Commercial buildings consist of some type of building frame or structure and an exterior cladding to cover the frame. The cladding material is usually applied as a *curtain wall* of brick, stone, concrete, aluminum, steel, or glass, or an exterior insulation panel. In some cases, reinforced concrete masonry (RCM) is the material of choice for commercial buildings of limited height.

The frame of a commercial building is designed to withstand certain loads and conditions. Architects and engineers will determine whether a steel frame or reinforced concrete frame is best suited for the building. Glass is a common cladding material for commercial buildings, although other materials are available for this purpose. In some cases, the entire building frame and cladding are concrete. There is very little wood used in commercial buildings because of the higher fire-resistive design standards.

Interior partitions are most often constructed of light gauge steel studs covered with sheetrock. Interior finishes include paint, wall coverings, carpet, tile, marble, granite, and acoustic ceilings.

Most commercial buildings have flat roofs covered with a bituminous membrane with gravel ballast, or some type of a vinyl or rubber covering. Commercial buildings with sloped roofs are often covered with pre-finished metal roofing.

Characteristics

Unlike the residential sector, commercial buildings are typically funded by corporations, agencies, or the government. Personal dollars are not involved and the owners are typically not as concerned with the day-to-day operations of construction. However, they are concerned with meeting the schedule and getting their operations up and running as quickly as possible. This need for speed to market has prompted many changes in *project delivery* that will be discussed later.

project delivery
A comprehensive process by which a building, facility, or structure is designed and constructed.

The primary focus in commercial building is actually the construction itself. If you are fascinated with tall buildings, towering cranes, and complex construction details, then commercial construction may be your niche. Depending on the size of the company, opportunities exist at the local, regional, national, or international levels.

Whereas residential construction requires an across-the-board understanding of the home building business, commercial construction requires a deep understanding of construction processes and techniques. Commercial contractors are rarely involved in the sales or marketing or land acquisition components of the project.

Industrial Construction

This sector of the industry is highly specialized and requires firms with vast resources and significant construction and engineering expertise. The number of contractors qualified to work within the industrial sector is limited. The project types included in this category are defined primarily by the production activities that occur within the facility. Manufacturing plants, electrical generating facilities, oil refineries, pipelines, steel mills, and chemical processing plants are all examples of industrial construction projects.

Means and Methods

Industrial buildings are often very basic in their exterior design. The building shell does not need to be very fancy for its intended purpose. The success of an industrial project is usually determined by how well the facility is able to perform relative to its production goals. In industrial construction, the processes that go on inside the shell constitute the real construction challenge. Unlike residential or commercial construction, the installation of equipment makes up a big piece of the industrial construction process. Massive boilers, reactors, and processors that need to be installed under strict quality standards and regulatory guidelines are what really count here.

Because of the complex process considerations, engineers are typically the lead designers on these types of projects. The means and methods associated with the construction of the building shell are quite simplistic; however, the installation of the equipment and process systems requires technological savvy, sophisticated knowledge, and great attention to detail.

Primary Materials

The building materials utilized in industrial construction are very similar to those used in commercial construction. Steel, concrete, and reinforced concrete masonry make up the primary components. These buildings often house specialized equipment, machinery, or process piping, and the interior finishes are usually quite stark for ease of maintenance. Often the concrete or block walls are simply painted, floors are left as concrete, and no ceiling finish is applied, thus leaving exposed piping and ductwork in full view. In some cases, special materials, such as glass piping or heat-sensitive tiles, may be utilized in the construction of industrial buildings.

Characteristics

This sector of the industry deals with building huge facilities that take many years to complete. In some cases, a project may be under construction for as long as 5 to 10 years and the possibility of the construction management team having to relocate is quite high. The funding for these projects is usually provided by private sources and the contract amounts are generally large. There are many international opportunities in industrial construction and anyone seeking a chance to travel abroad will most likely find it within this sector. Having an interest in international business, international law, or even world politics could be an asset for anyone considering this sector. And of course, fluency in a foreign language is always a plus.

Sometimes industrial projects are located in remote areas, even to the point where modern conveniences are in short supply. Depending on the facility type, there may be requirements for high security clearance and government oversight. It is very important that the engineers and construction managers on these projects work closely together because the consequences of poor communication can be serious.

In recent years, the opportunities for industrial contractors in the environmental arena have grown significantly. Hazardous-site cleanups and other ecological endeavors present special challenges that require the expertise of engineers, construction personnel, and scientists working together to address the problems.

Heavy Civil Construction

This sector of the industry impacts all of society in a very big way. Often referred to as horizontal construction, the heavy civil sector includes roadways, bridges, tunnels, dams, airports, and railways. Basically, any work that is associated with infrastructure, transportation, and how we move about involves the heavy civil construction market. Similar to the industrial sector, heavy civil projects are complex, usually high-dollar endeavors that take special engineering know-how. This market is huge and growing larger every day. The need for building and rebuilding of our nation's roadways, airports, sewage plants, and bridges is great.

These projects are typically designed by civil engineers and often the construction management team has a strong background in civil engineering as well. Heavy civil construction firms are generally very large operations that can offer opportunities nationally and internationally.

Means and Methods

Only a few trades are engaged in heavy civil construction compared to the other three sectors. There is no need for carpet layers or drywall finishers in this sector of the market. On the other hand, equipment and equipment operators play a huge role in the work of a heavy civil project. Heavy civil contractors make huge investments in equipment. Keeping the earth movers, excavators, scrappers, and trucks rolling is the name of the game for this sector of the industry.

Primary Materials

Asphalt, gravel, concrete, steel, and dirt make up the primary materials used in heavy civil construction. Most of us have witnessed highway road crews as they lay down new asphalt on our highways and streets. We watch as they bring in loads of gravel and rock dust before they place the hot asphalt and roll out the roadway.

Other heavy civil projects such as bridges and dams make use of large amounts of concrete and steel. For example, a dam project may require that a concrete-batching plant be constructed right on the building site in order to accommodate the quantities of concrete needed.

Characteristics

These projects are usually publicly funded and tend to last for a long time. Building miles of roads can take many years. It is not unusual for individuals involved in this sector of the market to move temporarily to where the project is located. There are also occasions when your work might require that you be located in isolated areas for long stretches of time. However, anyone intrigued by big machines, tractors, and excavators will be attracted to this sector. This sector of the market is the least affected by economic fluctuations, and therefore can offer a reasonable measure of job stability.

The Project Players

As our brief walk through construction history revealed earlier, the days of the individual master builder are long gone. No longer is it practical to expect one person to design, engineer, and build construction projects. Today's master builder is a collaborative team with diverse skills and expertise. There are many, many players involved and they all make a valuable contribution to the effort while at the same time adding to the complexity of the process. It is very important to understand the various roles and responsibilities of these many players as they influence the construction management process.

In addition to getting to know the primary players in the game, you need to know the secondary players involved and the various layers of influence and risks associated with their involvement. Understanding the intricacy of these relationships will help you appreciate the management function in construction.

Primary Players

The three principal players in any construction project are the owner, the designers (architects and engineers), and the contractor. Although these three parties are always involved in a project, the alignment and contractual relationships among them will vary depending upon the project delivery system utilized to deliver the project. Project delivery will be discussed in Chapter 2. Each of these parties provides distinct services and has specific accountabilities necessary to fulfill the building objectives.

Owners

program
A written statement that identifies and describes an owner or end user's needs and requirements for a facility. Every design starts with a program.

No construction would ever be accomplished without owners. They are the driving force behind the construction industry. Their demands for housing, commercial facilities, industrial products, and infrastructure are the chief motivation to build. After an owner determines need and decides to build, there are four primary duties that they are accountable for:

- Developing the *program* and outlining the needs and requirements of the end users

- Determining the quantity, extent, and character of the project by defining the scope of work
- Creating the overall budget for the project, including land acquisition (if necessary), development, design, and construction costs
- Providing the funding for the project and making periodic payments to the designers and the contractor

How an owner accomplishes these tasks is often determined by what type of owner they are. There are basically two types of owners—public owners and private owners. Public owners are typically government agencies such as the General Services Administration, the Army Corps of Engineers, or the state departments of transportation. These agencies represent the public and spend tax dollars to build courthouses, military bases, and federal highways. Private owners make up the bulk of construction spending and may take the form of an individual building a single home, a developer who builds speculatively, a small manufacturer enlarging operations, or a national firm that owns numerous facilities. Funding comes from private sources such as banks, investment brokers, and venture capitalists.

Design Professionals

There are two types of professional designers engaged in the construction process and each deals with different parts of the project design. Architects deal with the function, life safety issues, and aesthetics of the building, and engineers deal with the systems. They typically work together to complete the design function, with one or the other taking the lead depending on the type of facility being constructed.

I will use the term *designer* **throughout the text to imply either an architect or engineer.**

NOTE

The construction manager works with both the architect and the engineer on a regular basis throughout the construction process. The primary responsibilities of the designers are to:

- Assist the owner in developing the facility program and determining end user needs and requirements.
- Advise the owner regarding the image and character of the facility and establish broad design goals.
- Assist the owner in selecting products to fit the program and the budget.
- Advise the owner on special and aesthetic issues and generate graphic solutions to problems.
- Develop the final building plans, construction details, and specifications.

In order to better understand the distinctions between architectural design and engineering design, consider the human body. Just as a body has a particular functional design with arms, legs, and a head, as well as skin and hair to protect it from the elements, so does a building with various rooms, porches, stairs, an exterior cladding of brick or siding, and shingles or asphalt on the roof to keep it dry. The body has a skeletal system to keep it straight and upright, and a building has a structural frame to keep it straight and upright. The body has a circulation system to move blood and nutrients. A building has a plumbing and mechanical system to move water, waste, heat, and air conditioning. The body has a central nervous system to send energy to our legs and arms. A building has an electrical and communications system to send messages and deliver power to our offices and living spaces. Basically, architects deal with the arms, legs, hair, and skin, and engineers deal with the bones, blood, and nerves.

Architects

Architects are licensed professionals trained in the art and science of building design. They transform the owner's program into concepts and then develop the concepts into building images and plans that can be constructed by others.

Architects design the overall aesthetic and functional look of buildings and other structures. The design of a building involves far more than its appearance. Buildings also must be functional, safe, and economical, and must suit the needs of the people who use them. Architects also specify the building materials and, in some cases, the interior furnishings. In developing designs, architects follow building codes, zoning laws, fire regulations, and other ordinances, such as those requiring easy access by disabled persons. There are several specific roles within the typical architect's office that support the architectural design function.

Design architects   Design architects are the creators of the aesthetic solution—they are the concept and idea people. Although most design architects can only hope to achieve celebrity status, some become quite famous. As previously mentioned, we often recognize their names in association with their creations—Frank Lloyd Wright, Aalvar Alto, I.M. Pei, Julia Morgan, and Frank O. Gehry, to name a few. They are sometimes referred to as *signature architects*. Owners often seek them out because of their reputations. They are typically the senior associates or principal partners within the architectural firm. Their function first and foremost is to come up with the creative expression. They convey their ideas to their design staffs through sketches and schematic renderings. They do not typically engage in the actual production of the construction drawings. They are supported by architectural technicians and specification writers in the preparation of the final construction documents.

Architectural technicians   Architectural technicians are typically the drafters of the building plans. They are the ones who actually produce the drawings that are used for construction. They work from preliminary sketches and concept drawings provided by the design architects. However, the days of sitting at a drawing board with mechanical pencil in hand using a T square and a triangle are all but gone. Today drafters have become computer operators and produce their drawings electronically using CADD (computer-aided design and drafting) software.

Specification writers   Accompanying the plans for a new building is a written project manual referred to as the specifications. The plans and specifications compose the two parts of the legal contract for construction. The specification writer is responsible for spelling out the specific products and methods that are to be used on a project in order to ensure a particular level of performance and quality.

Engineers

Engineers are usually the lead designers for heavy civil and industrial projects. Engineers are regulated by professional licensing requirements that include a four- or five-year college program, a specific number of years of experience, and the passing of a professional licensing exam. However, in building design, they are most often hired as consultants by the architects. In this scenario, they have no direct contact with the owner.

There are many different engineering specialties; the most common ones associated with construction activities are described next.

Structural engineers   Structural engineers design the timber, concrete, or steel structural systems that support a building and basically hold it up to withstand the forces of wind, gravity, and seismic activity. They design the foundations, beams, girders, and columns that make up the skeleton of the structure.

Mechanical engineers   Mechanical engineers design the heating, cooling, ventilating, and plumbing systems within a building. They coordinate their efforts with the architectural design, the structural design, and the electrical design.

Electrical engineers   Electrical engineers design and calculate electrical loads and determine the circuitry, lighting, motors, transformers, and telecommunications needed for a building. They typically work closely with the architect to ensure that the owner's expectations are met and often coordinate their efforts with the mechanical engineer.

Civil engineers   Civil engineers design roads, bridges, tunnels, dams, site drainage, parking lots, runways, and water supply and sewage systems. Civil engineering, considered one of the oldest engineering disciplines, encompasses many specialties. They are the ones that take the bare land and excavate it, move it, drill it, and shape it to meet the needs of the architectural design and the construction. Site work is one of the most unpredictable and expensive aspects of any construction project, and good design makes all the difference in the world.

Landscape Architects

I am including landscape architects as a separate design professional because they are. Many people do not understand the distinction, but landscape architects are professionals licensed and regulated by an entity separate from building architects. Landscape architects deal with the building site and outside environmental issues surrounding the structure. They are involved with such things as plantings, sidewalks, retaining walls, and water features to enhance the project. Large architectural firms may employ landscape architects on staff and utilize their services in the overall design. Or the landscape professional may be hired directly by the owner or work under a separate contract with the builder.

NOTE Great landscape design can make an ordinary building look extraordinary. Likewise, an ill-conceived landscape design can make an extraordinary building look ordinary. Unfortunately, many owners fail to see the significance of this design element and shortchange the budget for landscape design.

Interior Designers

Not all projects will engage the services of an interior designer. They may be hired directly by the owner or be a consultant to the architect. They deal with the building's interior finishes or schemes and make decisions regarding furniture selection and placement, paint colors and accessories, light fixtures, window treatments, floor finishes, and ceiling treatments. The contractor may or may not have direct dealings with the interior designer.

Construction Professionals

According to the American Institute of Constructors, the term *constructor* is generally used to define the professional responsible for all construction activities whether he or she works as a general contractor, a construction manager, or a specialty contractor. The profession of constructor includes job titles such as, but not limited to, Project Manager, General Superintendent, Project Executive, Operations Manager, Construction Manager, and Chief Executive Officer. The constructor's job is to:

- Interpret the plans and specifications and prepare cost estimates and time schedules to meet the requirements of the owner.
- Determine and implement the best construction practices, means, and methods to satisfy the owner's requirements for time, cost, and quality.
- Oversee and manage all of the construction operations into a single, safe coordinated effort.

General Contractors

The general contractor, also known as the prime contractor, enters into a contract with the owner to deliver the construction project in accordance with the plans and specifications that have been prepared by the architects and engineers. They may or may not actually perform any of the actual construction work with their own forces. When they do, they are said to *self-perform*. When they don't, they arrange for subcontractors or trade contractors to perform the specialized craftwork such as excavation, concrete placement, painting, or plumbing. Today, more often than not, the general contractor maintains only a management staff and a field staff as permanent employees. The construction management staff includes estimators, schedulers, and purchasing agents while the field management staff consists of superintendents, foremen, field engineers, and lead workers. The work of the trades is performed under separate subcontracts with various specialty contractors.

Construction Managers

Construction managers may be employed by construction management firms, general contractors, architects, engineers, owners, or specialty contractors. The primary responsibility of the construction manager is to organize the project team to perform the construction management function that is the topic of this entire book.

Specialty Contractors

Specialty contractors are often referred to as subcontractors because they perform their work under a contract with another contractor (typically the general contractor) to do a portion of the contractor's work, as opposed to contracting directly with an owner. These subcontractors, in turn, may engage other subcontractors. Thus there can be several levels of subcontracting to a general contractor.

The Building Trades

It is important to include the trade workers as part of the construction professionals' discussion because, without them, there would be no construction at all. These are the men and women (plumbers, electricians, ironworkers, and so on) who actually perform the work. These skilled and semi-skilled workers are the construction industry's most valuable asset, although they are rarely recognized for their immense contribution. Unfortunately, too, their ranks are dwindling to crisis proportions despite relatively high compensation, due to decreased training opportunities, traditionally provided by labor unions and vocational schools. However, various trade associations such as the Associated General Contractors, Associated Builders and Contractors, and the National Association of Women in Construction have tried to pick up the slack by introducing educational opportunities through special initiative programs.

self-performed work
Construction work that is performed with the general contractor's own forces or labor. Work that is not subcontracted.

Secondary Players

Construction is second only to the restaurant business when it comes to high-risk business endeavors. Four out of five construction companies will go out of business during their first year. There are many factors for this. One of them is the power that outside parties have over the entire construction process and outcome. These secondary players, or what I call *layers of influence*, are beyond the immediate control of any of the primary players. I have divided these layers of influence into three levels.

First Level

This level of influence includes subcontractors, material suppliers, and equipment vendors. See the following graphic. This layer directly influences the outcome of a job in a serious way. Although this group is often directly connected to the primary players via a subcontract agreement or a purchase order agreement, they are primarily independent operators and not under the immediate control of the owner, the architect, or the contractor. And because they are not under direct control and yet provide vital services, they always add risks to the project. For example: A subcontractor is scheduled to start his or her portion of the work on a certain date but instead shows up three weeks later, delaying the startup of other related work and therefore delaying the completion of the overall project. Or a material supplier promises to deliver the concrete block for a commercial building on a Monday and your masonry subcontractor has a full crew waiting to start the work at 7:00 in the morning. The delivery doesn't arrive and the subcontractor goes off to start another job. The block delivery then shows up on Tuesday but the subcontractor is unwilling to return to your job until he finishes the one that he has already started.

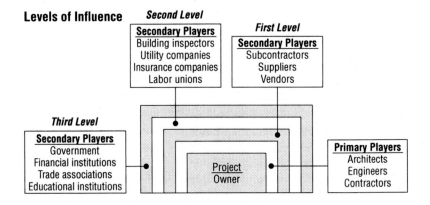

Levels of Influence

Second Level

This level of influence includes insurance companies, utility companies, bonding companies, building code officials, zoning, labor unions, and manufacturers. Although this level has no contractual connection or obligation to any of the three primary parties, they hold great influence over your project. For instance, a building inspector can shut down operations on a job for even the slightest code infringement, causing work stoppage for trades not even involved in the infringement. Or an insurance agent who fails to issue certificates of insurance on subcontractors in a timely fashion can put a monkey wrench in the administrative requirements and ultimately put the project schedule at risk. Or a strike at a manufacturing plant thousands of miles away can delay the delivery of your air conditioning units for a new retail store, delaying the completion of the job, delaying the opening of the store, and therefore costing the owner thousands of dollars in lost revenue for each day of delay.

Third Level

This layer of influence includes the courts and attorneys, local government, state and federal government, trade associations, education and training, bankers, and others. Like the second level mentioned previously, these parties do not have a direct link to the primary players, but do influence construction projects on a regular basis. Although the effects are not always immediate, actions and decisions by this group of players can have a significant impact on the whole industry, which eventually trickles down to the project level. For instance, government agencies that adopt policies or create new laws relative to such things as growth, wetlands, or endangered species are constantly having an impact on the construction industry. With the stroke of a pen, a project can be stopped dead in its tracks and millions of dollars can be at stake for the owner, the contractor, and even the architect, not to mention the eventual end users. Decisions to eliminate craft training and educational opportunities at vocational high schools and the decrease in labor union training have greatly affected the industry. The shortage of skilled workers immediately impacts the ability of the construction manager to deliver a quality product on time and within budget to the owner. It is the single most important issue facing the industry today.

Industry Image

In my estimation, construction is one of the most honorable professions that a person can pursue. However, the image of the construction industry is admittedly not always a positive one. As so often is the case, the negative aspects of this industry get the most coverage in the media and through word of mouth. The positive aspects—and there are many—are less often communicated, leaving us with the stereotypical images of construction. Practitioners who are all brawn and no brains, an unreliable workforce, a dangerous and dirty work environment, unscrupulous con artists posing as professional contractors, and entrenched discriminatory and sexist attitudes are some of the imagery conjured up regarding the construction industry. Don't get me wrong, the industry has its challenges; however, I find the industry to be filled with principled, hardworking, dedicated individuals, committed to building better communities. The industry may not have done the best job projecting its image in a positive light over the years, but that is changing. And as a teacher of the next generation of construction professionals, I can tell you that the future is looking very bright.

An Industry in Transition

Turning the image of the construction industry around is no easy task. Millions of dollars have been invested by several construction associations over the past several years in an effort to change the public's perception, and it appears to be paying off. The Associated General Contractors (AGC) has developed an exciting campaign called *Construction Futures*, an initiative designed to alter the current perception of the construction industry and to inform and educate youngsters, their parents, and teachers about the career opportunities that the construction industry has to offer.

The National Association of Home Builders (NAHB) created a public service campaign called *Home Builders Care* to recognize contractors who have contributed millions of dollars in cash, building materials, supplies, and countless volunteer hours to community charities through local community service projects.

Another effort, *ABCares*, is another national community service initiative undertaken by the Associated Builders and Contractors (ABC) to recognize chapters that contribute significantly to their communities.

NOTE   **Even the toy industry appears to be contributing to the rebuilding of the industry's image, although unintentionally, I'm sure. The *Bob the Builder* television franchise has sold millions of dolls, storybooks, and assorted toys in recent years. At the 2002 International Builders Show in Las Vegas, I picked up a new toy action figure named *Construction Jack*. I understand that the company has another action figure in the works called *Construction Jill*. Wow, there's a new message for little girls!**

It is hard to tell whether the efforts by the various construction associations have paid off, but it seems that there are clear signs that a new respect for the construction industry is emerging. The days of the individual master builder are long gone, but the new master builder, the collaborative team, is taking on challenges the likes of which have never been seen before, and the world is watching. The rebuilding of the Pentagon after September 11, 2001 is a good example. A project that was slated to take five years by federal government estimates was completed by September 11, 2002, in only 364 days by men and women determined to show what the American construction industry can do.

Technology

As with most industries, advancements in technology have revolutionized the way that we do business in construction. There are currently software programs available to assist with almost every management function in construction. Programs for estimating, scheduling, cost control, and project administration are common. Projects are managed using web-based "project integration" programs that allow all members of the team to exchange information, access building plans and specifications, process change orders, and even view construction activities and progress via a web cam from thousands of miles away. Building foundations and layouts are pinpointed using laser levels and GPS on a regular basis. Architects, engineers, and constructors can now develop three-dimensional and four-dimensional visual simulations of the building process right on their computer screens and conduct constructability reviews before the first shovel of dirt is ever turned on the job site.

The construction environment is becoming more and more complicated and the need for innovation is paramount. Not only has technology changed the way that we manage projects, but building materials, construction methods, and the projects themselves have become more sophisticated. Buildings are becoming "smart." Automated homes, offices, plants, and other facilities are using computers, networks, and programs to control specific operations such as temperature, airflow, lighting levels, and access.

Simply knowing how to swing a hammer or wield a power drill will not cut it anymore. It is not uncommon for even the smallest of construction firms to have laptop computers in the job trailer and PDAs (personal digital assistants) in every job foreman's pocket. Anyone who perceives the construction industry to be all brawn and no brains certainly has not visited a job site lately. "Toto, we are not in Kansas anymore!"

Globalization

Thirty years ago, 80 percent of the world's construction was being built in the United States and 20 percent was being built overseas. According to the U.S. Department of Commerce's *Construction Review* published in 1997, those numbers have reversed. Today, 80 percent of the world's construction is occurring on foreign soil and only 20 percent is occurring in the United States. This drastic shift is undoubtedly having an impact on the U.S. construction industry and those that are involved in it. With annual revenues in the $4 trillion range worldwide, more and more U.S. companies are pursuing international opportunities.

Each year, the weekly construction magazine *Engineering News Record* (*ENR*) publishes a list of the top 225 international construction firms. In 1994, only two

American contractors ranked among the first 20 on that list. In 1996, a total of 48 American firms made the list, accounting for 18 percent of total international construction revenue. No doubt that number has increased since 1996.

Today anyone working in the construction industry should anticipate a future involving an international experience. The world is getting smaller, and the demand for infrastructure and building programs for roads, dams, power plants, water and sewer facilities, mass transit, and even housing in emerging and third-world countries is immense. Individuals pursuing careers in construction management who are interested in the international market will undoubtedly have the opportunity to track that venture.

Diversity

There is no doubt that the construction industry in the United States is still a white- and male-dominated industry. However, the demand for construction managers is so significant that the only way the need can be met is by opening the doors to attract the best and the brightest to join in the effort to take on the building challenges around the world. And just as in other traditionally male industries, the face of construction is changing. As a professor of construction management, I have a chance to talk with recruiters from every sector of the industry and from all over the country. There is a conscious effort being made to bring diversity to the forefront of the profession and tremendous opportunities for women and minorities in the construction industry exist today.

NOTE **Estimates indicate that women account for approximately 10 percent of the construction industry. This is up from about 7 percent in the early 1980s and it appears that more women are finding their way to the management side of the business. In 1980, approximately 13 percent of all women in construction held management or professional positions in construction. In 2000 that number rose to 33 percent. Racial minorities also make up approximately 10 percent of the construction workforce, with 12 percent of those employed on the management side of the business.**

Making a Difference

There are not many professions where you can look around and actually see the difference that you are making in the world. In construction, the results of your work are right there for the whole universe to see. This became very apparent to me just as I was about to leave the construction industry and return to the university to complete a master's degree and doctorate.

In 1995, I left Virginia, where I had had my design and construction business for 10 years. On my last Sunday there, a woman from my church whom I did not know came up to me. She took my hand and, with tears in her eyes, thanked me for the wonderful contribution that I had made to the community. Her husband had worked for me as a subcontractor before his passing, and she spoke of how proud he'd been to be working on some of my buildings. Well, I too began to get teary-eyed, and when I left church I rode around that town and looked at the many homes, restaurants, and office buildings that I had designed and built. Until that day, I had never realized the impact that I and others make every day we go to work in construction. Knowing that I can return to that community 50 years from now and still view the fruits of my labor is a pretty awesome thing. The truth is that my work will still be standing long after I am gone—if not quite as long as the pyramids have lasted, at least long enough to impress my grand-children's grandchildren.

Career Opportunities

According to the U.S. Bureau of Labor Statistics, excellent employment oppor-tunities for construction managers are expected through 2010 because the number of job openings arising from job growth and replacement needs is expected to exceed the number of qualified managers seeking to enter the occupation. Employ-ment of construction managers is expected to increase about as fast as the average for all occupations over the next six or seven years. The number of wage and sal-ary jobs in the construction industry is expected to grow about 12 percent, com-pared with 15 percent projected for all industries combined. The bottom line is that the industry needs more construction managers than the universities can turn out. This is the case across the nation. As the level and complexity of con-struction activity continues to grow, so will the demand for qualified construction managers.

At my own university, approximately 200 companies have come to recruit our 65 to 75 construction management graduates each year for the past five years. It is not uncommon for students to receive 2 or 3 job offers upon completing their degree. Any construction management student who wants a job at graduation is practically guaranteed one in today's market.

NOTE

Advancement Opportunities

Construction managers may go to work for a number of different organiza-tions. On the private side, general contractors, construction management firms, architectural or engineering firms, developers, financial institutions, and large corporations may all hire construction managers. On the public side, various state and federal agencies, public schools and universities, departments of trans-portation, federal prison systems, and others may seek their skills as well.

As in any profession, advancement opportunities for construction managers vary depending upon an individual's performance, ability, and the size of the company they work for. The customary progression for a new construction management recruit is to start as a field engineer, then move to an assistant superintendent position, superintendent, estimator, assistant project manager, and then project manager. Within larger firms, highly qualified construction managers may eventually become top-level managers and executives, often moving to the vice president level or higher. Many construction managers will opt to branch out and start their own businesses.

Educational Offerings

The ideal construction management candidate is typically an individual who has a bachelor's degree or higher in Construction Management, Construction Engineering, or Construction Science, as well as practical experience working in construction. The work experience and hands-on knowledge of construction is as valuable as the degree. For this reason, many construction management students combine their formal university educations with paid internships while attending school. It is also not uncommon to find experienced field personnel pursuing their degrees in construction management as nontraditional older students.

Opportunities for education and training in construction management are numerous. As previously mentioned, the Associated Schools of Construction (ASC) lists about 94 colleges and universities offering four-year accredited degree programs in Construction Management or Construction Science. There are also a number of two-year colleges that offer construction management or construction technology courses as well as approximately 20 universities that offer a master's degree. In addition, several of the construction, engineering, and architecture trade and professional associations regularly host educational seminars on various construction management topics.

Typical course offerings in construction management include construction methods and materials, site surveying and layout, contract administration, construction documents, value analysis, cost estimating, scheduling, cost controls, accounting, business and financial management, building codes and standards, inspection procedures, engineering and architectural sciences, mathematics, statistics, computer applications, and information technology. Several of these topics will be discussed throughout this book.

Professional Affiliation and Certification

One of the easiest ways to get acquainted with the construction management profession is to become familiar with the various professional organizations affiliated with the industry. There are at least 250 organizations associated with construction and its practitioners. Two of these organizations offer voluntary certification programs for construction managers. Requirements combine a written examination with verification of professional experience.

American Institute of Constructors

The American Institute of Constructors (AIC) helps individual contractors who meet the requirements to achieve professional status through an examination and certification program. AIC is the certifying body for the designation of the Certified Professional Constructor (CPC) and the Associate Constructor (AC). The organization was formed in 1971 and serves the industry in a professional capacity similar to the professional organizations for architecture and engineering. You can learn more about the AIC at `http://www.aicnet.org`.

Construction Management Association of America

The Construction Management Association of America (CMAA) is dedicated to promoting the professional practice of construction management. The organization welcomes members from all construction and design disciplines as well as owners and various service providers to the industry. The CMAA offers professional designations through its Certified Construction Manager (CCM) program for individuals who complete their self-study course, pass the certification exam, and meet other requirements set forth by the organization. To learn more about the CMAA, go to their website at `http://cmaanet.org`.

Other Associations

Several other recognized professional associations warrant mentioning. Each of them offers training courses and seminars on various construction and construction management topics on a regular basis.

Associated General Contractors of America   Formed in 1918, the Associated General Contractors (AGC) is the oldest major organization serving the interests of general contractors. Their membership includes general contractors and specialty contractors as well as suppliers and service vendors such as insurance agencies, bonding companies, and technology merchants. You can learn more about the AGC at `http://www.agc.org`.

Associated Builders and Contractors   Associated Builders and Contractors (ABC) is a national trade association comprising contractor and subcontractor members who support a merit job philosophy. As such, members adhere to the belief that construction contracts should be awarded on the sole basis of merit regardless of labor or union affiliation. Their membership also includes material suppliers, vendors, and industry service providers. If you want to learn more about the ABC and the merit shop philosophy, visit their website at `http://abc.org`.

National Association of Women in Construction   The National Association of Women in Construction (NAWIC) was formed in 1955 in the state of Texas. They now have members in 49 U.S. states and 3 Canadian provinces.

NAWIC is dedicated to advancing career opportunities for women who are engaged in the construction industry. Their membership includes women working on the management and administrative side of the business as well as women who are working in the trades, such as electricians, carpenters, and welders. To learn more about NAWIC, check out their website at http://nawic.org.

National Association of Home Builders   The National Association of Home Builders (NAHB) is the largest of the construction associations with 211,000 members nationwide. Among their ranks are individuals from home building and remodeling companies of every size. A large percentage of their members come from related business venues such as building supplies, manufacturing, mortgage banking, real estate, and insurance. You can learn more about NAHB by going to their website at http://www.nahb.org.

Design-Build Institute of America   The Design-Build Institute of America (DBIA) is one of the newest professional organizations serving the design and construction industries. Founded in 1993, DBIA is dedicated to the practice of integrated project delivery, representing members of the entire project team: contractors, architects, engineers, and owners. In 2001, DBIA initiated a professional designation program recognizing design-builders as unique service providers in the industry. Individual practitioners who successfully complete the designation exam and meet other requirements of the program are recognized as Designated Design-Build Professionals, displaying "DBIA" after their names. To learn more about design-build, visit the DBIA website at http://www.dbia.org.

Project Management Institute   The Project Management Institute (PMI) serves individual members from around the world who are dedicated to advancing the practices and methods associated with professional project management. PMI has members from a wide variety of industries, such as information technology, business, engineering, pharmaceuticals, financial services, telecommunications, and construction. They offer a Project Management Professional (PMP) certification program that is recognized around the world. If you want to learn more about PMI, go to their website at http://pmi.org.

Terms to Know

base isolators

cofferdams

curtain wall

infrastructure

program

project delivery

self-performed work

slip forms

specifications

Review Questions

1. What is the name of the stone carvings dating back to the pyramids that contained the first written regulations pertaining to construction, commonly referred to as the first known building code?

2. By what specific measurement is construction used as an economic indicator for our nation's economy?

3. What are the four primary sectors of the construction industry?

4. Which building sector makes up the largest portion of the construction industry?

5. What is the name of the organization credited with promoting construction management as a legitimate and unique area of study at four-year universities?

6. What is the role of the owner on a construction project?

7. What is the name of the weekly magazine dedicated solely to the construction industry?

8. Name three associations affiliated with the construction industry.

9. What does LEED stand for and what is its purpose?

10. What two construction associations offer voluntary certification programs for construction managers?

Chapter 2

What Is Construction Management?

In This Chapter
- What makes the construction project unique
- What factors determine the success of a construction project
- What risks are associated with a construction project
- How risks are monitored and controlled
- What it takes to be a construction manager

In Chapter 1, you discovered that construction is about much more than just bricks and sticks or mud and mortar. You understand that buying construction is very different from buying cars or computers. Construction is complex, and there are many factors that influence the outcome of a construction project. The job of the construction manager is to take a set of written plans and specifications and a raw piece of land, and then coordinate all of the materials, manpower, and equipment necessary to guarantee the set price, schedule, and quality of the project—without any accidents or errors, regardless of weather conditions, interest rate fluctuations, acts of God, or any other unforeseen conditions. (Whew!)

Today the pressure for speedy delivery, cost efficiency, and high quality is immense. The success of any construction project depends on the men and women who plan, organize, and perform the work that transforms someone's dream into a reality. The process of constructing a building or a bridge does not happen in a factory under controlled conditions. It occurs in a dynamic environment where risk is inherent and the decision-making and problem-solving abilities of the construction management team are crucial to the success or failure of the project.

Let's now focus on the construction process itself and the specific management functions unique to that process.

Construction Management Defined

One of the best definitions that I have come across over the years is from Charles Patrick's book titled *Construction Project Planning and Scheduling*. According to Patrick, "Construction management (CM) entails the planning, scheduling, evaluation, and controlling of construction tasks or activities to accomplish specific objectives by effectively allocating and utilizing appropriate labor, material, and time resources in a manner that minimizes costs and maximizes customer/ owner satisfaction."

Although this definition explains the function of construction management, the discipline or profession of construction management is not quite so easy to understand. That's because construction management is not just a single task or activity. It comprises several tasks and is usually delivered by a construction management team. At the same time, an individual member of a construction management team performing even one of the CM functions is said to be doing construction management. Is it any wonder that the general public is by and large unaware of construction management as a distinct career?

If that isn't confusing enough, let's also consider the different ways the construction management function is offered as a service to the consuming public. In the most traditional sense, the construction management function is simply provided alongside the actual construction services. In other words, when an owner hires a general contractor to perform work for them, they get that contractor's construction management services as part of the package. The general contractor uses these skills to keep the project running on time, within budget, and in accordance with the plans and specifications provided by the owner's design professionals. However, if there are errors or omissions in the plans and specifications that were not discovered prior to construction, the contractor is not liable for any resulting cost overruns or time delays.

On the other hand, construction management may be contracted by the owner as a professional service separate from the work of the general contractor. In this case, part of the construction manager's job is to review the plans and specifications before construction begins. Doing so will prevent unwanted consequences and repercussions resulting from a lack of oversight by a construction professional. Construction management in these circumstances is usually provided as a distinct service or project delivery method.

I realize that much of this may seem a bit confusing right now, but later in the chapter I will spend time discussing the various project delivery methods and the functions of construction management. For now, I just want you to understand that many different people perform construction management services. This group of people includes general contractors, subcontractors, project managers, construction managers, construction estimators, general superintendents, job foremen, safety officers, quality control managers, and many other construction professionals. It takes a whole team of players to manage the construction project.

Throughout this book, when I use the term *construction manager* or *project manager*, or *constructor*, I am referring to any one of the entities that delivers construction management services: the general contractor, the construction management team, the construction management firm, or any individual construction manager trained in all aspects of construction management.

··
·· **NOTE** ···

The Construction Project

As discussed in Chapter 1, construction projects are extremely diverse and come in every size, shape, and flavor. However, there are some characteristics about construction projects that are common to all types, and these characteristics clearly distinguish them as unique from other industry sectors.

When we build a computer, or a piece of furniture, or even an airplane, we typically build a prototype first, then test it and work out the bugs before we put it into production. We do all of this under controlled conditions, using state of the art mechanics, robotics, and technology. These projects are usually built utilizing a relatively constant workforce, standard parts, and stable materials.

Now let's take a look at the construction project. First, every project is built as a one-of-a-kind facility, which means that each is built on a different building site, under variable weather conditions and particular environmental and topographical conditions. Each one is a prototype in and of itself. There is no testing it out first to make sure it works. Instead, the bugs get worked out as we go. Our workforce is primarily transient, practitioners of an assortment of trades moving from job to job, coming in and out of the process at various stages throughout the duration of the project. For the most part, our labor is still performed by the human hand—laying the brick, forming the concrete, and setting the steel. Finally, many of our materials, such as lumber, concrete, and plaster, are nature-made. They react to the heat, the cold, and the humidity on any given day.

In spite of these uncertainties and unique circumstances affecting the project, a construction manager is expected to deliver a high-quality facility on time, within budget, and accident free. That's one heck of a management challenge, to say the least! But let's identify exactly what it is that we are trying to achieve. The primary objective of the construction management function is the control of three main factors or values. They are time, cost, and quality. These three factors are commonly referred to in the industry as the *three-legged stool*.

However, there is actually one more very important factor, and that is safety. Construction can be a dangerous business and safety must be the foundation upon which all other values are placed, for without it the whole project is at risk.

Let's take a closer look at all the factors that influence the construction project and at how the construction manager considers each of them as part of the management challenge.

Project Values

In 1996, a group of owners, architects, contractors, and engineers gathered in San Francisco to discuss common goals and opportunities for collaboration in the building industry. This group formally organized themselves as the Collaborative Process Institute (CPI). During their discussions, they came up with what I think are the best descriptors of the factors that need to be managed and controlled on a construction project in order to produce a successful outcome for the owner and all parties involved. They referred to these factors as the *Six Dials of Project Value*: cost, time, quality, safety, scope, and function.

The Six Dials of Project Value

Cost   Time   Quality   Safety   Scope   Function

The idea is that each of these dials has a most advantageous setting for any given project and it is the project team's job to optimize these settings. As noted earlier, only the first four project values are within the traditional range of services provided by the construction management team: cost, time, quality, and safety. The last two, scope and function, are typically determined by the owner and their design team prior to the construction manager being involved. However, some project delivery methods bring the construction professionals onto the team early in the process so that they may assist with scope definition, overall function, and programming. I will discuss project delivery in greater detail later in this chapter.

NOTE   Although the Collaborative Process Institute (CPI) is no longer a functioning organization, their work and the ideas that came out of those first meetings are noteworthy and in my opinion reflect current trends in construction management. A copy of the CPI's "Collaboration in the Building Process" may be found on this book's web page on the Sybex website (www.sybex.com).

These dials of values and how they are monitored and controlled is illustrated in the following list. The Collaborative Process Institute describes them as follows:

Cost   It is essential to predict and control what the construction project will cost. Costs are established, targeted, and controlled by means of an estimate or budget. As the work progresses, expenditures for materials, labor, equipment, and subcontracts are tracked and measured against the estimates. The fundamental goal is to maintain costs within or below budget parameters. The construction manager who can minimize cost while maximizing overall value to the owner will optimize the cost dial.

Time   As the saying goes, time is money. For many projects, the speed with which the building can be brought on line is more important than almost any other factor. Time is monitored and controlled by a detailed schedule, breaking each item of work down into its component parts. Once all of the purchasing, fabrication, installation, and construction steps are identified, a time element is assigned to each step. The goal is to complete each of the work items within the time frame assigned.

The construction management team that can guarantee the schedule and actually beat it is invaluable to the owner.

Quality   Quality is the grab bag that covers all the aspects of the building not addressed by the other five values, such as aesthetic impact, user perceptions, appropriateness of building materials, and so on. Quality is monitored and controlled by a variety of means, including specifications, punch lists, inspections, tests, and user surveys. Special care must be taken to establish appropriate measures early in the project to focus attention and effort on the quality expectations of the team.

Safety   No matter how valuable a facility or structure may be, it is never more valuable than the health and welfare of the people who build and use the building. Care must always be taken to ensure that the building process, and the building itself, do not create unacceptable hazards to workers or users. These hazards range from risks during the building process (for example, falls, accidents, injury, and death) to risks from the completed buildings (for example, toxic gases, biohazards, and structural failure). Safety is best monitored and controlled proactively, by identifying potential risks and taking prudent steps to mitigate those risks.

Scope   Scope is monitored and controlled by means of an architectural program, which identifies the space needs and tracks compliance of the building design with those needs. An optimal scope outcome would match the end user's needs to the facility design over the life of the building with no gaps in between. The ultimate goal is high end user satisfaction.

Function   The best project teams try to meet all of the functional requirements of the end-user group. An optimal outcome would satisfy their short- and long-term needs, allowing for sufficient flexibility to adapt to changes in the market. Function is monitored and controlled by means of process flow diagrams and utilization analyses, which document the efficiency of the processes that will be performed in the completed facility.

NOTE When construction managers are engaged in the early stages of a project, they are often able to add value to the project by considering owner needs relative to the construction process. For example, a construction manager may recommend a phased approach to the construction if an owner needs to get a particular production line or function up and running before the completion of the entire facility. Good construction managers are great at solving these kinds of problems, and it is a smart owner who brings them on board to discuss end-user needs during the pre-design phase.

Keep in mind that these dials are all interconnected and that adjusting one will ultimately cause a change in the others. For example, if an owner requests that we crank up the time dial and complete the project earlier than we had contracted to do initially, then it is likely that the cost dial will also be turned up. Likewise, if an owner increases the project scope, then both the time and the cost dials will be turned up. So the job of the construction management team is to figure out how to best adjust, manage, and monitor these dials in order to optimize the performance of each value relative to the owner's requests. Throughout this book, I will focus on just how to do that for cost, time, quality, and safety.

Project Risks and Liabilities

Construction is a very risky business, for both the owner and the contractor. Part of the challenge is trying to place the risk in the hands of the party that can best manage that risk (see Table 2.1). That's why an owner hires a contractor to begin with—to shift the risks for the construction cost, time, quality, and safety over to someone trained to manage them. Once the risks are identified, understood, and analyzed, proper allocations can be made for reasonable schedules, estimates, and management plans.

Table 2.1   Risks Allocation Table

Type of Risk	Responsible Party		
	Contractor	Owner	Designer
Site conditions		X	
Weather conditions	X		
Project funding		X	
Subcontractor failure	X		
Job site safety	X		
Material deliveries	X		
Quality of the work	X		X
Delays in the work	X	X	

Table 2.1   Risks Allocation Table *(continued)*

Type of Risk	Responsible Party		
	Contractor	Owner	Designer
Defective design			X
Defective work	X		
Code compliance	X		X
Estimate errors	X		
Labor strikes	X		

Managing Construction Risks

Being a construction manager is something like being a scout sent out in front of the wagons to head off danger and forge a safe path to the intended destination. It is about anticipating all kinds of risks and responding in a proactive fashion to mitigate and control as many negative factors as possible in order to increase the odds of a successful outcome. The construction manager's job is to bring that project in on time, within budget, and in accordance with the owner's expectations regardless of how many surprises show up.

As discussed earlier in the chapter, many factors contribute to the unique nature of the construction project. These factors are also what make construction one of the most challenging and risky endeavors to pursue. I have already mentioned many of the obvious risks associated with construction projects—time, cost, quality, and safety—as well as some that are more unpredictable, such as the weather, a transient workforce, site conditions, and human error. But there are additional risks that may not seem to be related to construction at all, and therefore may be overlooked. Let's take some time to explore those.

For example, there are political risks, innovation risks, and organizational risks, to name a few. Building a new prison close to a residential neighborhood can put a builder in the middle of an ongoing controversy, and the constructor who takes on that project must be prepared to manage the public relations, media attention, and community resistance that may come along with it. All of these things take time to deal with, potentially causing significant delays and bad press that the contractor wasn't anticipating when she accepted the job. This is all part of the construction management function and it has nothing to do with lumber or bricks.

In another situation, an inexperienced construction manager might be tempted to take on a project containing electrical equipment operated by new state-of-the-art technology, all the while forgetting that he is just as responsible for the performance of these untested gadgets as he is for building the roof under which they are housed.

Or how about a builder working for a new owner who has never built anything before and lacks qualified personnel to respond to requests for information in a timely fashion? While the owner is trying to figure out what they want, the builder is at risk for time delays and cost overruns.

Although the goal is to find, flush out, and eliminate every possible snag and snafu in the way of a successful project, the reality is that bombshells can be dropped on any day on any project. Your job as a construction manager is to continually evaluate the situation, assess the risks, make decisions, and accept the responsibility for the results, right or wrong.

Scope Definition

scope of work
The parameters defining the overall extent of work to be included in a construction contract. The project scope is commonly communicated through construction plans and written specifications.

Writing a project scope or scope definition is the responsibility of the owner. The *scope of work* sets the parameters for the construction project and identifies the work to be done. Generally, the scope of work is presented in the plans or "blueprints" (so called because of the blueprint machines once used to reproduce them as white lines on blue paper) and in the written specifications, all of which are developed by the designer. The scope describes the building layout, site work, square footage, number of rooms, number of floors, types of materials (windows, siding, floor covering, roof, and so on), dimensions, special equipment, storage requirements, and so on.

The key to risk mitigation, for all parties, is to start with a really well-defined project scope. A poorly written scope will usually result in a poor response from the contractor. Obviously, a contractor can't plan for something that is not defined as a requirement of the project to begin with. A well-written scope, more than any other factor, will help reduce risks for all parties involved. It is critically important that the owner takes the time, does the planning, and solicits the professional help needed to do a good job before the project begins. It will pay off for everyone in the long run.

Project Delivery Methods

Anyone who has ever taken on a construction project is well aware that most projects display some cost overruns, time delays, and conflicts among the various parties. Of course, the object of the game is to mitigate these risks as much as possible. One of the ways we accomplish this is by choosing the right project delivery method to start with.

It is the owner who ultimately decides which project delivery method to use. Unfortunately, many owners are ill equipped to make a thorough assessment of the many factors that can impact project success relative to the owner's specific criteria. Too often they choose a traditional methodology simply because they are familiar with it. Ultimately, they end up accepting less than stellar results, not realizing that their decision for project delivery had set the stage for inefficiencies and trouble before the project even started. However, I am getting ahead of myself. I will provide some insight into project delivery selection criteria later in this chapter. For now, let's just focus on what project delivery is and how construction management plays into it.

What Is Project Delivery?

Project delivery is the process by which all of the procedures and components of designing and building a facility are organized and put together in an agreement that results in a completed project. The process begins with the compilation of needs and requirements of the owner spelled out in the architectural program. These needs and requirements are first expressed in preliminary plans from which initial material, equipment, and systems selections are made. With these selection decisions, the design becomes further refined until all design decisions are made and a final set of contract plans and specifications are completed. The owner then determines which procurement methodology (purchasing steps) to use to buy the construction services and the criteria that will be used to select the contractor. Finally, the owner selects which type of contract to employ. Once selected, the contractor goes about planning an overall strategy for delivering the project in accordance with the plans and specs that have been developed. All the parts and pieces of the agreement are put in place and the game plan is established.

This game plan also determines how the players will interact and communicate with one another over the course of the project.

Types of Project Delivery

There are basically three project delivery methods: design-bid-build, construction management, and design-build. Keep in mind that the functions associated with construction management are required in all three methods even though only one of them is actually named construction management. As I said earlier, this can get a little confusing.

These three project delivery methods differ in five fundamental ways:

- The number of contracts the owner executes
- The relationship and roles of each party to the contract
- The point at which the contractor gets involved in the project
- The ability to overlap design and construction
- Who warrants the sufficiency of the plans and specifications

Regardless of the project delivery method chosen, the three primary players—the owner, the designer (architect and/or engineer), and the contractor—are *always* involved. The traditional roles and responsibilities for the three parties were spelled out in Chapter 1, but keep in mind that the accountabilities and relationships change with the various project delivery methods, as I described in the list above. This will become clearer as you read the individual project delivery descriptions that follow. Each of these methods has specific advantages and disadvantages, and it is the owner's responsibility to assess the project delivery choices in relation to their project needs.

Design-Bid-Build

design-bid-build

A project delivery method in which the owner holds two separate contracts for design and construction. This method is often referred to as the traditional project delivery method.

Design-bid-build is commonly referred to as the traditional method of project delivery, and the traditional accountabilities apply. In this scenario, the owner first hires the architect or engineer to design the building or structure. The design professional prepares a design, moving through the three standard design phases: schematic design, design development (the design development drawings are often referred to in the industry as DDs), and finally contract documents (referred to as CDs). Under this arrangement, the design professional is usually selected on a qualifications basis and is typically paid a fee or a percentage of the building cost for his or her services. (Contract documents will be discussed in greater detail in Chapter 4, "The Construction Contract.")

After the plans and specifications are complete, the owner selects the general contractor who will provide the construction and construction management services. The most common means for selecting the general contractor under this method is by low price or low bid: several competing contractors estimate the project based upon the contract documents and the builder with the lowest price gets the contract. The general contractor typically subcontracts various sections of the work to specialty contractors. Under this method, the owner holds two separate contracts, one with the designer and one with the contractor.

In this arrangement, all dealings between the designer and the contractor go through the owner. There is no legal agreement between the designer and the contractor. This method is very linear in nature and the contractor does not have any input regarding the design of the project. The contractor is only responsible for carrying out the work as spelled out in the plans and specs and will utilize the various construction management functions to accomplish this task.

Design-Bid-Build Linear Approach

No contractor involvement

Design   Bid   Build

No overlap of design and construction

Under the design-bid-build method, the owner warrants the sufficiency of the plans and specs to the contractor. If there are gaps between the plans and specs and the owner's requirements, or any errors and omissions in the design, the owner is responsible for paying for those corrections. I mention this because the contractor is often the one who discovers the errors and submits the change orders necessary to correct the work. This is never a happy occasion for the owner. A constructability review, which will be mentioned later, can help prevent such surprises.

Construction Management

As you now know, *construction management* may be viewed from several different perspectives, and one of them is as a specific project delivery method. Under this method, construction management services are provided to the owner independent of the construction work itself. There are two options for the owner to consider under this method.

Option 1: Agency CM   The Construction Management Association of America (CMAA) defines *agency CM* as a fee-based service in which the construction manager is responsible exclusively to the owner and acts in the owner's best interests at every stage of the project. In this case, the construction manager offers advice uncolored by any conflicting interest because he or she does not perform any of the actual construction work and is not financially at risk for it.

This arrangement involves three contracts: one between the owner and the designer, one between the owner and the contractor, and one between the owner and the construction manager. The owner hires a designer and a contractor exactly as described under the design-bid-build scenario. In addition, the owner also contracts with a third party, a construction management firm that provides construction management functions but as an independent agent or representative of the owner.

The party responsible for the construction work is still an individual general contractor, and that contractor still carries out construction management functions relative to their internal requirements for managing the project to completion. In some unique situations, the owner may elect to bypass a general contractor and contract directly with several specialty contractors and allow the CM firm to manage each of them. These are called *multiple prime* contracts.

Option 2: At-risk CM (also called CM/GC)   The CMAA defines the *at-risk* CM project delivery method as an option that entails a commitment by the construction manager to deliver the project within a guaranteed maximum price (GMP). The construction manager acts as consultant to the owner in the development and design phases, but does the work of a general contractor during the construction phase.

construction management
The planning, scheduling, evaluation, and controlling of construction tasks and activities to accomplish specific objectives outlined in the contract documents.

agency CM
A construction management option in which the construction manager acts in the owner's best interests at every stage of the project, from design through construction. The construction manager offers advice and project management services to the owner but is not financially responsible for the construction.

multiple prime
A contracting methodology in which the owner bypasses the use of a general contractor and enters into multiple separate contracts with trade or specialty contractors for the various sections of the work associated with the project, such as concrete, framing, mechanical, and electrical work. Each of the specialty contractors involved becomes a prime contractor on the project.

at-risk CM
A project delivery method where the construction manager acts as a consultant to the owner in the development and design phases, but as the equivalent of a general contractor during the construction phase.

value engineering
A process in which various alternative approaches are evaluated and considered regarding design, product selection, or building system in an effort to provide the most efficient, cost-effective solution possible relative to value in response to the desires of the owner.

constructability reviews
A design review process in which experienced contractors and construction managers work with designers to ensure that the details of the design actually can be built in an efficient and cost-effective manner. The process entails review of materials, application, installation techniques, field execution, and building systems.

In this scenario, there are only two contracts, one between the owner and designer and one between the owner and the at-risk CM. Although this might seem like a tricky relationship to manage, owners are comfortable with it because the at-risk CM is also responsible for performing the construction and carries financial liability for bringing the project in on time and within budget. By contrast, under the agency CM model, the construction manager is not at risk for the budget, the schedule, or the performance of the work.

One of the great things about construction management project delivery is that it provides a contractual avenue by which the owner can bring the CM function into play early in the project planning and make direct dialogue with the design team possible. In these circumstances, the construction manager, acting on behalf of the owner, can contribute by providing *value engineering*, life cycle cost analysis, conceptual estimating and scheduling, and what is called *constructability reviews* during the design process and head off possible incompatibilities between design and construction, which typically result in cost overruns, time delays, conflicts, and legal claims down the road.

NOTE

One of the most frustrating things that happens with traditional design-bid-build project delivery is when the estimates all come in too high. Then the project goes back to the drawing board for redesign and is significantly delayed, leaving everyone involved deeply disappointed. The way to avoid this common occurrence is by using a project delivery method that allows for early contractor involvement and encourages a team approach.

Design-Build

design-build
A project delivery method in which there is only one contract between the owner and a design-build entity. The design-builder is responsible for both the design and the construction of the project. This method is often referred to as single-source project delivery.

The *design-build* methodology has grown significantly in popularity over the past ten years. It is often referred to as single-source project delivery and is the closest method we have to the master builder approach of old. In this arrangement, there is only one contract. The owner contracts with a design-build entity, which will be responsible for both the design and the construction of the project. Whereas design-bid-build has linear sequencing of the work, design-build often integrates and overlaps design and construction and allows for something called *fast tracking*. If you remember me stating earlier in the chapter how important time is for many clients, you will understand why design-build has become the project delivery method of choice for many owners today.

fast tracking
A practice utilized to speed up a job by overlapping the design phase and the construction phase of a project. Often applied in design-build or construction management project delivery.

Under the design-build method, the design builder warrants the sufficiency of the plans and specs to the owner. The design-builder is liable for any gaps between the plans and specs and the owner's requirements for the performance of the building. If there are any shortfalls, the design-builder picks up the tab.

One of the greatest advantages to design-build is the possibility for early contractor involvement. Under this method, all of the team players—the designers, the contractors, the material suppliers and manufacturers—have an opportunity to be in continuous communication throughout the project.

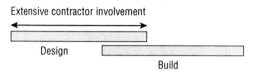

Design-Build Integrated Approach

Extensive contractor involvement

Design

Build

Overlapped design and construction

But what is a design-build entity, anyway? Where are the architect and the contractor in all of this? Actually, they're still two of the primary players, but how they organize themselves to do business is what differs. The design-build entity can be configured in three basic ways:

Designer and contractor partnership   In this scenario, two firms simply decide to work together on a single project with one of them at risk for the project. A construction firm and a design firm join forces to go after a project. One of the two partners takes the lead and actually enters into a contract with the owner to provide both the design and construction services. For example, under the contractor-led design-build model, the architect is hired by the builder (not by the owner as in design-bid-build) and the builder actually holds the contract to deliver both design and construction. If it is a designer-led design-build model, the opposite is true. The architect or engineer hires a contractor and is obligated for both the design and the construction. The partnership created is simply an agreement to work together. There is no new legal entity created under this setup. The second party is a subcontractor to the first but has no direct contract with or obligation to the owner. Contractor-led design-build is the most prevalent form practiced today.

Full-service design-build firm   This is probably my personal favorite when it comes to design-build, of which I am a big fan. In this model, the design professionals and the construction professionals work for the same firm, under the same roof. This situation permits no excuses for not communicating! One can just walk down the hall when a question or problem arises. You can imagine how efficient this process can be compared to the phone tag and e-mail lag problems that are common when team members try to communicate from a distance. Additionally, there commonly exists a higher level of trust among the various disciplines working under the same roof than what you would find under the other models. This, of course, adds to the efficiency.

Joint venture The joint venture configuration is similar to the designer and contractor partnership with one exception: the design firm and the construction firm actually create a legal entity, the joint venture, for the purpose of carrying out the design and construction of a specific project. Under this arrangement, both parties are at financial risk for delivering the project.

NOTE Teamwork and trust are really the keys to successful project delivery regardless of what method is used. Although the design and construction industry has historically been known more for its adversarial nature than for its collaborative spirit, things are gradually changing. The bottom line is that today's projects are simply too complex and too expensive to let petty issues and egos get in the way.

Trends in Project Delivery

It is important for anyone involved in, or planning to get involved in, construction management to fully understand the concept of project delivery, especially today. Today there is an increasing trend toward the more collaborative project delivery methods such as construction management and design-build.

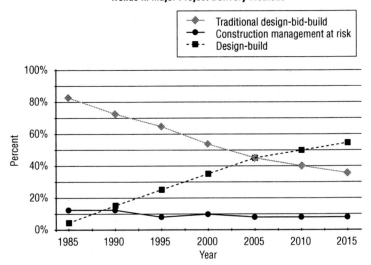

Trends in Major Project Delivery Methods

Bringing in construction professionals at the earliest planning stages of a project saves money in the long run and usually means that the project will be delivered earlier, with fewer conflicts and higher quality. Now that awareness of these benefits has become widespread, the role of the construction manager is expanding, and by most accounts this is a good thing. The following cost-influence curve highlights this fact.

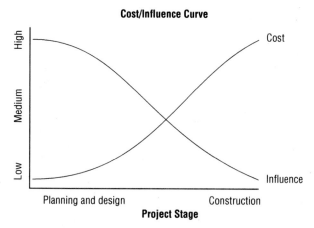

As you view the graph, consider the process of building a new home. It would be far less expensive to decide to add extra electrical outlets during the wall framing stage than it would be to make that decision after the drywall was up and the walls were painted. It would be even more cost effective to make that decision while the plans were still on the drawing board. Early contractor involvement helps flush out deficiencies in the design.

To some, bringing the contractor on board early in the planning stages may seem unnecessary and expensive, but if their input during design will help head off problems during the construction phase later on when making changes becomes very costly, then the money is well spent.

Project Delivery Selection

There are advantages and disadvantages to each of the project delivery methods I discussed. It is the owner's job to select the best project delivery method relative to the requirements for the project. Some factors that influence an owner's project delivery selection include cost, schedule, quality, design, risk tolerance, and construction expertise. Every project is different and there is not one single method suited to all situations or project types. It is very important to assess the goals for every new project being considered.

For example, if schedule is the most important criterion on a project, then selecting the design-build method would be the smartest choice because it is typically the fastest project delivery method. However, if high owner involvement in the design process is desired, then design-bid-build would be the better choice, because the owner hires the designer directly.

It is not the intention of this book to have you become an expert when it comes to project delivery, but I do want you to understand that just as scope definition has a significant impact on project risk, so does the project delivery method. The ability of the construction manager to discern the thoroughness of the scope definition and the suitability of the project delivery method goes a long way in mitigating risk from the start.

NOTE   To learn more about project delivery methods and selection, check out "Construction Project Delivery Systems—Evaluating the Owner's Alternatives" on the A/E/C Training Technology website (www.aectraining.com).

What Does a Construction Manager Do?

Okay, you are now aware of exactly what it is that you are supposed to be managing as a construction manager—cost, time, quality, and safety, right? And basically your job is to mitigate the risks associated with each of these factors and optimize project performance. But there's more. Before you have anything to manage, you must first compete for the opportunity to actually build the project. I haven't yet talked about one definitely critical task associated with construction management: actually getting the work in the first place. (Chapter 3, "How We Get the Work," is dedicated solely to this aspect of the process.)

So to clarify: the flow of events in construction management is to first get the work and then to do the work, and as we do the work, we must keep score by assessing our progress toward meeting the project goals for time, cost, and quality. Seven basic functions are performed to accomplish these three tasks. Some of them address only one of the primary tasks while others overlap and apply to more than one task. Although each of the seven functions is covered in Chapters 6 through 11, I want to introduce you to them now so that you can get an overall sense of just what construction managers do before I discuss what it actually takes to be one.

- Estimating the project
- Administering the contract
- Managing job site and construction operations
- Planning and scheduling the project
- Monitoring project performance
- Managing project quality
- Managing project safety

Construction Management Functions

The construction management functions are typically performed by a team of construction professionals trained in various aspects of the job. The experienced construction professional will be competent in all of the following management functions.

Estimating the Project

Given that cost is one of the major factors or values of the construction project, estimating is probably one of the most important construction management functions. Estimating entails the calculation and pricing of all materials, equipment, and man-hours needed to complete the work. We use estimating to get the work and also to help us keep score. In other words, we constantly compare the actual cost of the project with the estimated cost of the project and monitor any discrepancies. Significant variances are often the first sign of trouble and a good project manager takes immediate steps to determine the cause and mitigate the problem.

Administering the Contract

Contract administration (or project administration) is all about the "red tape" and paperwork associated with a construction project. As you might imagine, there are tons of reports, submittals, shop drawings, time cards, payroll records, change orders, inspection records, and numerous other documents that must be processed in order to manage a project as complex and expensive as a building, bridge, or highway. Basically, project administration deals with the management and handling of all the business affairs relating to the contract parties and their obligations. This function usually requires the effort of many different construction management personnel and is vitally important when it comes to doing the work and keeping score relative to our targets for cost, time, and quality.

Managing Job Site and Construction Operations

This is where all the action happens and we get to build something! This function considers every detail associated with the logistics of actually doing the work and getting it done. Think about all the activities and needs linked with workers doing their jobs: tools, equipment, traffic, parking, deliveries, storage, security, communications, signage, safety, trash, drinking water, lunch breaks, and so on. Right down to when to deliver, and where to place the portable toilet! These may be things that you have never thought of before relative to the construction project. But all of these things must be planned, organized, managed, and controlled on the job site in order for the construction to move forward in the most productive manner.

Planning and Scheduling the Project

Project planning is a critical component for successful completion of any type of building or structure. Planning is about organizing the activities that have to take place in a logical sequence in order to get the project from the groundbreaking phase (or earlier) to the occupancy phase, where the completed project can be used for its intended purpose. Scheduling introduces real time into the plan and is the tool used to communicate the scheme to all parties associated with the project. This function is all about doing the work as planned within a defined time span as well as helping keep score. The schedule is monitored and adjusted throughout the process.

Monitoring Project Performance

This is really one of the primary "keeping score" functions of construction management. There are two key components to controlling project performance: cost and time. Controlling is the process of measuring, monitoring, and comparing actual efforts with estimated inputs and adjusting the plan accordingly to get the project back on track for completion as intended. Estimates and schedules are the tools used to examine this progress.

Managing Project Quality

The quality standards on any project are established in the plans and specs prepared by the designer. Within these documents, specific measurable conditions are given. These include dimensions, tolerances, tests results, temperatures, and so on. It is the contractor's responsibility to see that all such quality standards are met and verified. In order for the builder to accomplish this goal, he or she must organize, institute, and adhere to a quality control plan. The quality control plan usually consists of a number of inspections, field tests, lab tests, and observations. It is very important that the contractor be able to document and report satisfactory compliance because only after the standards have been met will the owner accept the work and release payment.

Managing Project Safety

The ability to do work on a construction site is directly related to safe surroundings. Every construction manager is responsible for creating and maintaining a safe working environment. This function cannot be taken lightly. People get hurt and can even lose their lives on construction projects. This function, by necessity, must be a priority on every project regardless of size. The personal and economic costs associated with accidents, injuries, and deaths on the job site are clearly avoidable, and a proactive, rigorous approach to safety planning and management is one of the most important construction management goals.

Problem Solving and Decision Making

Although it is very important for a construction manager to be trained in all of the functions listed earlier, the two most important skills needed to succeed in construction management are decision making and problem solving. I'm sure you have determined by now that construction is not an industry for the weak of heart. The stakes are enormously high on every project and the environment is very unpredictable.

Throughout this book, I will provide Real World Scenarios to give you a little taste of the decision making and problem solving that relate to the various functions. What I want you to understand is that the solutions to many construction issues cannot be found in a book or relayed in a seminar—they are discovered by using critical and creative thinking skills and by being very resourceful.

Although being skilled in estimating, scheduling, or project administration will provide you the tools to evaluate and assess situations, it will be your ability to think on your feet, make tough decisions, and find solutions that may never have been tested before that will actually carry the day.

What It Takes to Be a Construction Manager

By this time, you are probably in one of three places. You are very excited about what you have learned so far, or you are not quite sure what to make of this thing called construction management, or you are wondering who in their right mind would ever get themselves involved in such a business! So before I take you any further, maybe this would be a good time to discuss exactly what it takes to be a construction manager.

General Requirements

The Bureau of Labor Statistics presents the following character synopsis in their *Occupational Outlook Handbook* when describing the necessary attributes of the construction manager.

> *Construction managers should be flexible and work effectively in a fast-paced environment. They should be decisive and work well under pressure, particularly when faced with unexpected occurrences or delays. The ability to coordinate several major activities at once, while analyzing and resolving specific problems, is essential, as is an understanding of engineering, architectural, and other construction drawings. Good oral and written communication skills also are important, as are leadership skills. Managers must be able to establish a good working relationship with many different people, including owners, other managers, designers, supervisors, and craft workers.*

Although this profile pretty much hits the nail on the head, so to speak, I would have to add a few more attributes to the list. I have found most construction managers to have a strong work ethic and an enthusiastic and highly motivated nature. They are tenacious and very results oriented. And, above all else, they are noted for being risk takers.

It is also very important for the construction manager to actually know something about building. It is much easier to manage a process when you have an appreciation for what it actually takes to get the work done, and believe me, you will have a greater appreciation for it after you dig a couple of ditches and manhandle some 90-pound sacks of mortar all day long. The best way to get this experience is simply to go out there and do the job.

Most companies look for individuals with both industry work experience and formal training or education in construction management. Therefore, it is not uncommon for construction management programs to require (or highly recommend) summer jobs and internships in the field for exactly this reason. I grew up in a family of carpenters and electricians so I was lucky enough to be exposed to the building side of construction very early on. Even if you have never been on a construction site before, it is very important to get this experience and not be intimidated by the environment.

NOTE

As a side note to women in particular: Women generally make excellent construction managers because of their innate ability to multitask. The one thing that may hold them back is their inexperience in construction. If you have a hard time landing that first hands-on construction job, try volunteering with such organizations as Habitat for Humanity or AmeriCorps.

Business knowledge is another factor that can really influence your capabilities and chances for success in construction management. After all, building is first and foremost a business, and all the criteria needed to flourish in business are required to flourish in construction.

And last but not least is having a good grasp of technology. An understanding of computers and software is vital to a career in construction management. Today, every function associated with construction management involves a computer application.

Typical Career Track

A typical career track for an entry-level construction manager might look something like this:

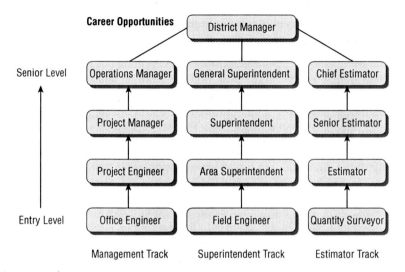

Career Opportunities

District Manager

Senior Level

Operations Manager | General Superintendent | Chief Estimator

Project Manager | Superintendent | Senior Estimator

Project Engineer | Area Superintendent | Estimator

Entry Level

Office Engineer | Field Engineer | Quantity Surveyor

Management Track   Superintendent Track   Estimator Track

Although there are many excellent companies to select from, I chose to use the Hensel Phelps Construction Company career path model because of their reputation for consistent performance and reliability. Hensel Phelps is consistently ranked among the top general contractors and construction managers in the nation by the *Engineering News Record (ENR)*.

Construction Management Job Descriptions

Job titles and job descriptions vary across company types and sizes, but most organizations will offer Field Engineer, Project Engineer, Superintendent, Project Manager, and Estimator positions. I have given a more extensive list next to try to give you a clear understanding of what it takes to become a full-fledged construction management professional and to give you some sense of the depth of knowledge and experience needed to achieve that goal. These descriptions were adapted from the Hensel Phelps Construction Company's website descriptions by permission and convey a typical chain of command scenario for a large, national construction firm.

> **Field Engineer**   This is an entry-level position. This individual works directly for the Project Superintendent. The Field Engineer (by title only; not actually an engineer) is responsible for project layout and dimensional accuracy of the project, interpretation of the project plans and specifications, communication with the craftspeople and subcontractors, jobwide

safety, production of detailed concrete form work drawings for field use, and the tracking and reporting of daily job production.

Office Engineer   This is an entry-level position. An Office Engineer (again, an engineer in title only) acts as the chief assistant to the Project Engineer and as support for the field. The Office Engineer's responsibilities include all procurement and timely delivery of materials to the project, review of shop drawings, processing of material submittals and requests for information, and assisting the Project Engineer.

Quantity Surveyor   This position is an entry-level position that works directly with the Lead or Senior Estimator on a bid. The Quantity Surveyor is responsible for estimating quantities of building materials, doors, and windows, and miscellaneous finishes. A basic understanding of construction and good plan-reading skills are prerequisites to this position.

Project Engineer   This position acts as the Chief Engineer on the project. The Project Engineer's position includes responsibilities ranging from development of bid packages to managing project schedules. A Project Engineer coordinates all shop drawings, reviews submittals, expedites deliveries, oversees project cost accounting, and processes owner and subcontractor billings. A Project Engineer is trained to successfully estimate and negotiate all change orders and direct the project administration. He or she supports the Project Manager and Area Superintendent in material deliveries, staff development, and overall project coordination. The Project Engineer plays an essential role in a successful project.

Area Superintendent   This position serves primarily on larger projects, assisting the Project Superintendent. The Area Superintendent supports development of the project schedule and pre-job planning, and accepts responsibility for a specific area of the project or phase of work. Responsibilities entail safety compliance, craft supervision and production, subcontractor coordination, scheduling, material handling, daily reports, quality control, and craft training.

Project Superintendent   The Project Superintendent is the company's representative with the responsibility and authority for daily coordination and direction of the project so that it is safe, within budget, on schedule, up to the company's quality standards, and satisfactory to the customer. To accomplish this, the Project Superintendent must conceptualize a plan to construct the project and ensure that the daily and weekly activities are consistent with this plan. The Project Superintendent and the Project Manager work together as a complementary team. The sum of their combined effort is greater than their individual efforts. The Project Superintendent concentrates most of her time on the daily and short-range direction of the project.

Project Manager This is the company's "management representative" who is responsible for the safe completion of projects within budget, on schedule, to the company's quality standards, and to the customer's satisfaction. It is their responsibility to initiate required action to achieve these objectives and to ensure that all project activities are consistent with contract documents and company policy. The Project Manager's duties vary as required to support the Project Superintendent and other personnel assigned to the project. The Project Manager's first responsibility is to support the effectiveness of the Superintendent and the project staff. Generally, the Project Manager concentrates on long-term planning, scheduling, and the identification and resolution of possible roadblocks and pitfalls prior to their having an impact on the project. The Project Manager is also responsible for ensuring that all logistical support is completed in a timely manner so that the Superintendent can concentrate on the daily and weekly direction of the company's resources and coordination of subcontractors.

Estimator This position is acquired after valuable years of field experience. The Estimator is a part of a project's estimating team and may be responsible for advanced quantity surveys of self-performed work such as concrete and carpentry work along with quantification of select subcontractor trades. An estimator learns more advanced estimating procedures along with the basics of pricing self-performed work. Additionally, the basics of bid closing are learned through shouldering the responsibility for specific sections of the bid.

Lead Estimator Lead Estimators work as members of the bid team on large, complex projects, or may be in charge of small to medium-sized projects in a support role. Lead Estimators are responsible for the survey and pricing of complex self-performed work. In this position, the Estimator learns to manage others to achieve goals and develops an understanding of the company's self-performed work production history, as well as the fundamentals of bid assembly, buyout, and subcontracting.

Senior Estimator The Senior Estimator reports to the Chief Estimator. The Senior Estimator is in charge of procuring an entire project. A successful procurement effort includes managing the bid team, developing the bid strategy, maintaining subcontractor relationships, and training other employees in the Estimating Department. The Senior Estimator is completely familiar with company production history and has a thorough understanding of subcontracting and procurement strategies.

Chief Estimator Reporting to the District Manager, the Chief Estimator is responsible for all estimating personnel and budget issues. Additionally, the Chief Estimator is responsible for identifying and tracking leads for future projects, and deciding which projects to pursue. The Chief Estimator is also responsible for reviewing all estimates.

As you can see, there are many levels of position and training involved in construction management. There is definitely a lot of room for advancement regardless of your starting level. Construction managers come from all walks of life and with every kind of background. There are many examples of high-ranking construction executives with major firms across the country who started out as laborers in the field when they were fresh out of high school. Today the training may be more sophisticated but the opportunities are just as ripe. It is not an easy accomplishment to achieve the Project Manager level in construction, but it is a very rewarding one.

Want to See if You Have the Right Stuff?

FMI Corporation is one of the nation's leading consulting firms to the construction industry. They have been conducting research and tracking construction management and manager success for over thirty years. Based on their research, I have put together a little fitness quiz. Just for fun, get out a pencil and respond to the following questions, using the instructions given. When you are all done, add up your responses, divide by the total number of questions, and note your average score. As you work through the quiz, keep in mind that there are no right answers.

Construction Management Aptitude Quiz

Use the following scale of 1–7 where 1 = Strongly Disagree, 2 = Disagree, 3 = Somewhat disagree, 4 = Neutral, 5 = Somewhat agree, 6 = Agree, and 7 = Strongly Agree, to rate your reaction to each statement.

1. I consider myself detail oriented and take pride in making sure that everything is done correctly.

   Strongly Disagree ⟶ **Strongly Agree**

   | 1 | 2 | 3 | 4 | 5 | 6 | 7 |

2. I have strong written communication skills.

   Strongly Disagree ⟶ **Strongly Agree**

   | 1 | 2 | 3 | 4 | 5 | 6 | 7 |

3. I have strong verbal communication skills.

   Strongly Disagree ⟶ **Strongly Agree**

   | 1 | 2 | 3 | 4 | 5 | 6 | 7 |

4. I am good at meeting with people and finding new opportunities.

    Strongly Disagree ———————————▶ **Strongly Agree**

    1   2   3   4   5   6   7

5. I usually do whatever it takes to get the job done, even if it means working long hours.

    Strongly Disagree ———————————▶ **Strongly Agree**

    1   2   3   4   5   6   7

6. I have a good sense of humor.

    Strongly Disagree ———————————▶ **Strongly Agree**

    1   2   3   4   5   6   7

7. I like to look at problems in a systematic way, making sure that all aspects have been taken into account.

    Strongly Disagree ———————————▶ **Strongly Agree**

    1   2   3   4   5   6   7

8. I am very creative and am likely to find unique approaches to problems.

    Strongly Disagree ———————————▶ **Strongly Agree**

    1   2   3   4   5   6   7

9. I listen to what other people say and am willing to incorporate other people's suggestions into my plans.

    Strongly Disagree ———————————▶ **Strongly Agree**

    1   2   3   4   5   6   7

10. I like to work on projects that are visible and out there for the whole world to see and touch.

    Strongly Disagree ———————————▶ **Strongly Agree**

    1   2   3   4   5   6   7

11. I would rather work outdoors than in an office.

Strongly Disagree ————————➤ Strongly Agree

1   2   3   4   5   6   7

12. I enjoy taking on risky projects, and I don't mind if there's some downtime between project activities.

Strongly Disagree ————————➤ Strongly Agree

1   2   3   4   5   6   7

13. I don't mind getting dirty at work.

Strongly Disagree ————————➤ Strongly Agree

1   2   3   4   5   6   7

14. I am more concerned about my own happiness in my choice of career than I am in what other people think of my choice.

Strongly Disagree ————————➤ Strongly Agree

1   2   3   4   5   6   7

15. I like to compete.

Strongly Disagree ————————➤ Strongly Agree

1   2   3   4   5   6   7

16. I do not take rejection personally, and I look at failure as an opportunity to learn.

Strongly Disagree ————————➤ Strongly Agree

1   2   3   4   5   6   7

17. I do not give up easily.

Strongly Disagree ————————➤ Strongly Agree

1   2   3   4   5   6   7

18. I like working in teams and with people of diverse backgrounds.

Strongly Disagree ⟶ **Strongly Agree**

| 1 | 2 | 3 | 4 | 5 | 6 | 7 |

19. I am able to prioritize and balance working on several tasks concurrently.

Strongly Disagree ⟶ **Strongly Agree**

| 1 | 2 | 3 | 4 | 5 | 6 | 7 |

20. I believe that there is always a solution to any problem and am willing to negotiate until a satisfactory solution can be found.

Strongly Disagree ⟶ **Strongly Agree**

| 1 | 2 | 3 | 4 | 5 | 6 | 7 |

So how did you do? The nature of the questions should give you a pretty good insight into the type of characteristics that tend to show up in the most successful construction managers, at least according to FMI. If your overall score averaged a 4.0 or higher, you are probably well suited for a career in construction management. Remember: the industry is filled with every kind of personality and character type. There are so many positions to fill and functions to perform in construction management that it takes a variety of skills, aptitudes, and characteristics to get the job done. But one thing is sure: every day is different in construction, and you could spend a lifetime learning all there is to know about the industry. So let's continue on the journey and begin to take a look at what this career is really all about.

Terms to Know

agency CM	design-build
at-risk CM	fast tracking
constructability reviews	multiple prime
construction management	scope of work
design-bid-build	value engineering

Review Questions

1. Distinguish between construction management as a function and construction management as a project delivery method.

2. Identify at least three characteristics that make the construction project unique from other industry sector projects.

3. Name the four primary project values to be managed, monitored, and controlled.

4. Why is scope definition so important in the construction process?

5. What is meant by the term *project delivery*?

6. Identify the three primary project delivery methods and discuss how they differ contractually.

7. Explain how agency CM is different than at-risk CM.

8. What is meant by the term *fast tracking*?

9. Name the three basic ways in which a design-build entity may be configured.

10. Identify the seven functions of construction management.

Chapter 3

How We Get the Work

In This Chapter

- How the contractor tracks down projects to bid on
- How the bidding process works
- How the constructor prepares for the competition
- The different criteria used to determine the winners
- The various factors considered before competing

Before we can start managing any project, we must have a project to manage. To get a project to manage, the contractor must first find projects to bid and then win the opportunity to build them. Finding and getting work is a crucial factor in the success of a construction firm. Obtaining information about upcoming projects is a big part of the overall marketing effort of the construction company.

Some companies can boast of a certain number of negotiated projects that are just handed to them because of reputation or prior dealings with a happy client. However, in the majority of cases, contractors must compete for their work and their livelihood. In the old days, this competitive process was pretty straightforward. But today it has become quite complex and the strategies employed to win the project require abilities that were not needed before, such as negotiation, presentation, team building, and communication skills.

The construction industry has always been a very competitive business, and today the competition has become even more aggressive. The stakes are higher and the margins are lower, and the skills that must be employed are at a different level. Today all aspects of your game must be operating at full capacity in order to win projects. Owners are much more sophisticated and make much greater demands. But the game is indeed a challenging one and the rewards can be significant.

Finding the Work

Like most industries, construction firms must battle for their share of the market. The bulk of a company's workload will be secured through a rigorous price bidding competition. But even before a contractor decides to compete, he or she must first do some reconnaissance work and determine where the projects are, what they entail, and when they will be put out for bid.

The first step in the process is to determine who is preparing to build new projects and when they will be ready to start. It is imperative that the contractor find and maintain a relatively constant stream of potential jobs in order to stay in business. For a construction company to be successful, it must engage in an intelligence-gathering effort—scoping out new work and keeping an ear to the ground, so to speak, regarding project design starts and capital improvement campaigns among investors and the corporate world. An uninformed contractor who does not find out about a project until it has already broken ground with equipment and materials being delivered has missed an opportunity to win that project. The bottom line is that there are more contractors competing for the work than there is work to compete for, and any missed opportunity is a mistake.

I do not mean to imply that a contractor should go after every single job out there, but he or she must know about what is coming up in order to decide which ones are worth pursuing. Later in the chapter, I will discuss several factors that are considered when deciding whether to compete for a project.

Although almost every member of the construction management team shares in this task at some level, it is typically the senior estimators, senior managers, and business development personnel who are charged with this most important assignment.

Marketing Efforts

The recognition of construction management as a vital and valuable service relative to the construction process has opened the door for genuine marketing efforts among the most successful construction firms. Today most construction companies have a marketing arm in-house whose sole function is to be on the watch for upcoming projects. The marketing efforts are no longer limited to persuading owners to put them on the bid list so they can compete for the contract. Today, as construction management services become more and more sophisticated, the real effort is focused on convincing owners that they should bring the construction management team on board early to assure the greatest chances for project success. As you learned in Chapter 2, "What Is Construction Management?," the earlier the construction manager is engaged in the design and construction process, the greater the benefit to the owner and the overall construction process. Opportunities for value engineering and constructability reviews as well as budgeting and scheduling during design are just a few of the benefits of early CM involvement. Conveying these benefits to the owner is a high priority of the marketing personnel within the construction firm.

Although contractors are familiar with and accustomed to competing for the work they get, the game has changed in the last few years. They now understand that what they have to offer is extremely valuable in the overall scheme of things, and an opportunity to negotiate rather than compete is a major goal of today's construction firms.

Rules of the Game

Although the competitive environment is changing in the construction industry, there are still some rules associated with the game that remain the same. Public contract laws have required the selection of building contractors solely on the basis of lowest responsible bid. For years, many private owners adopted similar procedures for buying construction services, and it was rare for a private owner to consider any other option for buying construction other than the same method that was mandated for public work. Interestingly, today, legislative reforms have resulted in both public and private owners having a few more options available to them. Much of this chapter will address those options. However, before getting into those options, let's first take a look at the aspects of the contracting laws that remain the same.

Public or Private Domain

In Chapter 1, "The Construction Industry," you learned that construction projects are classified as either public or private by virtue of how they are funded. Public schools, highways, and government buildings are examples of projects funded with taxpayer dollars. On the other hand, building types such as retail outlets, private offices, private schools, and apartment complexes are usually financed by private sources.

Public Projects

When public funds are being used to sponsor a project, there are certain regulations that must be followed when it comes to bidding for the job and awarding the contract. The *open bid* process must be used. In open bidding, the project must be publicly advertised in newspapers and trade journals, and any contractor is allowed to submit a bid.

open bid
A competitive bidding requirement for all public projects. An open bid is one that is advertised publicly and allows any qualified contractor to submit a bid on the project.

Although the logic behind the open bid system is understandable, there are some worrisome problems that go along with it. For example, with open bidding, the owner cannot restrict the number of contractors who will participate in the competition, and they must allow all comers, even if the contractor's technical or financial capabilities are questionable.

There are a few preventive measures associated with public work to safeguard the public from problems regarding contractor competency or financial capability. The law requires contractors who compete for public projects to post three bonds: a bid bond, a performance bond, and a labor and material payment bond (also called a payment bond). These bonds are issued by a surety company and act somewhat like a form of credit. Although the surety does not actually lend the contractor money, it uses its financial resources to back the obligations of the contractor. For example, the bid bond assures the owner that if the contractor is the low bidder, he or she will indeed enter into a contract with the owner. However, if the low bidder simply cannot go forward with the contract, then the owner can award it to the second highest bidder with the surety stepping in to cover the difference between the two bids. The owner is protected from having to pay the higher price. Likewise, if the contractor is unable to perform the work as promised or fails to pay his or her suppliers and subcontractors, the performance and payment bonds kick in, and the surety pays for completion of the work done by another contractor. Obviously, the contractor must have an excellent reputation and show evidence of sound financial standing before any surety will give its backing, so this safeguard is a pretty reliable one. However, given the risky nature of construction, things can go wrong, and in reality no one ever wants to see this safeguard used if it is at all avoidable.

Prequalification is another process available for use in the public domain if an owner chooses to employ it. This helps with weeding out those contractors who are not qualified to bid the project in question. The contractor community has mixed views regarding prequalification. Some applaud it for placing the competition on a more even keel, while others abhor it as being unfair and an invasion of privacy.

prequalification
The process in which an owner, based upon minimum financial, management, and other qualitative data, determines whether a construction firm is fundamentally qualified to compete for a certain project, or class of projects.

Private Projects

Private owners are not restricted by the rules set forth in open bidding. They may solicit bids from whomever they choose. In other words, bidding is "by invitation only." The owners often send out an *Invitation for Bids* in letter form to a select number of contractors. They may choose contractors with whom they already have good working relationships, or handpick contractors who have a reputation for quality and performance relative to the project type. Under this

Invitation for Bids
A notification sent to a selected list of contractors, furnishing information on the submission of bids on a private project.

closed bid system, the owner has much more flexibility. They can narrow the qualification criteria and limit the number of contractors who are allowed to compete. However, it is not unusual for private owners to instigate the same safeguards mandated by law under public contract laws. Prequalification, bid bonds, performance bonds, and labor and material payment bonds are common requirements of contracts for private work as well.

closed bid
Used with private projects and is not open to the public. Bidding is by invitation only, via an Invitation for Bids, to a selected list of contractors.

Sources of Information

All construction projects are advertised in one form or another. How they are advertised differs depending on whether the project is public or private. Public projects are typically advertised in newspapers or trade journals. They are also advertised in various government publications such as *Commerce Business Daily* or online governmental bid and request-for-proposal listing services such as GovernmentBids.com.

Most contractors subscribe to some type of electronic construction news service. Electronic news services are one of the easiest ways to keep up with projects that are coming up for bids. For a nominal service fee, these services provide up-to-date information on the status of projects from concept to completion. This allows the construction firm to anticipate work, pick and choose which jobs to go after, and develop an overall bidding strategy. McGraw-Hill Dodge Reports is one of the more popular services available. The intent of these services is to provide accurate, in-depth project information. Both public and private jobs are advertised in the reports, which convey the status of construction projects from the feasibility stage to the completion of the project.

Another type of public notice, the *Advertisement for Bids*, contains all of the pertinent information that a contractor would need to know in order to pursue a job. The types of information typically included in an advertisement are as follows:

Advertisement for Bids
A public notice, usually published in newspapers, trade magazines and journals, providing information regarding bidding procedures for public projects.

- Project name and description
- Project location
- Owner name and address
- Architect or engineer name, address, and contact information
- Bid due date and time
- Where to access the plans and specs
- Project duration with anticipated start and completion dates
- Bonds required

◆ Restrictions on bidders

◆ Project budget or anticipated price range

ADVERTISEMENT FOR BIDS

Sealed proposals will be received by ABC School District at the Central Administration Building, 1111 Penny Lane, Paso Robles, CA, until 2:00 p.m., April 1, 200__ for a

New Administration Building
(located at 101 Schoolhouse Circle, Paso Robles, CA)

at which time and place, they will be publicly opened and read.

A cashier's check or Bid Bond payable to the ABC School District in an amount not less than five (5) percent of the amount of the bid, but in no event more than $10,000, must accompany the bidder's proposal. Performance and Payment Bonds and evidence of insurance required in the bid documents will be required at the signing of the contract.

Drawings and specifications may be examined at the office of A.B. Architects & Associates, 2000 Ponderosa Street, Atascadero, CA and at the Jackson County Builders Exchange.

Bid documents may be obtained from the Architect upon deposit of $75 per set, which will be refunded in full on the first two sets issued to each general contract bidder submitting a bona fide bid, upon return of documents in good condition within ten days of bid date. Other sets for general contractors, and sets for subcontractors and dealers, may be obtained with the same deposit, which will be refunded as above, less the cost of printing, reproduction, handling, and distribution.

Bids must be submitted on proposal forms furnished by the Architect or copies thereof. Incomplete bid proposals will invalidate the bid proposal and the bid will be rejected and returned to the bidder. The right to accept any bid, or to reject any or all bids and to waive all formalities is hereby reserved by the ABC School District.

A pre-bid conference will be held on Friday, March 15, 200__ at 1:00 p.m. on the site of the proposed project. All bidders are required to attend the conference.

In addition to subscribing to construction news services or depending on public advertisements, the private sector looks to established relationships with the design and business community at large for impending projects and bid opportunities. When I was in business, I made a habit of making monthly phone calls or lunch dates with various business leaders and designers just to scope out opportunities that might be on the horizon. It was not uncommon for an architect with whom I may have had a good working relationship to contact me when he or she got a new design project, giving me a heads-up regarding potential work for the future.

Construction management personnel contact owners and designers on a regular basis to inquire about upcoming projects or the status of projects already on the drawing boards. They also look for news articles and stories about facility expansions and new enterprises emerging, and then follow those leads with letters of interest and company brochures. This is all a part of the marketing effort. Even craftspeople have grown accustomed to being in on the intelligence-gathering effort, especially during slow economic times. Without this effort to keep finding new work, a construction company cannot survive.

The Competition

One of the reasons I always liked the construction business is that I love to compete. I like the idea that I have the opportunity to pit my team's skills, talents, know-how, and ingenuity up against another team's to solve a problem, with one side being declared the victor. When it comes to getting the work in construction, it is very much a high-stakes game. As a matter of fact, the game carries on long after you are announced the winner—all the way through to the end of the project. That will become evident to you when I get to the "keeping score" aspects of construction management. In the end, what will ultimately determine whether you are a winner of this game or not is whether you have met the owner's expectations for price, schedule, and quality—and on top of that, whether you have made a fair profit as planned.

Competitive Bidding Process

The purchasing of construction services is often referred to as procurement. Procurement signifies the purchasing steps that the owner takes to obtain goods and services. The most prevalent procurement method used to buy construction services is competitive bidding. Anyone who has ever gotten work done on their car or had their roof repaired is probably familiar with the competitive bidding process. The old adage is to get three prices on the work and award the job to the lowest bidder.

The competitive bidding process has been used to buy construction for a very long time. It came into play in a big way during World War I and World War II. Government contracts for both commodities and services were numerous during that time, and taxpayers were supplying the revenue to make those purchases. Competitive bidding was implemented to reduce the risk of fraud, favoritism, and undue influence and to reassure taxpayers that their tax dollars were being spent properly.

Although this method has worked fairly well for the construction industry for a long time, satisfaction has begun to wane, and new procurement methods are on the rise. There is a big change taking place in the construction industry, and today there are several ways in which to compete. Let's take a closer look at the options.

·······················
·················· ***NOTE*** ··············· Everyone understands that competition can be a powerful tool for maximizing the value of a dollar. However, construction can no longer be viewed as a simple commodity. Projects are very complex, and the ability to perform, not just low price, should be a compelling criterion for contractor selection. Poor management of the process will result in a delayed project or a project over budget or both, and no one can afford that.

How We Play the Game

How the game is played is really at the discretion of the owner. As discussed in Chapter 2, the owner decides which project delivery method they will employ for their project. Their choice ultimately sets the stage for the competition. There are really only two competition criteria used to determine the winner of the game: price, qualifications, or a combination of both. Each of the project delivery methods is designed around one or more of the criteria.

Competition Criteria and Project Delivery

In traditional design-bid-build, price is the primary criterion used to determine who will win the project. Basically, the contractor who submits the lowest price will be awarded the contract. With construction management (specifically, agency CM), qualifications become the main factor in determining which CM firm will win the competition. And with at-risk CM and design-build, a combination of price and qualifications are considered when selecting the winning team. The following graphic illustrates the connection between project delivery method and selection criteria. Although there are exceptions to these standard practices, for the purposes of this book, I will stick with the more common situations.

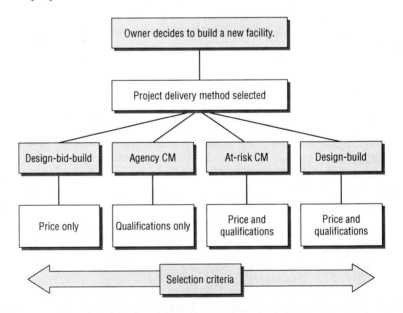

Selection Methods

Once the owner determines which project delivery method and corresponding competition criteria they will use, the framework for the actual selection process has been set. There are basically three selection methods utilized for purchasing construction and construction management services:

- ◆ Low-bid selection
- ◆ Best-value selection (BVS)
- ◆ Qualifications-based selection (QBS)

Each of these selection methods uses a different solicitation instrument to advertise the project. For example, low-bid selection, which is most commonly associated with traditional design-bid-build project delivery, utilizes the Invitation for Bids (IFB). Best-value selection utilizes a *Request for Proposals* (RFP), and qualifications-based selection employs a *Request for Qualifications* (RFQ). These solicitation instruments are what the contractor responds to in an effort to win the project. Each of these instruments is designed to measure the appropriate criteria associated with the analogous selection method. The way in which the contractor prepares to compete for the work differs with each of the methods. Table 3.1 reflects the relationship between the criteria, selection method, and solicitation instrument for all three competitions.

Request for Proposals (RFP)
A solicitation document, written by the owner, requesting pricing and a technical solution for design and/or construction services.

Request for Qualifications
A document issued by the owner prior to an RFP to solicit contractor or design-builder qualifications. The RFQ may be used by the owner to shortlist potential proposers, or it may be used by itself as the final competitive submittal employed in qualifications-based selection.

Table 3.1   Selection Methods

Criteria	Selection Method	Solicitation Instrument
Price only	Low-bid selection	Invitation for Bids (IFB)
Qualifications only	Qualifications-based selection (QBS)	Request for Qualifications (RFQ)
Qualifications and price	Best-value selection (BVS)	Request for Proposals (RFP)

In the past several years, owner preferences have shifted from the traditional low-bid selection method to more frequent use of the best-value selection method (design-build and at-risk CM). However, traditional design-bid-build is still the selection method of choice for a majority of owners.

Each of the selection methods represents a different kind of competition and the steps required to move through the process vary. Because the market is wide open now for any one of these methods to be utilized, it is important to be familiar with each of them.

Low-Bid Selection

The low-bid selection method is all about price, and it is still the most common way for contractors to get their work. It all starts with a set of contract documents. (Contract documents will be discussed in detail in Chapter 4, "The Construction Contract.") The main components of the contract documents are the plans and specifications prepared by a design professional. The plans and specs describe the overall scope of the project in great detail. They are like a set of written instructions for how to build the project. Under this selection method, the plans and specs are classified as being 100 percent complete, meaning that the architect has taken them through the final stages of design before putting them out for bids. In other words, all bidding contractors bid on a single design, making for an "apples versus apples" competition. The object of this game is for all competing contractors to evaluate the plans and come up with a price based on their own unique strategies for doing the work.

responsive bid (or proposal)
A bid or proposal package that meets all of the requirements of the solicitation instrument.

notice to proceed
The owner authorizes the contractor to begin work on a project on a particular day or as soon as possible. This notice is linked to the duration of the project.

Each contractor thoroughly reviews the plans and specs and then prepares an estimate for the cost of the project. The estimate includes all of the materials, labor, equipment, subcontracts, overhead, and profit necessary for the job. The estimates are then compiled into a sealed bid form and are due to the owner on a particular day and at a particular time. The sealed bids are opened and the contractor with the lowest *responsive bid* will be awarded the job. An official contract will then be executed between the contractor and the owner. Shortly thereafter, a *notice to proceed* will be issued by the owner providing the go-ahead for construction. This flow chart identifies each of the steps in the process.

Contractor   **Owner**

Obtain the plans and specs. → Review the plans and specs. → Prepare the estimate. → Tabulate the bid. → Submit the sealed bid. → Owner opens the bids. → Low bidder is announced. → Contract is awarded. → Give notice to proceed. → Construction begins.

Low-bid Selection Method

The low-bid selection method is characterized by a very standardized procedure. All competing contractors pretty much follow the same steps for arriving at their bids. Let's walk through these steps one at a time to get a better sense of the way the game is played.

Obtaining the Plans and Specs   Once the contractor selects a project to bid on, he or she must then get copies of the plans and specs. The Advertisement for Bids or Invitation for Bids typically stipulates how the contractor can obtain the plans and specs. They are normally available from the architect's or engineer's office. There is usually a limit on how many sets of documents may be distributed to each contractor, and a refundable deposit is required to check out the documents. The contractor is often limited to two sets of drawings; the deposit amount varies from as little as $10 to over $150 per set.

Although the number of sets available for each contractor may seem like a minor detail, it is actually quite significant in terms of managing the bid preparation process. Today, most general contractors subcontract out a majority of the project's work to specialty contractors. Each of these subcontractors must also review the plans and specs so they can submit their price quotes to the general contractor. Obviously, two sets of documents are not sufficient to get the job done when there are dozens of subcontractors who will be submitting price quotes to the prime contractors. For this reason, most design firms also place drawings at local plan service centers during the bidding period. These centers are usually managed by various trade associations or builders exchange groups. The subcontractor typically reviews the documents right at the facility and does not check them out, so no deposit is required. Clearly, it is very important for all interested parties to have access to these documents.

Reviewing the Plans and Specs   This is a very important step in the process. Even though the plans and specs have been obtained, no commitment to bid has fully been made. Not until a complete and thorough review of the documents has been made should a commitment be made. There are many factors to consider when deciding whether to proceed with the bid. At this stage, the primary consideration is the quality of the documents themselves. The main purpose of these documents is to convey the overall scope of the project and what exactly it is that the contractor is responsible for. If the scope definition has been communicated well, it will allow the contractor to do a much better job of coming up with an accurate estimate. If the drawings are poor, then the contractor (and the owner, for that matter) is at greater risk and must try to anticipate the gaps while still remaining competitive. Although reputable designers make every effort to produce quality documents, it is virtually impossible to create a perfect set of plans, free from errors or omissions. Generally, the better the set of drawings, the closer the bids will be. Poor sets of documents may result in an erratic set of bids.

....
.... **NOTE** .... In today's very competitive market and with today's complex construction projects, the quality of the plans and specs is of the utmost importance. Quite frankly, the quality is slipping, which is another reason why other selection methods are growing in popularity.

Preparing the Estimate   Although Chapter 6, "Estimating Project Costs," will deal exclusively with this very important function, I want to give you a sense of how it plays into the bidding process. After the contractor scans the plans and specs to get a good feel for the job and decides that indeed he or she will go forward with the bid, a much more thorough examination takes place in order to quantify all the parts, pieces, and people necessary to build the project. Think about planning a vacation. You must come up with all the items you are going to need to have a successful trip: money, passports, reservations, transportation, medications, clothes, toys, beach towels, and so on. You try to anticipate everything you might need. This is similar to doing an estimate—except that with an estimate, the stakes are much, much higher if you forget something!

Tabulating the Bid   Once all the quantities for materials, equipment, subcontractors, and labor are determined and added up, prices are applied and a total cost is calculated. The contractor adds the necessary overhead for managing the project and a profit for the firm's efforts and comes up with a total price for the job. This price is then reviewed by senior management and a final bid is agreed upon. This bid is eventually recorded on the bid proposal document supplied by the owner and goes into a sealed envelope with the job name and contractor name written on the outside of the envelope.

Submitting the Bid   Usually, a member of the contractor team hand-delivers the sealed bid to the location designated in the bid advertisement. It is crucial that the bid be turned in prior to the cut-off time. For example, if bids are due in the architect's office at 2:00 P.M. on a particular date, it must be there by 2:00. If a bid is received at 2:01 P.M. on that day, it is automatically disqualified. Exceptions to this hard-and-fast rule are very rare.

Although one would think that the contractor's bid tabulation would take place long before the due date and time, the reality is that the final bid number is rarely ever available until literally the last minute. I have spent many hours in the bid room of my office on bid day adjusting numbers right up until five minutes before the bid is due. The normal course of events is that the final bid number is called into the contractor's on-site person (often referred to as the runner) at the bid delivery location. The runner then frantically writes the number on the bid document, seals the envelope, and hands it to the official receiving the bids, who then notes the exact time of receipt.

Why Would You Do It This Way?

I know you must be wondering why anyone would put themselves through such a stressful ordeal, but that is exactly how the game is played. Why would someone wait until the last minute to submit their bid? Ah, but remember, this is a low-price competition. Keep in mind that the material suppliers, vendors, and subcontractors are competing against each other as well, and they too are changing their prices right up until the last minute, trying to gain a strategic advantage by discounting their bids at the very last second. If you expect to win at this low-bid game, then you must be prepared to play it the same way as everyone else.

Opening the Bid and Announcing the Low Bidder   The bid opening is when everyone learns who the apparent low bidder or winner is. Sometimes this occurs immediately after the bids are received and is an event that is open to the public. Most public projects require a public bid opening. The bidding contractors typically have a representative present at the opening (often the runner mentioned earlier). The bids are announced and recorded on an official bid tabulation sheet, similar to the one shown here.

Bid Tally Sheet
Project: Administration Building Complex
ABC School District, Paso Robles, CA
Date: April 1, 200__

Bidder	Rank	Base Bid Amount	Addenda Noted #1	Addenda Noted #2	Sub List	Bid Bond	Noncollusion Affidavit	Insurance Confirm	Experience Certification
1. Acme Construction	5	$6,789,900	Yes	Yes	Yes	Yes	Yes	Yes	Yes
2. Basic Builders, Inc.	1	$4,900,000	Yes	Yes	Yes	Yes	Yes	Yes	Yes
3. Quality Plus Contractors	3	$5,678,100	Yes	Yes	Yes	Yes	Yes	Yes	No
4. Build-It-Best Construction	4	$6,100,500	Yes	Yes	Yes	Yes	Yes	Yes	Yes
5. Hammer Head Construction	2	$5,250,850	Yes	Yes	Yes	Yes	Yes	Yes	Yes
6. Superior Construction, Inc.	6	$6,940,000	Yes	Yes	Yes	Yes	Yes	Yes	Yes

NOTE

At a public bid opening, the selection committee is careful to announce the low bidder as the apparent low bidder. The selection committee needs time to review all submitted documentation to determine whether the contractor with the lowest bid actually complied with all of the requirements of the solicitation. Typical additional requirements include bid bonds, noncollusion affidavits, certificates of insurance, and subcontractor lists. If any of the required documents are missing or are found to be in error, then the bid may be deemed nonresponsive and disqualified. In such an event, the job would go to the next lowest responsive bidder.

The Bid-Running Challenge

To give you some sense of just how tense this common procedure actually is, let me describe what the operation was like before the invention of the cell phone. On bid day, I would send someone to the bid location several hours before the bid time and have them commandeer the closest telephone to the bid depository location and guard it with his or her life. We would synchronize all watches with the official clock on-site. Then we would time just how long it took our point person to run (and I mean run, hence the nickname *runner*) from that telephone location to the desk of the person receiving the bids. We would deduct the run minutes from the official bid time and calculate up to the absolute last minute when we must finalize our bid number. Today, with cell phones, the runners can be standing next to the depository desk when they receive the final call. But don't think it is any less stressful (or exhilarating, depending on how you look at it). The final bids are often still determined during the last few minutes of the competition. Anyone who works a bid on bid day has to have nerves of steel because, as stated before, the stakes are very high, as are the opportunities to make a mistake.

Awarding the Contract   Once the smoke clears and the victor is finally determined, the owner and the contractor enter into an official agreement. This usually occurs several days after the bid opening. Several other submittals are often required before signatures actually reach the paper. For example, it is not uncommon for the owner to request a proposed schedule and schedule of values from the contractor before the agreement is signed. These documents become an official part of the contract. (More will be said about these two items in Chapter 7, "Contract Administration.")

Basically, the agreement stipulates the responsibilities of the parties as they embark upon the construction of the project. At this point, the contractor and construction management team are essentially obligated to fulfill the requirements of the contract in accordance with the plans and specs for the agreed-upon price submitted in the bid.

Giving Notice to Proceed   The contract is signed and all of the legal paperwork is in order. However, the actual start of construction does not take place until one more document is executed. That document is an official notice from the owner to proceed with the work. The notice to proceed is an important document in that it starts the clock running for the construction. As previously indicated, time is often a critical factor with any project and there must be an official start and end to the job in order to measure performance, especially when penalties are assessed for late completion.

One of the challenges of the construction manager is to actually be ready to start the job when the official notice to proceed arrives. Remember, at this point we have not thoroughly planned the job, we have simply priced the job in order to win the competition. Having been awarded a contract, we now have to very quickly mobilize a project team and all of the apparatus that goes along with that. Think of it as trying to deploy troops to a new engagement on a moment's notice, and imagine all the planning needed to accomplish that. The average building contractor bids on many jobs a year, not knowing exactly which ones they will win. Once the win is announced, the construction manager must revisit the bid, check the availability of resources, and begin to develop an overall strategic plan, setting the stage for the rest of the game, ensuring an ultimate win in the end.

Beginning Construction   Now it is time for part two of the game to begin! All of the work that it took to get the job in the first place will now be passed on to the construction management team. The estimates that were calculated during the bidding process will now be used as benchmarks for managing the performance throughout the duration of the job. The skills of the entire construction management team will come into play and carry the job to the finish line.

Although competitive low bidding is still the dominant method used to determine contract award in construction, the best-value approach is gaining popularity as the procurement method of choice, even in the public sector. Today approximately 70 percent of all public projects are delivered using a best-value method.

NOTE

Best-Value Selection

This competition is very different from low-bid selection in numerous ways. For one, in this game, the judges consider qualifications as well as price when determining a winner. When applying the best-value selection method to design-build project delivery (which is the most prevalent application of this selection method), the owner may choose to evaluate the design as part of the qualifications criteria. In other words, the design is not 100 percent complete when the competition begins, as it is in design-bid-build. So part of the team's challenge is to design, or complete the design, as a requirement of the competition. As you learned in Chapter 2, design-build project delivery makes use of an interdisciplinary team of contractors and designers and features a single-source responsibility.

best value
Any selection process in which proposals contain both price and qualitative components, and the award is based upon a combination of price and qualitative considerations.

So unlike low-bid selection, where the fundamental premise is to compare price based on a single design (or compare apples with apples), the premise under *best value* may actually compare different designs and their correlated prices (like comparing apples and bananas). It is an absolutely fascinating game to play, in my opinion, and is gaining ground as the selection method of choice in many sectors.

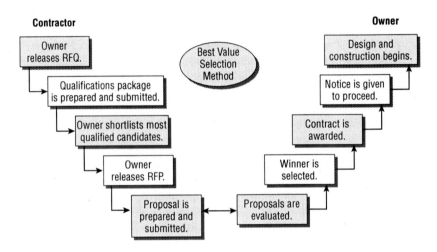

Just as with low-bid competitions, there are several steps to take when playing this game. However, the steps are very different in that the best-value method is not solely a bidding game. Qualifications, which may entail any number of factors, are also solicited, and may even include a technical proposal component consisting of the project design.

Releasing Request for Qualifications (RFQ)   Similar to the low-bid method, the project is typically advertised through all the usual channels. However, the advertisement is not an Invitation for Bids. Instead, it all starts with a Request for Qualifications, followed by a Request for Proposals. (Sometimes the two solicitations are combined.)

Qualification factors commonly include experience, financial and bonding capabilities, record of design and technical excellence, staff expertise, project organization and management plans, quality control plans, and budget and schedule performance. The owner can ask for any criteria they want. They can ask for information on safety records, the use of women- and minority-owned business affiliates, individual team member credentials, and so on.

shortlisting
Narrowing the field of offerors through the selection of the most qualified proposers on the basis of qualifications.

Preparing the Qualifications Package and Shortlisting Candidates   In response to the RFQ, the contractor or design-build team prepares a package that is submitted to the owner by a certain date and time specified in the advertisement. The qualifications packages are received and reviewed by the owner. The owner often puts together a jury panel made up of several representatives and stakeholders to judge the submittals. The panel selects preferably three, but not more than five, of the best-qualified contractors or design-builders in a process called *shortlisting*. The shortlisted competitors are then invited to respond to the Request for Proposals. No pricing is involved at this stage.

Releasing Request for Proposals (RFP)   The RFP, prepared by the owner, is a very important document in that it will represent the legal requirements and criteria for the entire project. The RFP includes information regarding the owner's program, budget, schedule, and other requirements associated with the project. As previously stated, the plans and specs may not be 100 percent complete at the time of the competition under the best-value selection method. Final design schemes and cost proposals are solicited from the shortlisted contractors or design-builders.

Preparing the Proposal   The team of designers, builders, and estimators develops the design for the project along with a corresponding price. The team prepares drawings, written specifications, and sometimes a physical model as their response to the RFP. This package, often referred to as the *technical proposal*, along with the separate *price proposal* constitutes the total response to the RFP. This is a far cry from simply submitting a bid under the low-bid model. As you can imagine, the work involved under this method is much greater and significantly more costly. It is not unusual for contractors and design-build teams to spend $20,000 and even upwards of $200,000 in the preparation of these proposals. Contractors in this game play to win or they don't play at all. That's why the shortlisting component of the competition is so critical. Limiting the competition to only three or four opponents increases your odds and makes the investment worthwhile.

technical proposal
The part of a design-build proposal that contains the conceptual design for the project. May also include information regarding schedule, team makeup, and overall management plan for the project.

price proposal
The part of a design-build proposal that stipulates the price at which the design-builder will provide the design and construction services necessary to complete the project.

Submitting the Proposal   Although there is a specified date and time for the receipt of the proposals, there is not an immediate opening of the proposals. As you might imagine, it takes time for the jury to review all of the materials submitted by the participants. The initial review period can be two weeks or more. It is not unusual for the owner to request the design-build teams to make in-person presentations to the selection committee before making a final contract award. This way, the panel has the opportunity to ask for clarification on any items that are not clear concerning the proposals.

Evaluating the Proposals and Selecting the Winner   Under the best-value selection method, an evaluation panel or jury is appointed by the owner. This panel usually consists of individuals who will ultimately be associated with the new facility. For example, if the project were an elementary school, you might find a school board member, the principal, a teacher or two, the maintenance supervisor, and the director of facilities on the jury.

There are numerous ways in which to evaluate the responses to the RFP. The proposals are evaluated on the basis of quality, functional efficiency, aesthetics, price, and other factors. The technical proposal components and the price component are scored separately.

weighted criteria
An evaluation method used in best-value selection in which maximum point values are assessed for qualitative and price components of a proposal. Contract award is based upon the highest total points earned.

One of the most common methods for scoring the technical proposals is called *weighted criteria*. Basically, the owner ranks each of the criteria relative to its importance to the project. Then each jury member assesses a score to each team for each criterion. The weighted criteria are multiplied by the score for each factor and a total score is calculated.

Table 3.2 illustrates how an evaluation matrix with criteria and weights works. When price is part of the competition, a similar scoring occurs relative to price. The price score and the weighted criteria score are added together and the proposal with the highest score wins the competition.

Table 3.2   Weighted Criteria Evaluation Matrix

Best Value Proposal	Team A		Team B		Team C	
	Score	Points	Score	Points	Score	Points
Design Solution (Weight 10)	4	40	3	30	5	50
Financial Capability (Weight 8)	3	24	4	32	5	40
Energy Efficiency (Weight 6)	5	30	4	24	3	18
Management Plan (Weight 10)	5	50	4	40	4	40
TOTAL POINTS		144		126	148 WINNER	

Scoring: 5 = Excellent; 4 = Good; 3 = Fair; 2 = Poor

Awarding the Contract   The winner of the best-value competition enters into a contract for two things: the design of the project and the construction of the project. This is quite different from low-bid selection. Whereas in low-bid the plans and specs are part of the contract, with best-value the plans and specs are nonexistent or not complete yet, and therefore cannot govern the contract at this point. What does govern the work of the contract are the requirements of the RFP, the technical proposal, and the price proposal. Just as with the low-bid process, several days usually pass before a contract is actually signed.

Giving Notice to Proceed   The notice to proceed document under best-value selection is very similar to that issued under low-bid selection. The difference is that with best-value selection, the notice is to start the design process followed by the construction.

Beginning Design and Construction   Some design has to be completed before construction can begin. But as you learned in Chapter 2, a portion of the design and construction may be overlapped in order to speed up the entire process.

Although the steps set out above describe the best-value selection method when used with design-build, keep in mind that best-value may also be used with design-bid-build project delivery. When used with design-bid-build, design is not a factor in the competition. The design is already complete and presented in the RFP. The participating contractors compete on qualifications and price only; design is not one of the criteria being judged.

NOTE

Qualifications-Based Selection

There are no limitations to using qualifications-based selection (QBS) for construction in the private market. Basically, any private owner could decide to ask a number of contractors to compete on qualifications only. However, our society is so accustomed to low-bid selection for construction that QBS is not a common occurrence in the building industry, even though most architects and engineers have always been selected this way. For public projects, there's actually a statute that prevents architects and engineers from competing on price. The Brooks Act (1972) requires that qualifications-based selection be used by federal design and construction agencies to purchase architecture and engineering services. Price quotations are not a consideration in the selection process. Prices are negotiated after the selection has been made on the basis of demonstrated competence and qualifications.

The qualifications-based selection process is often utilized for agency CM and design-build project delivery on a regular basis. There are some jurisdictions that even allow this method to be used for public projects. When it is used, the process basically follows the first steps outlined earlier under the best-value approach, except that price is not a factor. In other words, a Request for Qualifications is advertised, with proposers responding with qualifications packages. An evaluation matrix similar to that shown for the best-value matrix in Table 3.2 is used to evaluate the competitors, with the high scorer winning.

You Get What You Pay For

The presumption behind the Brooks Act is that we don't want professionals who are responsible for the public safety to be the low bidder. After all, you wouldn't select your doctor based on the lowest price, would you? Based on the same logic, you would not select your architect on the basis of being the cheapest practitioner. On the other hand, construction has historically been viewed as a commodity, so competition based on price seemed appropriate. But today, construction requires skills far beyond the trades—it requires professional management to handle all of the regulatory bureaucracy, entitlement, contract administration procedures, procurement, contract negotiations, estimating, scheduling, cost control, quality assurance, safety mandates, and so on. In my opinion, construction management is just as much a profession as architecture and engineering, and qualifications should also be the primary discriminator.

NOTE   Qualifications-based selection is sometimes called direct selection. Basically, an owner simply decides that they want to work with you because of your reputation and past performance. This is a position that many contractors strive for: an opportunity to be recognized and selected for the quality and professionalism of their work.

Making the Bid/No Bid Decision

As you can probably tell, the task of finding and getting work in the construction industry is an ongoing challenge and takes a lot of effort. Regardless of which type of competition that contractors engage in, the decision to bid or not to bid is not one to be made lightly. A great deal of time and effort is spent in preparing a detailed estimate or a technical proposal with no guarantee of winning the job.

Finding jobs to bid on or propose is one thing, but deciding to invest the time, money, and effort it takes to win them is another. Numerous factors must be weighed before you go forward with the effort. There are some jobs that you do not want to get. The construction manager must discern which jobs are worth going after.

There are many motivations for bidding work. The most obvious has already been stated: to stay in business. But just as in any competition, it is best to pick your battles wisely. Table 3.3 outlines a number of common factors that contractors consider before making the decision to bid or not bid on a particular project.

Table 3.3   Making the Decision to Bid

Factor	Considerations
Who the owner is	Some owners are known for being easy to get along with and others are known for being difficult. Those who have a reputation for being controlling, highly litigious, or difficult to please have a harder time getting contractors to bid their work.
Who the architect is	There are architects who are noted for the quality of their plans and specs and architects who are noted for poor quality documents. Contractors stay away from architects with reputations for producing poor quality plans and specs.
Location of the project	If the project is located close to the contractor's office, this usually gives him a strategic advantage. He is familiar with the local labor market, and job site overhead can be kept to a minimum. If the project is far away, then the expense to run the job goes up and the labor market is unknown and therefore a higher risk.
Present workload	The contractor's workload always has an impact on when to bid and when not to bid. When there is plenty of backlog, contractors are pickier regarding which jobs they go after. On the other hand, when work is slow, contractors will usually bid on jobs that they would otherwise stay away from just to keep their operations going.
Technical aspects of the job	The contractor has to assess her technical expertise and ability to manage and supervise the work relative to the technical complexity of the work itself. Whenever contractors decide to bid on work with materials, equipment, or systems that are new to them, they take on greater risk.
Is it a high-profile project?	There are reasons to take on a high-profile job and reasons to stay away from them. Obviously, if the contractor wants to increase his own visibility and reputation, taking on a high-profile project is one way to do that. In other circumstances, such visibility may have a downside, especially on a project that is controversial to begin with.

Table 3.3   Making the Decision to Bid *(continued)*

Factor	Considerations
Type of project	Contractors often become specialists in certain types of work and scout for those kinds of jobs specifically, wherever they may be located.
Size of project	Contractors are generally limited as to the size of the project that they can go after because of their bonding capacity. Larger companies are attracted to the larger projects. Smaller companies look for the smaller projects.

The bidding process is getting more competitive and profit margins are getting thinner. For this reason, the marketing effort in construction is ever increasing. Companies are positioning themselves as reputable leaders in the industry and pressing for opportunities to negotiate directly with owners, bypassing the very expensive and risky bidding process altogether—and it is working. As owners become more interested in high-performance results over low price, many construction firms are increasing the percentage of work performed under negotiated contracts versus low-bid contracts.

A Final Note

The primary construction management function associated with getting the work, regardless of which selection method is used, is the estimating function, which will be discussed in great detail in Chapter 6. In my opinion, this is probably the single most important function in the process. Without good estimating skills, a construction company won't be in business very long. Estimates that are consistently too high will result in a lack of work, and estimates that are consistently too low will result in jobs losing money—and either scenario will eventually lead to the company going out of business. It is no wonder that one of the highest ranking positions in construction management is Senior Estimator. These positions often lead to a Director or Vice President position in the construction firm.

Terms to Know

Advertisement for Bids

best value

closed bid

Invitation for Bids

notice to proceed

open bid

prequalification

price proposal

Request for Proposals

Request for Qualifications

responsive bid (or proposal)

shortlisting

technical proposal

weighted criteria

Review Questions

1. Why is open bidding required on public projects?

2. Name a tool used to reduce the number of bidders on a public project and increase the quality of the contractor pool.

3. What is the purpose of a labor and materials payment bond?

4. Identify the notice document that informs the public of upcoming construction projects funded with taxpayer dollars.

5. Name the three selection methods used to buy construction services and identify the solicitation instrument used for each one.

6. Which procurement method is the most commonly used today and what is the selection criteria used to determine the winner?

7. What is the name of the official document that the owner uses to notify the contractor to start construction?

8. Name the two primary selection criteria categories considered when using the best-value method.

9. Describe how the weighted criteria evaluation process works.

10. List at least three factors that are commonly considered before deciding to bid on a construction job.

Chapter 4

The Construction Contract

In This Chapter

- The various documents included in the contract
- How the contract documents impact the construction
- The standard protocols used when preparing the contract documents
- The various types of contracts used for construction

Wow—you survived the bidding competition and were announced the winner. Great! Now what? Well, now it's time to look closely at what exactly you're accountable for. What you're accountable for is outlined in the contract, but what makes up the contract in construction is a little more complicated than, say, the contract for buying lawn service. A construction contract is an agreement between the owner and the contractor and is enforceable by law. Generally, the contractor agrees to perform a service for some consideration or payment. There are many documents that make up the construction contract.

Up until now, I have been referring to the "plans and specs" as the contract documents. The contractor is responsible for delivering the project in accordance with the plans and specs. However, it is time to get into the nitty-gritty of exactly what is meant by that common term. This chapter examines all of the procedural and administrative details of the construction contract.

The consequences of failing to understand the obligations of the contract are significant, and every construction manager must be completely familiar with what constitutes the contract for construction. The bottom line is that every aspect of the project will be controlled by these documents and the work of the contractor will basically be judged by them.

The Contract Documents

The contract for construction is made up of much more than just a simple agreement form. Although an agreement form is eventually executed between the owner and the contractor, there are many more documents that direct the construction of the project and responsibilities of the parties. All of these documents taken together make up the construction contract and they are referred to as the *contract documents*.

Under most circumstances, the contractor is not involved in the actual design of the project. The contract documents are the medium through which the architect or engineer communicates the design intent to the contractor. Therefore, you can certainly understand just how important it is that the documents be as complete and free from error as possible.

There are two major components to the contract documents: the drawings and the project manual. The drawings basically define the quantity of the work—the length, the width, the area, the volume, and so on. The project manual, which includes the specifications, defines the quality of the work. The construction team must fully familiarize itself with these documents before bidding a job and should know them inside out before proceeding with construction. The components of the contract documents are discussed in detail here.

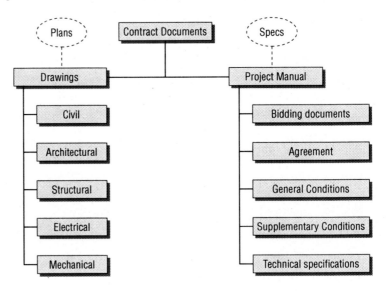

The Drawings

If I were to choose the most basic skill necessary for anyone involved in construction, it would be the ability to read construction drawings. Anyone who has ever built a house is probably very familiar with the consequences of failing to understand exactly what is in those darn drawings. They are filled with symbols and abbreviations generally unknown to the public at large, and many of the lines on the sheets are meaningless to the layman. Yet every one of those symbols, abbreviations, and lines represents an instruction to the builder.

The drawings are a graphical set of directives prepared by the architects and engineers in order to communicate the wishes and desires of the owner. They are the single most important communication tool employed by the industry to convey the work of the contract. They are critical to the process and their quality is of utmost importance.

Prior to the Renaissance, the master builders communicated their design intent by building models and drawing sketches to help explain what they wanted the builders to do. During the Renaissance, architects decided that they could simply make drawings and write instructions on paper to communicate their desires. The process went from the idea of showing the builders how the work was to be done with a model to telling them how to do it with plans and specs.

Today, models are being reintroduced to supplement building plans with the use of 3D and even 4D (4D includes time) computer modeling. These are very sophisticated programs. The fact is that buildings and structures are so complex today that it is almost impossible to figure out all of the intricacies of the building process in a two-dimensional mode. In most of life, history has a way of repeating itself, and design and construction communication is no exception. I predict that, in the not too distant future, two-dimensional plans will be completely obsolete and electronic modeling will become the communication tool of choice for all building projects. But, in the meantime, it is important for anyone interested in construction management to understand what exactly constitutes a set of construction drawings.

Drawing Production

Back in the old days, the plans or drawings were often called "blueprints." That term came from the way in which documents were printed: produced by hand using lead pencils or ink and reproduced using blueprint machines. The paper used to reproduce the drawings was actually blue paper and all of the lines on the paper printed in white. The printing process used today produces blue lines on white paper and the correct term for the drawings is actually "bluelines." However, many people still refer to the drawings as blueprints.

Most drawings today are actually produced electronically using computer-aided design and drafting software known as CADD, and the prints are produced on digital plotters using multiple ink colors. So the expression "back to the drawing board" is actually passé, because when redesign must take place, today it actually means back to the computer.

Drawing Size

Drawings can range in size from a three- or four-sheet set used to build a simple house, up to a monstrous set of over 100 sheets required to build a magnificent structure such as the Cathedral of Our Lady of Angels in Los Angeles. Obviously, the bigger the project, the bigger the set of drawings.

NOTE

A single drawing sheet can range in size from 24˝ × 36˝ to 36˝ × 48˝ to even larger sizes. Trying to manhandle some of the larger drawing sets can actually be physically challenging.

One of the great advantages of CADD is the capability to manage all of the drawings electronically. Today, a 100-sheet set of drawings weighing forty pounds or more can fit on one CD-ROM disk and be carried in your pocket.

The users of these drawings (contractors, subcontractors, and vendors) must be able to find the information that they are looking for as easily and quickly as possible. Standardization of the documents facilitates ease of use, and helps maintain a consistent quality of graphic communication. Therefore, standard protocols have been established for organizing drawing sets and for organizing each sheet.

Organization of the Drawings

As you can imagine, a lot of information must be conveyed to the construction team when trying to build a complex facility. Although the architect is the lead designer on a building project, and is accountable for providing the architectural design for the facility, he or she does not do all of the work alone. Various engineers are hired by the architect to assist with specialized areas of design, such as civil engineering, structural, mechanical, and electrical design. The architect is in charge of coordinating all of these efforts and is responsible for compiling the final set of design documents. Therefore, the drawing set is organized by the various types of designs required to fully communicate the extent of the construction (such as civil drawings, architectural drawings, structural drawings, and so on) and they are numbered accordingly for easy reference.

perspective drawing
A three-dimensional drawing representing width, length, and height of a structure.

Most sets of drawings start with a cover sheet providing general information about the project. For example, the project owner is noted, as are the architect, the engineers, and sometimes even the financier. The location of the project is often noted on the cover sheet as well, using vicinity maps and subdivision plats. Sometimes a *perspective drawing* of the building is also shown on the cover sheet. After the cover sheet, it is common to order the drawings in accordance with a standard protocol. That standard protocol calls for the civil drawings to be placed directly behind the cover, with architectural, structural, mechanical, and electrical drawings to follow.

Civil drawings   These drawings are usually prepared by a civil engineer working with the architect and describe all items of work associated with the site. The site work includes such things as grading, demolition, excavation, site utilities, streets, curbs, and gutters and their details. Sometimes landscaping is also included under this section. The civil drawings are typically numbered as C1, C2, C3, and so on.

Architectural drawings   The architectural drawings are prepared by the architect and usually constitute the bulk of the set. They describe the overall aesthetics of the facility, including project size, shape, and appearance. Detailed information regarding dimensions, materials, and quality are graphically depicted through the architectural drawings. The architectural work includes such things as floor plans, exterior elevations, and sections; door, window, and finish schedules; and architectural details. These drawings are numbered A1, A2, A3, and so on.

Structural drawings   The structural drawings are prepared by a structural engineer working as a consultant to the architect. Coordination between the architecture and the structure is very important. Good synchronization here can help avoid expensive conflicts down the road during construction. The structural drawings identify the major components making up the structural frame of the building, such as columns, beams and girders. The structural engineer also provides the structural calculations, which analyze the vertical loads as well as lateral loads consisting of wind and earthquake loads. These drawings are typically numbered S1, S2, S3, and so on.

Mechanical drawings   The architect will hire a mechanical engineer to prepare the mechanical drawings. The mechanical work splits between two major support components for any building—the plumbing and the HVAC (heating, ventilation, and air conditioning). The plumbing portion of the drawings typically includes information describing the installation of water lines, sewer lines, and gas lines. The HVAC portion of the drawings covers ductwork, air handlers, compressors, and other equipment associated with climate control. Fire protection can also be included with the mechanical drawings. The mechanical engineer also provides heating and cooling calculations used to determine the required capacity of the heating and cooling equipment and the requisite energy compliance forms to demonstrate that the building complies with energy-efficiency requirements. The mechanical sheets are numbered M1, M2, M3, and so on.

Electrical drawings   The electrical engineer, working as a consultant to the architect, prepares the electrical drawings. The electrical work includes all of the rough wiring, transformers, and panel boxes, as well as receptacles, switches, and light fixtures. Communications and computer wiring are also included in the electrical drawings. The electrical engineer provides calculations to determine the proper wire size, conduit size, and over-current protection device (fuse or circuit breaker) capacity. These drawings are numbered E1, E2, E3, and so on.

NOTE   Although the construction manager is not expected to be an expert technician in all facets of the construction, he or she must be able to interpret and understand all of the work described in the different drawings. This is no easy task, and it can take years of experience before one becomes knowledgeable in all areas.

Types of Drawings

As previously mentioned, fundamental to construction and construction management is the ability to read and interpret the plans. Within every set of plans there are specific types of drawings that help the reader obtain a better understanding of the construction. Because so much information must be communicated to explain how the structure is to be built, each layer of drawings becomes more and more specific, emphasizing greater detail. There are four basic types of drawings that can be used to communicate the intent of the design and construction. They are plans, elevations, sections, and details.

Plans   A plan view is a horizontal "cut" or slice through the entire building. Every set of construction drawings includes at least one plan view of the building. That's why we often refer to the drawings as plans. Often there are several different plan views incorporated into the drawings. For example, foundation plans, floor plans, and framing plans are common elements of a quality set of drawings. Most plans are drawn using a $1/4''$ scale, but some large buildings must be drawn at a $1/8''$ scale in order to fit on the drawing sheet.

NOTE   A $1/4''$ scale means that every $1/4''$ measured on the drawings represents $1'$ in true dimension. Because there are 12 inches in a foot, the building will actually be 48 times (4×12) larger than the drawing itself. The architect uses a special measuring rule called an architect's scale to lay out drawings.

Elevations   Elevations depict what the building or structure looks like from the outside. All four sides of the building are typically shown in elevation. They are usually drawn to a ¼″ scale depending on the size of the project and the size of the sheet being utilized. Again, sometimes a ⅛″ scale might need to be employed. The elevations are often named according to which direction the exterior wall faces. The South Elevation of the building is the wall that faces south.

Sections   Section drawings are used to present a deeper understanding of the design at certain key spots in the plan or elevation. A section drawing represents a vertical "cut" through the building from top to bottom. There are usually several section drawings included in a set of plans. They are very helpful in trying to visualize exactly how all of the parts and pieces come together at a particular point in the structure. These drawings are often drawn using a ½″ scale, but may need to be downsized to a ¼″ scale if room on the sheet is limited.

Details   Detail drawings depict portions of the building "blown up" in scale to help explain finer elements of the design. They are drawn very large, comparatively speaking, utilizing 1″, 1-½″, or even 3″ scale. They are particularly helpful for viewing connections, intersections, special features, or tricky construction details.

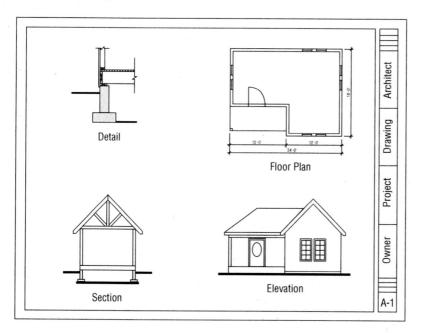

Again, given the amount of information that must be conveyed in these documents, it is not unusual for there to be discrepancies between the various levels of drawings. As a matter of fact, it is so common that specific guidelines are often established in the General Conditions to the contract provided in the project manual to address the problem.

Typically, the more-detailed drawings take precedence over the more-general drawings if there is a conflict between the drawings. In other words, the detail drawings take precedence over the sections and the sections take precedence over the plans. For example, a foundation plan might indicate that the concrete footings are 24 inches wide and 10 inches deep. But the wall section shows that the footings are 24 inches wide by only 8 inches deep. The wall section would take precedence over the foundation plan and the footing would be presumed to be only 8 inches deep. However, it should be noted that the specifications take precedence over the drawings altogether.

Obviously, the opportunities for error in interpreting these documents are numerous. It is the construction manager's job to try to eliminate the conflicts before the construction ever starts. Unfortunately, the pace of the work after winning the contract award is usually fast and furious, and the project team must be constantly on the lookout for such discrepancies in the plans and specs in order to avoid costly mistakes.

Project Manual

The project manual is the second part of the contract documents. This is the part that is often referred to as the "specs." Although the technical specifications do make up the bulk of this manual, a number of other documents are included in the book. The project manual contains all the written construction documents about the structure to be built. Those documents include the bidding requirements, contracting requirements, and written specifications for every detail of the building.

Whereas the project plans provide the graphic instructions for the builder, the project manual provides the written instructions. These instructions deal with many of the "red tape" or administrative items associated with the building project. And, believe me, there is a lot of red tape involved when building a construction project.

Understanding, organizing, coordinating, and managing all of this red tape is actually a primary function of the construction manager. And remember, the ability to fulfill the requirements addressed in these documents and in the drawings is what will be judged if there is a problem on the job. There are typically four primary sections in the project manual:

- ◆ Bidding documents
- ◆ General Conditions
- ◆ Supplemental Conditions
- ◆ Technical specifications

Let's take a look at each of these sections and consider how they relate to the construction manager's job.

Bidding Documents

The first section of the project manual provides information regarding the bidding process. There are four documents included under this heading:

Advertisement or Invitation for Bids   This item usually appears at the very beginning of the project manual. The information found within these documents was covered in Chapter 3, "How We Get the Work." Basically, the IFB acts as a notice to interested parties regarding the project and the requirements for bidding.

Instructions to Bidders   This section includes specific instructions regarding the bidding process and goes into much more detail than the Invitation for Bids. Although many of these instructions are pretty standard, it is always wise for the construction manager or estimator to review the document thoroughly. In addition to the basic information regarding the project, the Instructions to Bidders also includes:

◆ Procedures for submitting questions and obtaining clarifications regarding the contract documents.

◆ Information regarding *addendum* receipt and inclusion as part of the contract documents.

◆ Rules concerning bid submission including bond requirements, bid opening, rejection of bids, and notification of successful bidder. Rules pertaining to bid withdrawal would also be disclosed.

◆ The expectations for post-bid deliverables including such items as the schedule of values, cash flow projections, the construction schedule, payment and performance bonds, or any other documentation requested by the owner prior to the signing of the contract.

addendum
A change or addition to the contract documents issued after the documents have been released but before the bids are due.

Bid forms   The actual forms that need to be filled out when submitting the bid are included in this section of the manual. The bid or proposal form includes information regarding the bid price, completion date, subcontractors, alternate pricing if requested, and receipt of addendum. Some projects require specific verification regarding special requirements. For example, the project may require Minority and Women's Business Enterprise participation. In this case, an MWBE compliance certification form would be included with the bid forms.

Agreement form   A copy of the contract form is also included in the project manual. This is the document that will actually be signed by the parties after the contract is awarded. There are different types of contracts that may be executed, and the builder must know which one is going to be used. The various contract types are discussed later in the chapter.

General Conditions

The General Conditions is one of the most important documents associated with the contract for construction. In essence, it sets the ground rules for the playing of the game. The responsibilities of each of the parties are clearly delineated and the specific terms of the contract are defined in this section of the manual. It is vital that the contractor know exactly what is contained in this section. In the following, I identify the standard clauses that typically appear in the General Conditions and give a brief description of each:

General Provisions   This section provides fundamental definitions for the contract, the work, and the drawings and specifications. It also clarifies the ownership, use, and overall intent of the contract documents.

Owner Responsibilities   This section stipulates the information and services that the owner is required to supply. It also identifies the owner's right to stop the work and the owner's right to carry out the work.

Contractor Responsibilities   This section lays out the obligations of the contractor regarding construction procedures and supervision of the work, labor and materials, warranty, taxes, permits, fees and notices, schedules, samples and product data, and cleaning up.

Administration of the Contract   This section assigns duties to the architect for the administration of the contract. Specific clauses dealing with the architect's responsibility for visiting the site and making inspections are included. The section also addresses how requests for additional time and claims and disputes will be handled.

Subcontracts and Subcontractor Relations   This section deals with the awarding of subcontracts to specialty contractors by the general contractor for portions of the work.

Construction by Owner or Others   This clause deals with the owner's right to perform some of the construction work with his or her own forces or to award separate contracts to other parties besides the general contractor.

Changes in the Work   This section explains how changes are to be authorized and processed. This is a very important clause in the contract because changes in the work are one of the areas of greatest contention between the owner and the contractor.

Time and Schedule Requirements   Time is always an important factor on any project. This section defines project startup, progress, and completion relative to the specific project schedule. It also addresses issues associated with delays and extensions of time to the contract.

Payments and Completion   This section is very important because it identifies how the contractor will be paid. It specifies how applications for progress payments are to be made. It also deals with the withholding of payments and failure to pay issues.

Protection of Persons and Property   This section addresses concerns for safety of both the owner's property and the people on the project. It deals with specific issues such as the handling of hazardous materials and emergencies, as well as overall safety programs and requirements.

Insurance and Bonds   This section deals with insurance and bonding requirements of the parties.

Uncovering and Correction of Work   This clause has to do with acceptance of the work by the architect (as agent of the owner). It stipulates how and when the contractor is responsible for uncovering and/or correcting any work deemed unacceptable.

Miscellaneous Provisions   This section addresses various miscellaneous matters such as typical successors and assigns issues, tests and inspections, and interest on delayed payments.

Termination or Suspension of the Contract   There are reasons for terminating a contract and either party has the right to do so under certain conditions. This section deals with the conditions under which parties may terminate or suspend the contract.

There are many standard General Conditions that have been developed by various trade and professional organizations. The most common among these is the General Conditions published by the American Institute of Architects, AIA Document A201. The advantage to using a standard form such as the A201 is that most contractors are already familiar with it and it has been tested in the courts.

NOTE

Supplemental Conditions

The Supplemental Conditions or Special Conditions usually deal with matters that are project specific. In other words, they are considerations beyond the scope of the standard General Conditions and serve as an augmentation to the terms laid out in the General Conditions. Examples of some project-specific information that may appear in these conditions are listed here.

- Soils and soil-testing information provided by the owner
- Survey information provided by the owner
- Materials or other services provided by the owner
- Job signage requirements

- Traffic control and pedestrian safety requirements
- Phasing or special schedule requirements
- Requirements for security
- Temporary facilities and sanitation requirements

Technical Specifications

Technical specifications make up the bulk of the project manual. Whereas the bidding documents, General Conditions, and Supplemental Conditions deal primarily with the administrative aspects of the contract, the specifications deal more directly with the construction. They are used in conjunction with the plans and describe the detail that cannot be conveyed by the graphic depictions alone. The specifications identify the requirements of the project relative to the labor, materials, equipment, and procedures needed to accomplish the work of the contract. The plans and specifications taken together are intended to aid in pricing the job as well as performing the work. The primary purpose of the specifications is to clarify and describe the following aspects of the job:

- Quality of materials
- Standard of workmanship
- Methods of installation and erection
- Quality control and quality assurance procedures

Between the drawings and the specifications, every material and every installation that goes into building a project must be identified and specified. That includes everything from the concrete and steel in the foundation to the smallest knob on a drawer front. As you might imagine, this task is a massive undertaking. Fortunately, an organizational structure has been developed to assist designers and contractors in keeping track of all of this very important information and presenting it in a logical order. The information is organized into a master format consisting of 16 standard divisions. This format was developed by the Construction Specification Institute.

Construction Specification Institute

The Construction Specification Institute, or CSI, was founded in 1948. The CSI serves all of the major disciplines involved in the building design and construction industry. Although they have developed many tools to assist the industry, one of the most important is the specifications organizational structure known as the MasterFormat.

The MasterFormat is the most widely used system for project manuals and specifications. This format also becomes the reference framework for construction product information, market data, and pricing databases. This standardized format for specifications fosters clearer communication among designers and builders and all the other project players as well. That makes it much easier to meet the owner's requirements for time, budget, and quality, which is the whole point to begin with.

CSI MasterFormat

This guide is used by virtually every practitioner in the design and construction business. All work in construction is organized and managed under this format. It is not only used for organizing and communicating design data and information, but is also used to organize estimates and track project costs. The Master-Format is something that every construction manager must be familiar with. The 16 standard divisions of the MasterFormat are listed next. I have also identified a few examples under each category to help you recognize the work of each division.

Division 1: General Requirements   Includes overhead items directly associated with the project such as job trailers, supervision, field testing, security fencing, and project clean-up.

Division 2: Site Work   Includes items such as site demolition, erosion control, grading, excavation, site utilities, tunneling, fences, gates, irrigation, and landscaping.

Division 3: Concrete   Includes such items as cast-in-place concrete, concrete forms, reinforcing steel, concrete finishing, and concrete curing.

Division 4: Masonry   Includes items such as brick, concrete block, glass masonry units, stone, and mortar.

Division 5: Metals   Includes items such as steel beams, girders, columns, ornamental iron, metal decking, and pipe railings.

Division 6: Wood and Plastics   Includes items such as rough carpentry, interior trim, cabinets, shelving, and stairs.

Division 7: Thermal and Moisture Protection   Includes items such as insulation, roofing, waterproofing, gutters, downspouts, flashing, and caulking.

Division 8: Doors and Windows   Includes metal doors and frames, wood doors, overhead doors, storefronts, windows, skylights, and glass.

Division 9: Finishes   Includes items such as drywall, paint, acoustic ceiling, carpet, wall coverings, and tile.

Division 10: Specialties   Includes items such as flagpoles, toilet partitions, fire extinguishers, and bathroom mirrors.

Division 11: Equipment   Includes items such as kitchen appliances, range hoods, medical equipment, and recreational equipment.

Division 12: Furnishings   Includes items such as draperies, art, murals, bookcases, pews and benches, stadium seating, plants, and planters.

Division 13: Special Construction   Includes items such as swimming pools, tennis courts, kennels, and security systems.

Division 14: Conveying Systems   Includes items such as elevators and escalators.

Division 15: Mechanical   Includes plumbing, heating, ventilating, and air conditioning items such as water piping, waste piping, plumbing fixtures, valves, furnaces, air handlers, compressors, and duct work.

Division 16: Electrical   Includes items such as electrical wiring, transformers, light fixtures, computer wiring, communications, sound, and video.

CSI Numbering System

The CSI utilizes a five-digit numbering system for organizing various work items under each division. The first two digits represent the division of work. The next three numbers represent what is referred to as broad scope and/or narrow scope divisions or levels. Here is an example:

Division 4: Masonry

04000	General Information		
04200	Masonry Units		
		04210	Clay Masonry Units
		04220	Concrete Masonry Units
		04270	Glass Masonry Units

The CSI system is very sophisticated. Some architects make full use of the system when putting together their project manuals and others may limit the level of detail provided. Regardless of the extent, knowledge of the CSI organizational framework will help the construction management team quickly and easily access the information they need, when they need it.

Section 06100
ROUGH CARPENTRY

PART 1 – GENERAL
1.01 Description
A. Section Includes: Provision of all lumber, framing, rough hardware and blocking as indicated in the contract drawings.
B. Related Sections:
1. Section 03100 – Concrete Formwork
2. Section 06195 – Prefabricated Wood I-Joists

1.02 References
A. Requirements of GENERAL CONDITIONS and DIVISION 1 apply to all Work in this Section.
B. Published Specifications standards, tests, or recommended methods of trade, industry, or governmental organizations apply to Work in this Section.

1.03 Submittals
A. Shop drawings of all specially fabricated rough hardware.

1.04 Product Delivery, Storage and Handling
A. Provide proper facilities for storage of materials to prevent damage to edges, ends, and surfaces.
B. Keep materials dry. Where necessary, stack materials off ground on level flat forms, fully protected from weather.

1.05 Job Conditions
A. Environmental Requirements: Maintain uniform moisture content of lumber at not more than 19 percent before, during, and after installation.
B. Sequencing, Scheduling: Coordinate details with other Work supporting, adjoining, or fastening to rough carpentry Work.

PART 2 – PRODUCTS
2.01 Material
A. Rough Carpentry
1. Sills on Concrete: Foundation grade redwood or pressure-treated Douglas Fir.
2. Lumber: Studs, plates, beams, joists, posts, and blocking – Douglas Fir No. 1.
B. Rough Hardware
1. Nails: Common wire, typical. At exposed conditions and with pressure-treated lumber, use hot-dipped, galvanized nails.

2.02 Source Quality Control
A. Lumber shall bear grade trademark or be accompanied by certificate of compliance of appropriate grading agency.
B. Plywood shall bear APA grade trademark.

PART 3 – EXECUTION
3.01 Examination
A. Examine areas to receive rough carpentry Work and verify that spacing, direction, and details of supports are correct to accommodate installation of blocking, backing, furring, and nailers.

3.02 Installation
A. Studs, Joists, Beams, and Posts: Install all members true to line. No wood shingle shims are permitted. Place joists with crown up; maximum $1/4$-inch crown permitted.
B. Nail joints in accordance with applicable requirements of the CBC Table 23A-II-B-I unless otherwise shown or specified.

3.03 Field Quality Control
A. The Owner's Testing Agency shall:
1. Inspect erected timber framing as required to establish conformity of Work with Drawings.

The specification sample provided illustrates a very simple area of work for a very simple project. Compound the level of detail in this sample about 10 to 20 times and you might get a sense of just how much information the construction manager *must* pay attention to in order to ensure that the project will be built in accordance with the contract documents, on time, and within budget.

Many of the directives posted in the specifications, especially those associated with the execution of the work, are standard operating procedures for experienced contractors. However, the specifications establish the expectations for quality and contractor performance, and all work will be measured against them. It is an awesome challenge, to say the least. If you had any doubts about how demanding a construction manager's job is, this close look at what constitutes the contract for construction should dispel them!

All of this detail, along with the drawings, General Conditions, and Supplemental Conditions, make up the part of the contract that tells us "how" we are to do the project. But there is another piece to the contract that addresses the "how much" element of the agreement. This important component can be structured in a number of ways, and you need to understand all of them.

Contract Types

Just as the owner makes the decision regarding the type of project delivery to be employed, the owner also determines which contract will be utilized for the project. Generally, which form is used depends upon the type of project and the amount of risk that the owner is willing to accept. It is important that the construction manager be familiar with each type. There are four basic types of construction contracts: lump sum, cost-plus-fee, guaranteed maximum price, and unit cost. All of them contain the standard sections that I described earlier; however, they differ in two fundamental ways:

- How the contractor's price is quoted to the owner
- How risk is allocated to each of the parties

Lump Sum Contracts

change order
Requests made by the owner to add or subtract features to the scope of the project resulting in changes to the contract.

Lump sum contracts are the most common type of contract, especially for building construction. Under this arrangement, the contractor agrees to complete the work specified in the plans and specs for a single fixed amount of money. From the owner's standpoint, this is probably one of the safest contracts because cost is known up front. However, that is assuming that the plans and specs from which the contractor's estimates are made are accurate. Once the contract is signed, both parties must live with the terms of the contract, and any flaws, errors, or omissions in the plans and specs will result in a *change order*. Change orders result in extra work and/or extra time, both of which result in extra cost to the owner. And although most owners are adamant about "no change orders" when they bid the job, it is completely unrealistic to assume that the contract documents will be flawless; change orders should always be anticipated for design-bid-build work utilizing a lump sum contract.

On the other hand, if there are cost overruns associated with the work that have nothing to do with errors or omissions in the design, but instead are the result of poor management, rework, or even weather, then the contractor must suffer the loss with no additional compensation from the owner. Likewise, if superior performance by the construction management team results in a cost savings, then the contractor will solely benefit from that savings. Table 4.1 illustrates the various scenarios.

Table 4.1   Lump Sum Contract

Contract Amount	Actual Cost	Contractor Impact	Owner Impact
$2,000,000	$2,029,000	Contractor suffers a $29,000 loss.	No impact, as the contract amount remains the same.
$2,000,000	$1,990,000	Contractor earns an additional $10,000.	No impact, as the contract amount remains the same.

Cost-Plus-Fee Contract

Under a cost-plus-fee contract (also referred to as *time and materials*), the owner reimburses the contractor for all actual costs associated with the work plus a fixed fee or percentage of the cost. This type of contract is often utilized in situations where it is difficult to define the scope of the project accurately, or when time is of the essence and construction needs to start before the full plans and specs are complete.

For the contractor, this type of agreement guarantees a profit on the job regardless of project cost. However, the owner is at significant risk under this arrangement because there is no limit set for the project cost and the contractor really has no incentive for minimizing that cost. For this reason, it is very important that the owner clearly spells out upfront exactly which costs will be reimbursed and which costs will be viewed as part of the contractor's fee. For example, labor, materials, equipment, and subcontracts are always reimbursed. But soft costs such as overhead and supervision may be disputed as reimbursable expenses.

time and materials
Another name for a cost-plus-fee contract. These are the two cost factors that are reimbursed under a cost-plus-fee contract. Time equates to the cost of the labor, and materials equates to the cost of the building products used in the construction.

Another important consideration for both the owner and the contractor with a cost-plus-fee contract is the amount of paperwork involved. Each billing requires a full accounting of exact project costs with receipts. This adds a tremendous administrative burden to both parties. The construction manager must prepare the bill and the owner or architect must review and approve the bill. All of this extra work adds overhead expense on both sides and must be accounted for. Table 4.2 illustrates this scenario for a $2,000,000 budget.

Table 4.2   Cost-Plus-Fee Contract

Actual Cost	Fee as % of Cost*	Contract Amount	Contractor Impact	Owner Impact
$1,994,500	$99,725	$2,094,225	None. The contractor still earns a 5% fee.	$94,225 over budget amount of $2,000,000.

* Presuming a 5% fee

Guaranteed Maximum Price Contract

guaranteed maximum price (GMP)
A contract methodology in which the contractor is reimbursed for actual costs of materials, labor, equipment, subcontracts, overhead, and profit up to a maximum fixed price amount. Any costs over the maximum price shall be borne by the contractor. Any savings below the maximum price will revert to the owner. This type of contract is often implemented when design is less than 100 percent complete.

The *guaranteed maximum price (GMP)* contract is a variation of the cost-plus-fee contract and has become very popular, particularly with owners using design-build project delivery. This contract contains the best features of the lump sum and cost-plus-fee contracts. (See Table 4.3.) The guaranteed maximum price offers a firm cap on the overall contract price and at the same time stipulates that the owner is obligated to pay only actual costs plus a fee. Under this scenario, the owner is protected by the guarantee of a maximum price and yet receives the benefit of any realized savings. It also allows for an early start of construction because the pricing of the job can occur before plans and specs are 100 percent complete.

Table 4.3   GMP Contract

GMP Contract Amount	Actual Cost Plus Fee	Contractor Impact	Owner Impact
$2,000,000	$2,029,000	Contractor suffers $29,000 loss.	No impact. The contract amount remains the same.
$2,000,000	$1,990,000	No impact.	Owner receives benefit of $10,000 savings.

When using a GMP contract, a smart owner often provides an incentive to the contractor for working as efficiently as possible by agreeing to split any savings with the contractor. The owner may offer splits in the 60/40 range or even 50/50 range. However, even without shared savings, there is still a great incentive for the contractor to perform well. Any time a contractor can return money to an owner, the odds for repeat business go way up.

NOTE

Unit Price Contract

Unit price contracts are used when the work to be performed cannot accurately be measured ahead of time. Unit pricing is common for heavy civil and highway-type projects. Even though engineered site plans and specs are prepared for this type of work, it is very difficult to make exact quantity estimates because the material we are working with is not something we can physically count off like bricks or steel beams. The material quantities are much more imprecise (such as dirt or the removal of dirt) and the work is often performed by large equipment such as bulldozers or backhoes instead of by installers such as electricians or carpenters.

For this reason, the owner typically provides fixed quantities for the contractors to apply their unit pricing to. This arrangement provides for a competitive bid situation via unit prices even though the exact quantities cannot be accurately determined from the plans and specs. For example, the owner could provide quantities for excavation, pipe laying, and backfill. The contractor would quote a dollar amount per cubic yard for soil excavation, a dollar amount per linear foot of piping laid, and a dollar amount per cubic yard of backfill installed and come up with a total bid based upon the quantities that the owner provided.

The risk to the owner under this contract method is obvious. See Table 4.4 for an illustration. If the owner's quantities vary greatly from the actual requirements of the job, then the owner will be responsible for the additional costs. The final price for the project is not known until the work is complete. The only sure thing about this approach is that the unit costs for each item of work remain the same throughout the project.

Table 4.4   Unit Price Contract

Work Item	Estimated Quantities*	Contract Unit Prices	Bid Amount	Actual Quantities	Final Cost
Trench Excavation	14,000 CY	$5.25	$73,500	13,500 CY	$70,875
8" Pipe	1,750 LF	$18.24	$31,920	1,750 LF	$31,920
Engineered fill	4,500 CY	$22.50	$101,250	4,700 CY	$105,750

Table 4.4   Unit Price Contract   *(continued)*

Work Item	Estimated Quantities*	Contract Unit Prices	Bid Amount	Actual Quantities	Final Cost
Backfill	9,500 CY	$4.00	$38,000	9,800 CY	$39,200
TOTAL			$244,670		$247,745

* Provided by owner

Terms to Know

addendum

change order

contract documents

guaranteed maximum price (GMP)

perspective drawing

time and materials

Review Questions

1. What two major components make up the contract documents?

2. When did architects first begin to use drawings to communicate their design intent?

3. What does CADD stand for?

4. There is a particular way in which the drawings are organized in a set of drawings. Identify the order of drawings in a typical set of plans.

5. What is the difference between a plan view and a section view in a set of drawings?

6. Name the four primary sections of a project manual.

7. The CSI MasterFormat is broken down into how many divisions?

8. Under which CSI division would you find building insulation?

9. Name the four basic types of construction contracts.

10. Under a guaranteed maximum price contract, what happens if the actual cost is less than the guaranteed maximum contract price?

Chapter 5

Project Stages

By now, it should be very clear to you that the construction project is a complex undertaking and numerous people, activities, and requirements are involved to accomplish the goals set forth by the owner. Obviously anyone involved in construction management must be familiar with the stages in the overall process in order to move the project from concept to occupancy and utilization by the end user.

The overall design and construction process is very linear in nature and requires a systematic, comprehensive approach. Each of the stages is unique, and specific management techniques and skills are needed to keep everything on track. The project team works together in a coordinated effort, hoping that the ball doesn't get dropped and nothing falls through the cracks. After all, there is a lot at stake and everyone looks forward to a successful completion of the project.

It is time to take a look at just what the design and construction process entails. This chapter focuses on the stages of the process and the tasks associated with each of them.

The Design and Construction Process

Even though the construction process is complex and often overwhelming, there really is a method to the madness. The design and construction of buildings, bridges, and roadways follow a consistent linear path from initial concept to occupancy. We move through the process one step at a time, eventually arriving at the successful delivery of the construction project. These stages are as follows:

- Design
- Pre-construction
- Procurement
- Construction
- Post-construction
- Owner occupancy

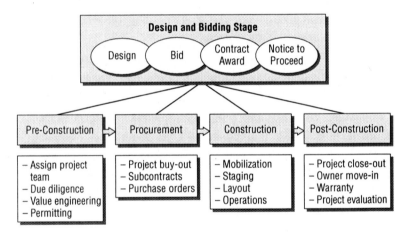

The Design Stage

Every project starts with a design, and the design process involves an intensive study and a lot of considerations. Architects and engineers basically take ideas combined with certain requirements and develop the two into comprehensible plans and specifications that are used to construct the new building or facility. Traditionally, contractors are not directly involved in the design process unless the project delivery method is design-build or CM. But whether or not they are involved in this stage, good contractors are aware of what occurs during this first step in the project sequence.

In addition to aesthetics, the design stage is about function and layout. But the ultimate purpose of the documents is to communicate graphically to the contractor what to build, and in some instances how to build it. There are four steps to the design process:

◆ Programming and feasibility

◆ Schematic design

◆ Design development

◆ Contract documents

These steps are sequential and build on one another. As the designers work through the process, they move the design from concept to detailed drawings. Let's consider each of these steps one at a time.

Programming and feasibility   Programming is typically done prior to the design process, and engages the owners and end users to clarify needs, goals, and objectives for the facility. Some of the information that comes out of the programming stage is the overall building size, the number of rooms and their adjacencies, how the spaces will be used, who will be using them, and what the requirements are for their function. The owner will inform the designer about what they like and what they don't like. Often the project budget is also discussed during programming, and it is the designer's responsibility to try to carry out the design with this budget in mind. That's where the feasibility comes in. Obviously, if the final design comes in over budget, then adjustments must be made to the original design. Unfortunately, this happens more often than not.

Schematic design   Schematic or conceptual design is the first step of the creative process. These drawings consist of rough sketches identifying general spaces and adjacencies, shapes, circulation patterns, orientation, and perhaps massing. The design team starts to consider such things as materials, sizes, colors, textures, and other aesthetic factors. At this point, the design is far enough along for the design team to outline preliminary specifications and estimates.

Design development (DD)   The design development stage is where much of the detail work gets done. A great deal of research and investigation takes place regarding the use of materials, equipment, and systems that will go into the facility. The specifications become more developed at this stage, and more accurate pricing can now take place. It is during the design development process that value engineering and constructability reviews are typically performed.

working drawings
The final detailed drawings used for construction. Also called contract documents.

Contract documents (CDs)   The final detailed drawings (along with the final specifications) are called the contract documents. These drawings may also be referred to as *working drawings* because they are the plans that the builder will actually use for construction. You are already familiar with the makeup and significance of these design documents and know that they indeed constitute a major component of the legal contract. These are the documents that are used to solicit bids and pricing from the contractor. The quality of these documents will impact the quality of the pricing. If a significant design feature is not presented in the drawings, then it will not be priced by the contractor. And although we often refer to the contract documents as 100 percent complete, the truth is that they rarely are; all parties must be prepared for the changes that will inevitably arise as the project goes forward. Managing these changes can make up a large part of the construction management challenge.

Codes and Compliance Issues

One of the major responsibilities of the design team is to make sure that the design meets all building codes and complies with various statutory regulations such as environmental impacts. In the overall scheme of things, this task can sometimes turn out to be the most frustrating for all parties involved. Throughout the design process, the plans are submitted to the appropriate planning, zoning, and building authorities for plan checks and compliance reviews. This process can take weeks, months, or—yes—even years. There are indeed projects that get tied up in the red tape and political bureaucracy of planning commissions and town councils and take an eternity to see the light of day. Fortunately, the contractor is usually not involved until after the final design stage, when all that remains is to obtain the building permits. But even this process can take weeks or months depending on the number of resubmittals that must take place and the workload of the particular jurisdiction. Once again, the quality of the contract documents relative to code compliance will influence the ability of the contractor to expedite the permitting process.

Bidding Stage

The design phase culminates with the competitive bidding stage. The drawings and specifications are complete and now it's time to select the builder and award the contract. The architect produces multiple sets of documents for distribution to the contractors during the bidding stage. The architect also sends several sets to the building department for a plan check. The plan check by the building department occurs at the same time that bidding is taking place among the selected contractors.

The competitive bidding process and contract award were discussed in Chapter 3, "How We Get the Work." Traditionally, the architect coordinates the bidding procedures and assists the owner in making the contractor selection.

A notice to proceed is issued to the winning contractor and now the work that will transform the design into reality begins.

The Pre-Construction Stage

Up to this point, the only members of the construction team who have been involved with the project are the estimators. Now with contract in hand and a notice to proceed from the owner, it is time to bring on the rest of the team. This is when the estimators pass the job over to the project manager. The project manager is the captain of the construction management team. This is most likely the first time that the project manager has seen the job, so the quality of the information passed from estimator to project manager is very important. Keep in mind that cost control is one of the most crucial components of the construction management task, and poor transfer of information here will result in significant headaches for the construction management team down the road. I will discuss estimating and its importance in detail in Chapter 6, "Estimating Project Costs."

The project manager's job at this point is to set the course of action and put together the team that will carry this project through to satisfactory completion for all parties involved. This is the pre-construction stage (also referred to as job startup), and it is all about planning. I can't say enough about how important this step is. Unfortunately, often this pre-construction phase is fast and furious because of schedule constraints, and finding the time needed to create a fully thought-out plan of action can be very difficult. As I said earlier, receiving the notice to proceed is something like receiving orders to deploy troops and equipment in an urgent military maneuver; time is of the essence, and you don't always have the people or the resources that you need right at the moment when you need them. Most construction managers will tell you that job startup and job closeout are the two most difficult processes to manage. Let's take a look at some of the tasks associated with the startup or pre-construction process.

NOTE The key to good project planning is the ability to anticipate potential problems before they become actual problems. It is very important that the project manager take the time to completely familiarize himself or herself with the project goals and come up with a plan that will ultimately meet the owner's expectations for time, cost, and quality, while still realizing a fair and equitable profit for the construction firm.

Assigning the Project Team

One of the very first tasks that must be taken care of by the project manager is putting together the project team. Depending on the size and complexity of the job, the typical construction project will have a project manager, contract administrator, general superintendent, maybe an assistant superintendent, and at least one field engineer. The on-site project team is supported by the office management team in the form of estimating, contract administration, accounting, job costing, and payroll.

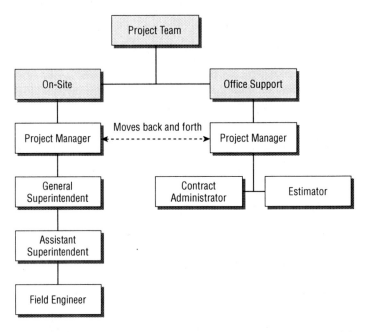

Construction project managers are often accountable for more than one job at a time. It is not uncommon for them to be running two or three projects simultaneously, visiting each one at appropriate intervals. Superintendents and field engineers are assigned to only one job at a time and typically remain on-site for the duration of the project. Once the project is complete, the team will disband and individual members will be assigned to various other sites as needed.

Having the right project team makes all the difference in the world when it comes to a smooth-running job. The members must get along, support each other, and be able to work together under stressful conditions. The construction site is a unique environment—sometimes a tough environment—and the team must be up for the challenge. I have seen projects where as many as 100 different craftsmen were trying to do their job under intensely difficult conditions: cramped spaces, inadequate resources, and limited time. Tempers get short and frustration runs high. If you are a member of the management team, you had better have a relatively high "emotional intelligence quotient" because your ability to be flexible and responsive will far outweigh any benefits from being rigid and reactive. Let's take a closer look at the individual team members and consider their respective roles.

Project manager (PM)   As stated earlier, the project manager is the captain of the team. Project managers usually have extensive experience in construction and a broad background in all aspects of the management process. Although the size of the company and the size of the project ultimately influence the specific duties of the PM, generally the PM is charged with four fundamental management tasks: assembling the best possible team for the project, developing the overall project schedule, setting up the cost control system, and establishing a quality control plan. The PM guides and directs the project team and monitors the schedule, cost, and quality, making adjustments as needed to bring about a successful outcome.

The project manager's accountability is twofold: they must see to it that the obligations spelled out in the contract documents are met to the owner's satisfaction, and they must also make sure that the project runs as efficiently as possible, taking advantage of every opportunity to save time and money to ensure a fair and reasonable profit to the construction firm.

Contract administrator   This person assists both the project manager and the superintendent with many of the details of the contract—especially the general and supplemental conditions of the contract discussed in Chapter 4, "The Construction Contract." For example, the contract administrator may process progress payment applications, change orders, or submittals on behalf of the project manager. The contract administrator must be completely familiar with the contract stipulations and provisions and accustomed to working with all of the common forms, policies, and procedures.

Superintendent   If the project manager is the captain of the team, then the superintendent is the first lieutenant. The superintendent is responsible for coordinating all of the construction activities on-site and keeping the project on schedule. The superintendent must be very knowledgeable when it comes to construction methods and details, because he or she is in charge of all direct labor and subcontractors and must ensure that the work complies with the requirements of the contract documents. The superintendent must also manage the flow of materials, deliveries, and equipment to create the most efficient and productive environment possible. And, of course, safety planning and management is a major function that the superintendent is responsible for.

The superintendent is the daily point of contact for the owner and must maintain good working relations with all of the owner's representatives. Sometimes this can be the most challenging aspect of the job; however, it is a critical one. Nothing can turn a job sour more quickly than having the wrong superintendent on the job. The days of the rough-and-tumble construction superintendent are long gone. Today the man or woman in charge of running the job on-site must be as much a diplomat as a construction expert.

Field engineer   This entry-level position is usually the first step to becoming a project manager. Field engineers are responsible for handling much of the paperwork that passes through the field office. They are usually assigned the tasks of processing and tracking requests for information (RFIs), submittals, and shop drawings. (These three processes will be discussed in detail in Chapter 7, "Contract Administration.") They may also assist with the project layout, payment verification, subcontractor coordination, and any other tasks assigned to them by the superintendent. Although the field engineer is an entry-level position, the role is a vital one on every project. (By the way, field engineers are not necessarily licensed engineers. The term *field engineer* is simply a job title.)

Once the project manager has established the project team, he or she needs to bring everyone up to speed as soon as possible, especially the superintendent. The PM and superintendent will usually spend several hours or even days together planning for the project—developing schedules and strategies for a successful outcome. It is important that they become as familiar as possible with the drawings, the specs, the project scope, the budget and schedule, subcontractor bids, and every other aspect of the job. Once the work starts, it can speed along like a runaway train, and the captain and first lieutenant had better have a really good plan in place to keep it on track!

NOTE

The superintendent's role is a critical one. In years past, the supers came up from the ranks, first working in the field as a laborer or craftsman. Today a superintendent is more likely to be a college graduate with a degree in civil engineering or construction management who has a particular bent toward the construction operations side. A good superintendent is worth his or her weight in gold, and supers actually are often among the highest paid members of the team.

Due Diligence

Due diligence is not a term that is proprietary to the construction industry. Many industries understand the concept. In simple terms, due diligence is the process of identifying any problems or areas of concern that exist so that those problems can be factored into the decision making that takes place during the pre-construction stage. Surprises increase risk and are not welcome during construction—they hinder the work progress, impacting the schedule, the cost, and in some instances even the quality of the job. Bottom line: Surprises should be avoided at all cost.

unforeseen conditions
Unknown physical conditions at the site that were not anticipated by the owner or the contractor.

Site investigation   Although due diligence can be performed with any section of construction work, product, or procedure, the one area of construction where due diligence is of utmost importance is with site work. Site work deals primarily with site clearing, grading, and excavating and is generally considered one of the most risky divisions of work. Surprises such as hidden geological problems, hazardous material, or historical remnants may be discovered after the job begins. Anything that the contractor can do to mitigate *unforeseen conditions* associated with the site should be done before the work begins.

Soil testing and engineering   One of the most reliable practices utilized to eliminate surprises associated with subsurface conditions is soil testing. Owners should insist upon these tests being conducted and designers should ensure that the reports are made part of the Supplemental Conditions to the contract. The conscientious contractor will use the information in these reports to properly price the job and conduct the work. This information is commonly used by civil and structural engineers to design various site improvements and foundation systems as well.

However, even a soils report may contain flawed data. Some owners, in an effort to cut costs up front, rely on old reports and information. The results can be disastrous. It is often the classic case of an owner or designer being penny-wise and pound-foolish, and the courts have seen more than one case where such tactics have resulted in millions of dollars in claims.

Value Engineering

Value engineering is a process that may or may not be conducted during the pre-construction phase, depending primarily upon which project delivery method is being used. In the low bid, design-bid-build scenario, the owner is not really asking you for this evaluation. However, in the more integrated collaborative approaches, it is often a matter of course to conduct value engineering analysis as the design is being developed. In my opinion, value engineering is actually one of the most valuable services that a construction management team can deliver.

In this process, a thorough analysis is conducted of the design, products, and materials and their application, installation, and execution to determine whether the proposed design solutions are really the best solutions relative to their cost. The purpose of value engineering is to optimize resources to achieve the greatest value for the money being spent. The designers, contractors, building trades, engineers, manufacturers' representatives, and end users are engaged to brainstorm the best possible solutions. A project team that can propose creative and cost-effective solutions can really shine, and adds tremendous value to the overall project.

One of the most underutilized resources available to the design team in the development of their solution is the engagement of the field personnel who actually install the systems, equipment, and products specified and the end users who actually use the facility every day. They can provide great insight into what works and what doesn't work but are rarely ever called upon to join in the design team discussions.

Real World Scenario

Getting Burnt by Bad Information

Recently, a custom home builder friend of mine was building a beautiful custom home on a Santa Barbara hillside in California. When pricing the grading and excavation for the bid, the contractor relied on the grades and elevations in the site plan provided by the architect. After getting the project, the contractor proceeded to lay out the house according to the site plan. The contractor presumed that the architect had performed the proper due diligence in preparing the drawings. Unfortunately, when the contractor started to lay out the house, he discovered that there was not enough hilltop to support the foundation of the house and massive amounts of fill dirt had to be brought in to build out the bank. Talk about big surprises!

When the contractor asked the architect where he got his information for the site plan, the architect indicated that it was from aerial photographs. The accuracy of site grades presented in an aerial photograph can be counted on only within a five-foot (plus or minus) range at best. When you are trying to situate a rather large house on top of a relatively small hilltop, five feet makes all the difference in the world. The contractor relied on the information that the architect had provided and therefore was not liable for the error. However, the architect failed in the due diligence process and, unfortunately, the owner was left to pay a significant price. The contractor, being the bearer of the bad news, was put in a very uncomfortable position, and vowed that he would never again trust the site information provided in the contract documents without first doing checks and reviews for himself. If he had known that the site plan elevations were taken from aerial photographs instead of being ascertained by standard surveying practices, he would have anticipated a large margin of error and would not have proceeded with the project until all information provided in the site plan could be verified. This was a costly lesson for all involved and delayed the job considerably.

Permitting and Inspection Process

As mentioned earlier, before construction can begin, building permits must be issued by the local building authority. This is probably the single most crucial aspect of the pre-construction process. Although the owner may secure building permits before the project is let out for bids, in most instances this task is typically handled by the construction management team. If this task is mismanaged, the entire project is at risk for failure.

Time is of the essence on virtually every construction project. A delayed permit has caused many a contractor's hair to turn gray before its time. Unfortunately, even when the contractor is on top of the permitting process, circumstances beyond their control may throw a monkey wrench into the works. For example, new compliance requirements or revised building code regulations will typically cause the process to be deferred.

The construction management team must be vigilant in pursuing timely building permit release. The building permit establishes the inspection schedule for the project. The number of inspections required depends upon the building authority jurisdiction and project type. It is very important that the superintendent be fully aware of the inspection requirements connected to the project. More information regarding inspections will be presented in Chapter 8, "Construction Operations and Job Site Management."

The Procurement Stage

To procure means to buy or obtain. The procurement stage of construction management is often referred to as "buying out" the job or purchasing the labor, materials, and equipment needed to complete the project. A great deal of the construction management function has to do with managing contracts—contracts to secure the labor and trades needed to perform the work, and contracts to secure the materials and equipment that will be placed on the project. The two primary instruments associated with this effort are subcontracts and purchase orders.

The procurement operation can be a very simple process handled on a local basis by the superintendent, or it can be a major department or division within the construction company whereby purchases are made on a regional or national level. Some projects warrant a combination of both approaches. In the home-building business, for example, the very large national companies typically have procurement departments that purchase labor and materials for hundreds of homes at a time, securing the best prices available on a national basis. On the other hand, on a high-rise office complex or other large commercial project, the superintendent may purchase small quantities of miscellaneous materials, such as lumber for wood blocking from a local building supply, or hire local labor for a small contract item, such as caulking. However, larger material purchases such as steel framing might be made by the estimating, purchasing, or procurement department back at the main office. It depends on the size of the job and the size of the construction organization running the job. Either way, project procurement constitutes much of the direct cost associated with the construction project. Let's briefly look at the two primary instruments used to manage this part of the work. Each will be discussed in greater detail in Chapters 6 and 7.

Subcontracts

Today, very few general contractors self-perform the construction work that actually builds the structure or facility. General contractors buy trade labor through subcontracts. During the bidding process, various trade contractors offer up bids for various sections of work. These bids (usually the lowest of the submitted bids) are what get placed into the general contractor's price to the owner in the contractor's bid. At this point, there is no contract between the general contractor and the trade contractor. There is just an offer of services (sometimes including materials) at a specified price. Once the general contractor is determined to be the winner of the job, he or she will select which trade contractors to hire to do the work of the project. A subcontract is executed with each of these trade contractors. A big part of the project team's job is to manage each of these subcontracts—to see that all of the conditions of the contract are adhered to and that the work is performed in accordance with the plans and specifications. This process will be explained in detail in Chapters 6, 7, and 8.

NOTE   When selecting subcontractors, price is only one of the factors to consider. Many general contractors have determined that it is sometimes better to forgo the low bidder and choose a subcontractor with a reputation for excellent service and dependability, even if their price is a little higher. It is not unusual for general contractors and subcontractors to develop strategic alliances based upon past experience.

Purchase Orders

Almost every business is familiar with the concept of purchase orders. A purchase order is an agreement between a vendor and a customer to provide certain products that meet a particular specification for a specified price. Purchase orders work in construction the same way they work in other businesses.

As you know, there are hundreds of products and materials that go into building a new structure or facility. Keeping up with all of these orders and delivery dates is an awesome challenge, but a critical one. Order mishaps and delayed deliveries have caused many jobs to suffer costly consequences for the contractor and the owner.

One strategy used by contractors to better manage this process is assigning a member of the project team to function as the purchase order expediter. This person's responsibility is to focus on the procurement schedule relative to construction progress and to track purchase orders and deliveries. Failure in this area can be devastating to the success of the project. This topic will be revisited in Chapters 7, 8, and 9, "Project Planning and Scheduling."

The Construction Stage

Once the work is ready to start, the superintendent will call for a pre-construction meeting with all of the subcontractors and major material vendors. This meeting essentially establishes the ground rules for working together. The superintendent also uses this opportunity to go over issues such as work sequencing, work hours, material storage, quality control, site access and many other pertinent topics.

These first meetings on-site help set the tone for the whole project. It is important to establish an environment of trust and cooperation right up front. Starting out on the wrong foot by being overly demanding and rigid does not make for a pleasant working relationship down the road. Remember, every construction project brings together a new group of people, most of whom are working together for the first time. There is a tremendous amount of coordination among the trades that must take place during construction, and the really good superintendents know that they must spend almost as much time building relationships as they spend building the facility. Chapter 8 provides much more detail relative to the management of the day-to-day operations associated with the construction phase of the project.

Mobilization

Mobilization is all about setting up and getting ready to start construction. Construction cannot begin until all of the proper personnel, materials, and equipment are in place. This is a very important part of the process because it sets the stage for all that is to follow. The mobilization activity is often discussed under Division 1 of the specifications referenced back in Chapter 4. Some of the activities that should be done during the mobilization process are:

- Set up field office.
- Set up temporary storage facilities.
- Secure the site.
- Organize adequate parking and site access.
- Develop a materials and handling plan.
- Secure temporary electric, water, and telephone service.
- Arrange for trash and debris removal.
- Provide and place portable toilets.
- Install job signage and barricades.
- Assemble survey and layout personnel.
- Confirm testing agencies and personnel.
- Establish job site management systems.
- Establish safety programs and protocol.
- Obtain and pay for all required permits.

Staging and Layout Plans

Mobilization addresses all of the activities that we must accomplish in order to start the construction. But where are we going to put all of these materials, equipment, mobile office facilities, trash dumpsters, portable toilets, storage trailers, and the like? The superintendent must formulate and diagram a site layout plan and staging strategy that will provide the highest productivity and efficiency of movement. You will get a much closer look at this requirement in Chapter 8, including some of the factors considered when making site layout decisions. For right now, just keep in mind that the organization and layout of the overall project site will indeed impact just how well the construction proceeds.

Construction Operations

The heavy equipment operators are moving dirt, the concrete finishers are pumping concrete, and the steel erectors are setting beams and girders. There are cranes hoisting equipment and trucks delivering materials and workers making noise and stirring up dust everywhere. To the innocent bystander, this scene may appear quite chaotic, but to the knowledgeable observer, this is what construction is all about. This is where it all happens. All of this apparent chaos is actually a well-orchestrated effort directed by one of the most valuable players on the construction management team—the superintendent, often with support from an assistant superintendent and at least one field engineer.

The pace is hectic, the stakes are high, and it is one of the most exciting environments to be a part of. Whether your project is a highway, a manufacturing facility, a hospital, or a home, you get to literally have a hand in the building of society, the building of a nation—the fruits of your labor will be right there for the whole world to see for generations to come.

The on-site project team must be very familiar with all elements of construction. Lots of questions and requests for information are going to arise regarding the intent of the plans and specifications, and it is the project team's job to obtain the answers and clarify confusing aspects of the work to keep things moving forward. The team works together to sequence all activities and coordinate all efforts by the various building trades, material suppliers, building inspectors, and safety officials, adjusting the schedule as they go.

Table 5.1 highlights some of the typical work items associated with various building elements. Keep in mind that each work item may require the coordination of several building trades and numerous materials. For example, a standard foundation can include excavation, formwork, fill, reinforcing, concrete, masonry, anchors, and imbeds. Every project requires the management and coordination of hundreds of materials and activities on the job site daily, not to mention all the people and personalities involved. It's an awesome challenge, to say the least!

Table 5.1   Building Elements and Work Items

Building Element	Work Included
Site work	Clearing, grading, utilities, layout, landscaping, irrigation, paving, exterior concrete
Foundations	Excavation, standard foundations, special foundations, slabs on grade
Basement construction	Basement excavation, basement walls, basement floors, waterproofing, perimeter drains, backfill
Superstructure	Floor construction, roof construction
Exterior closure	Exterior walls, exterior windows, exterior doors

Table 5.1   Building Elements and Work Items *(continued)*

Building Element	Work Included
Roofing	Roof coverings, flashings, roof openings
Interior construction	Partitions, interior doors, specialties
Staircases	Stair construction, stair finishes
Interior finishes	Wall finishes, floor finishes, ceiling finishes
Conveying systems	Elevators, escalators, moving walkers, material-handling systems
Plumbing	Plumbing fixtures, domestic water distribution, sanitary waste, rainwater drainage, special plumbing systems
HVAC	Energy supply, heat-generating systems, cooling generating systems, control and instrumentation
Fire protection	Fire protection and sprinkler systems, standpipe and hose systems, fire protection specialties
Electrical	Electrical services and distribution, lighting and branch wiring, communication and security systems
Equipment	Commercial equipment, institutional equipment, vehicular equipment, other equipment
Furnishings	Fixed furnishings, movable furnishings
Special construction	Special structures, integrated construction, special construction systems, special facilities
Selective building demolition	Building elements demolition, hazardous compounds abatement

The Post-Construction Stage

You might think that once the construction is complete, the job is over. Not quite. Just as when you cook and serve a magnificent dinner for a roomful of people, you still have to clean up afterward. The post-construction stage is the cleanup stage. It is very important that this stage be handled with as much energy and enthusiasm as the project startup and operations, because a slipup here can have costly consequences down the road. And you always need to remember that no matter how well the first 90 percent went, if you make mistakes and drop the ball during the last 10 percent of the job, that's all the owner will remember. The team still has a number of tasks to manage before they can call it a wrap.

Project Closeout

The final step in the construction process is the project closeout. As previously stated, along with project startup, this step often becomes the most difficult to manage. This is the stage where all the loose ends get taken care of as the construction team readies the facility for occupancy by the end users. This is the time when the contractor turns the building over to the owner. However, before the owner actually takes possession of the facility, there are a number of sequential steps that must be performed by the contractor. The construction management team must complete the following list of final standard procedures before they can celebrate the completion of a job well done:

- Project punchout
- Substantial completion
- Final inspection
- Certificate of Occupancy
- Commissioning
- Final documentation
- Final completion

As you might imagine, project closeout can often be a time of great stress and anxiety on the part of the construction management team and the owner's staff. The owner is anxious to move in and the project team is usually anxious to move on to the next job. It becomes especially stressful if the owner schedules some major event such as a "grand opening," or with school construction, the start of a new academic year. The dates for these events are established way in advance and there is usually very little wiggle room if things aren't going well for the contractor as the job moves toward completion. This is when the management of the project becomes a real challenge and creative strategies come into play in order to meet the critical deadlines. The school buses will be arriving with children whether the contractor is ready or not.

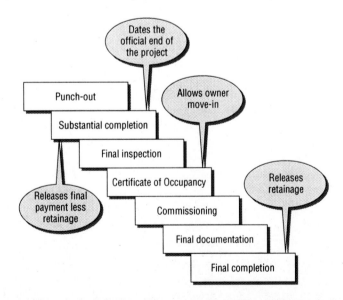

Project punchout   At the end of every project there are always minor items of work that must be taken care of. They may include little items that have been overlooked, such as the installation of a robe hook or doorstop, or minor repairs or adjustments, such as replacing a cracked floor tile. Each of these items must be addressed before the project is acceptable to the owner. The project punchout activity is managed through a project *punch list.*

punch list
The minor adjustments, repairs, and work items that must be done before substantial completion can be achieved. The list is prepared jointly by the owner, architect, and contractor. The architect confirms completion of each item on the list.

The punch list contains all of the work items remaining to be done to complete the project. The list is a compilation of observations noted by the owner, designer, and contractor as they conduct the formal project walk-through. The challenge for the construction management team is to summon all of the various trades involved to return to the project to adjust, fix, or complete the multitude of small items that need attention. As you might guess, this is not an easy task—most subcontractors are well on their way to starting their next job and would really rather not be bothered by some little nuisance work item. However, to the owner, attention to these small things makes all the difference in the world. And the completion of the punch list is of considerable importance to the general contractor because the completion of the list ultimately leads to the release of the final payment. Delay in this stage of the project is of no minor consequence. Just how this challenging task gets managed will be discussed in greater detail in Chapter 7.

Project completion   Every project has a beginning and an end. The notice to proceed defines the start of the project. However, there are two steps to defining the end of the project.

Substantial completion   *Substantial completion* is the first step. Substantial completion occurs after the punch list work has been completed and is approved by the architect. At this point, the architect determines that the new facility can be utilized for its intended purpose and actually issues a formal Certificate of Substantial Completion. This date is very important because it marks the official end of the project and establishes the beginning of the warranty period. Now all payments due to the contractor are released, with the exception of a small percentage called retainage. (Retainage will also be addressed in more detail in Chapter 7.)

substantial completion
The point at which all punch list work has been completed and the owner can occupy or take possession of the new facility.

Final completion   Final completion is accomplished after all remaining contract requirements have been met, such as the issuance of all final paperwork and documentation (warranties, product manuals, and so on). This step is also certified by the architect and sets up the release of all remaining payments due to the contractor.

Certificate of Occupancy   After the architect issues the Certificate of Substantial Completion, the contractor or the architect will call for the final inspection by the building official. The building official then issues a Certificate of Occupancy (CO). This regulatory device signifies that all life safety code requirements are met prior to anyone occupying the building. The primary concern is that the building be safe to occupy. The owner cannot move in until this certificate is issued. Sometimes a conditional CO can be issued allowing the owner to occupy a portion of the facility prior to completion of the entire facility.

Commissioning   When you buy a new car, you need a little instruction about its design and workings before you can operate it. Likewise, there are many areas of operation throughout a new facility that need to be explained to the owners. This process is called *commissioning* and may be conducted by the general contractor, by subcontractors under the direction of the general contractor, or by the architects or engineers involved in the project.

First, commissioning is a process of testing systems and equipment to make sure that they are all working properly before turning the facility over to the owner. This process can be as simple as running the dishwasher or testing the air conditioner in a new home, to starting up huge turbines in a hydroelectric facility.

The second part of the commissioning task deals with training the owner's personnel in the operation and maintenance of the equipment and systems installed in the new facility. Because the contractor is accountable for the equipment and its operation at least during the warranty period, it is a very important part of project closeout and should not be shortchanged. It is in the contractor's best interest to make sure that all owner staff charged with operating the new systems are up to speed regarding their function and receive the proper operation manuals.

Final Documentation   Sticking with the car analogy, when you buy a new car, it is customary to find an owner's manual in the glove compartment. When you build a new facility, there is also a set of documents delivered to the owner that might compare to an owner's manual, except that the product is substantially larger and more complex than a car. Some of the documentation associated with the turnover of a new facility include:

- Warranties
- Operation manuals
- Inspection and testing reports
- *As-built drawings* or record drawings

Pulling together all of this paperwork for distribution at the end of the project can be one of the most tedious aspects of the job. For this reason, it is always helpful to have a good contract administrator on the project team. The management of this effort is discussed in further detail in Chapter 7.

---

commissioning
A process of testing and checking all equipment and systems within the facility at the end of a project to assure proper functioning and operation. May also include the training of owner personnel in the operation and maintenance of the equipment.

as-built drawings
Record drawings completed by the contractor and turned over to the owner at the end of the project identifying any changes or adjustments made to the conditions and dimensions of the work relative to the original plans and specifications.

Owner Move-in

Finally, you have moved through all the stages of the process and have turned the keys over to the owner. This is always an exciting time for the owner. Keep in mind, though, that with all the moving-in activities come dings, dents, and scrapes to the new finishes. That's why it is customary for the contractor to inventory any spare parts and surplus materials associated with the project, such as a partial gallon of paint, a half box of floor tiles, or a few ceiling tiles, and leave them behind. With these extra materials, the owner's maintenance personnel can make the touch-up repairs that are inevitable when furniture and equipment are being pushed around and shoved into place.

Warranty Period

Most construction contracts contain warranties. From a legal standpoint, there are two types of warranty that the construction professional must be concerned with: express warranties (written into the contract) and implied warranties (established or required by law). Express warranties deal mostly with the workmanship and installations. Examples of express warranties routinely included in construction contracts are:

- ◆ A warranty that work will be performed in a good and workmanlike manner
- ◆ A warranty that materials will be new and of good quality
- ◆ A warranty that the work will conform to the requirements of the contract documents

Implied warranties in construction deal primarily with the products, materials, and equipment installed in the new facility, such as appliances, equipment, or other goods typically installed by subcontractors. Most of these are what are commonly referred to as manufacturer's warranties. However, the contractor is liable to the owner if the product fails. In such a case, the contractor will first look to the subcontractor and then to the manufacturer to back up the warranty. Examples of implied warranties common in construction are:

- ◆ A warranty of fitness for a particular purpose (that the goods will serve the buyer's intended use)
- ◆ A warranty of merchantability of goods (that the goods will be of at least average quality and conform to any labels or advertising about the product)

As noted above, the warranty period starts immediately after the Certificate of Substantial Completion has been issued by the architect. Most contracts require a one-year minimum warranty or correction period on most installations on the project. Many products carry a manufacturer's warranty longer than that. It is in the contractor's best interest to be very familiar with the warranty requirements of the contract from both a management and a legal perspective. The actual project team will most likely not be directly involved in the management of any warranty work on the project, but they will set the stage for the implementation of that activity by compiling, preparing, and distributing all warranty documentation to the owner at the end of the project. This can actually be a daunting task given the number of subcontractors involved and the various equipment installed, but it is one that must be coordinated nonetheless.

NOTE

It is very important for the contractor to communicate a clear distinction between punchout and warranty. If this line gets blurred even in the slightest, it will cause a nightmare for the construction management team. Obviously, there will be minor items of work that show up after the punch list is complete. However, they should be addressed under the warranty provisions. No new items should be added to the punch list after the final walk-through. Otherwise there will be no end to the punchout operation and the contractor will never achieve substantial completion.

Project Evaluation

This is the last step in the post-construction stage. Project evaluation is an opportunity for the construction management team to debrief the project and consider what worked and what didn't work. This very valuable step allows the lessons learned to be passed on to other project teams. Information regarding subcontractor and vendor performance, equipment glitches, inspection snafus, or owner-relations issues are all grist for the mill. Unfortunately, this important step rarely gets executed. The team members are all off to the next job and the wisdom never gets communicated to the organization as a whole. This is one habit that I always tried to institutionalize within my own company and that I believe should be developed as standard operating procedure for construction firms. I will discuss project evaluation in greater detail in Chapter 10, "Monitoring Project Performance."

The Successful Project

Whew! Finally! We adjusted the last doorknob, delivered the last warranty, and turned over the keys. But wait a minute—just because the owner moves in and takes occupancy of the facility doesn't mean that the contractor's job is done. For one thing, the contractor must organize a plan to address warranty items and callback issues in a systematic and timely fashion. Secondly, it is always in the contractor's best interest to stay connected to the client and make sure that they are satisfied with the final product.

Ongoing communication and contact after the owner moves in should tie right back into the overall marketing strategy for the company. It costs a lot less to stay connected to a customer that you already have than it does to woo a new one, and we all know that word of mouth is the best advertising you can have.

Of course, if the owner isn't satisfied, that will also influence your market. So before moving on to the details of the various functions of construction management, let's analyze what constitutes a successful project.

Measuring Project Success

There are really two perspectives when it comes to measuring the success of the project. First, did the project meet the requirements of the owner for aesthetics, function, cost, quality, and time? And second, did the contractor make a fair profit as planned? If the answer to both questions is yes, then the project team can acknowledge a win all around. However, there are many steps involved in delivering a project from an idea to occupancy—and many people involved, as well. Sometimes this process goes smoothly; other times, the process is a long, bumpy ride. There are many factors that influence the outcome but there are fundamentally two criteria that contribute to the overall success: good design and excellent construction management.

Let me put it this way: even the best construction management team will have a hard time delivering a bad design to the owner without painful change orders and schedule delays. However, even a great design runs the risk of suffering under the leadership of a mediocre construction management team. Either way, I hope you can grasp how important it is for the owner to make smart choices all along the way by selecting the best design and the best construction team available. Squeezing the design team up front by low-balling their fee in an effort to save money will only prove to be extremely expensive when the design has to be remedied in the field. Likewise, unrealistic expectations regarding schedule, cost, or quality frustrate the construction team and often result in needless conflict and dissension.

Terms to Know

as-built drawings	substantial completion
commissioning	unforeseen conditions
punch list	working drawings

Review Questions

1. Name the four fundamental stages of the construction management process after the design stage.

2. What are the four distinct stages of the design process?

3. How does the quality of the design drawings impact the quality of the construction?

4. In relation to construction, what is meant by the term *due diligence*?

5. What are the two procurement instruments used to buy out the construction job?

6. Name at least three positions that make up the members of the on-site construction management team.

7. What occurrence marks the official end of the project?

8. What is the name of the tool used to keep track of and manage the completion of all of the loose ends, minor repairs, adjustments, and missing items at the end of the project?

9. What is value engineering and what is its purpose?

10. Why is it important to have a clear distinction between the project punchout and the warranty period?

Chapter 6

Estimating Project Costs

There are always two questions asked by a client considering an investment in construction: "How much?" and "How long?" Estimating responds to the first question. Very few projects can go forward before the cost of the construction has been determined.

Estimating is a distinct function in the construction management field, and unlike some other jobs in construction, the estimator's role is pretty specific. The estimator's primary focus is costs. They have the awesome responsibility of accurately determining the price of the project, while maintaining a competitive edge in the marketplace. Projects are won or lost by the efforts of the estimator. However, no matter what your job or position is in the construction company, you need to understand the estimating process as well.

After reading this chapter, either you will decide that this is one position that you will avoid at all cost (no pun intended) or you will be drawn to it like a magnet. That is the response in the industry as well. Either way, you will understand the process and discover just how important estimating is to construction management.

Estimating project costs requires a methodical approach, yet at the same time demands certain finesse. This chapter introduces you to both aspects and walks you through the steps necessary to build a construction estimate from the ground up.

What Is an Estimate?

An estimate is an educated guess. We are all familiar with estimates. We have obtained estimates for work on our car, for getting our house painted, or for closing costs on a mortgage. And most of us have actually engaged in doing an estimate. We've guessed or estimated how many jelly beans are in the jar at the local county fair, or calculated how many gallons of paint we need to paint the living room. The main difference between these simple estimating activities and the estimates used to price construction is complexity and what's at stake. When you estimate how many gallons of paint are needed to paint your living room and you are off by one or two gallons, the stakes are pretty small. But when you estimate the cost to build a nuclear plant, or a superhighway, or a hospital, or even a house, the stakes are much, much higher.

The estimate is a summary, based on the best information available, of probable quantities and costs of materials, labor, equipment, and subcontracts to complete a project, including taxes, overhead, and profit. It is the number used to develop the project bid price. The bid price is what goes in the contract, and the contract obligates you to perform all work needed to complete the project in accordance with the plans and specifications.

The consequences of any errors or omissions in the estimate are borne by the contractor, and the contractor will not actually know what the true cost of the construction is until the project is complete. If the estimated cost is equal to or greater than the actual cost, the project makes money for the contractor. If the estimated cost is less than the actual cost, the contractor loses money on the project.

As you can see, estimators have an awesome responsibility. First, they must come up with an accurate, but competitive estimate that will win the job. Second, their planning and calculations set the stage for the overall management targets for the entire project. Once the estimator turns the project over to the project manager and his or her on-site team, the estimator shifts to a support role and really has no direct management duties associated with the day-to-day operations.

Every time a contractor estimates a job and submits a bid, he or she is taking a risk. It is a high-stakes gamble and there are many factors that may influence the outcome. The construction management team is on the front lines to manage this risk to a successful outcome.

NOTE   When a job goes bust for the contractor with significant cost overruns, there is often an internal argument regarding who is to blame. The project manager may point to a bad estimate as the source of the failure. But the estimator may turn around and accuse the on-site team of poor management resulting in the overruns. This finger-pointing is usually a futile effort; the time would be better spent looking at specific areas of overrun and analyzing them, line item by line item, to see what mistakes should be avoided on the next project or estimate.

Simple Estimate: How Many Gallons of Paint?

You have decided to repaint your living room. You want to go buy the paint but you must first figure out how much you need. What types of information will be required to make this determination? Based on that information, how many gallons will you need and how much will it cost?

Basic Information

One gallon of paint covers 350 square feet (SF). Each gallon of paint costs $27. The room is 16´ × 14´ with an 8´ ceiling, one door (3´ × 7´), and three windows (each 3´ × 4´).

Specification

Paint all walls and ceiling with two coats of paint, one color only. Do not paint door, windows, or trim.

Process

Ceiling area = 16´ × 14´ = 224 SF

Wall area = [16´ + 14´ + 16´ + 14´]8´ = 480 SF

Deduct openings: Door = 3´ × 7´ = 21 SF and [3]3´ × 4´ = 36 SF

Total square feet: 224 + 480 − [21 + 36] = 647 SF

Total gallons of paint:

647 SF × 2 coats of paint = 1294 SF

1294 SF ÷ 350 SF per gallon = 3.63 gallons

Must purchase 4 gallons × $27 = $108 plus tax.

Note: Labor, preparation materials, and equipment are not included (ladders, brushes, rollers, masking tape, drop clothes, clean-up).

Every person in construction management must be familiar with the estimating process, but not everyone in construction is suited to be an estimator. It takes special skills and aptitude to be successful at this very important role in construction management. Let's consider exactly what it takes to be good at this job.

Characteristics of a Good Estimator

I started my career as an estimator, and I think that it is one of the best ways to really learn the business. As an estimator, you have to learn to "build" the project mentally before you can price it. You must decide upon the construction approach and make decisions all along the way as to how the facility will be built. As an estimator, you develop a tremendous understanding and knowledge of construction products, productivity, and process. In my opinion, no one knows the project as well as the estimator. I used to walk onto the site and be able to tell in an instant if something was off in the layout or missing altogether. After all, I had already built the project in my mind and was aware of every detail associated with the construction.

People in the business either love estimating or hate it. I love estimating. Once you are an estimator, it sort of gets in your blood and you end up having the capacity to estimate anything. You begin to think in terms of chunks of time and cost. You walk into a room and can immediately estimate the size of it without any measuring device because of what you know about products and dimensions. The acoustic tiles, the floor tiles, the wall panels, the doors, the windows—all of these items provide hints for you to use to ascertain dimensions without having a measuring tape.

The estimator is probably one of the most important people in construction management. Without them, the rest of the team wouldn't have much to do because they wouldn't have any jobs. There are specific skills and characteristics that are common among estimators:

- Reads contract documents well
- Is knowledgeable about construction techniques
- Is familiar with typical job conditions
- Is familiar with construction products
- Has good visualization skills
- Follows instructions explicitly
- Is creative, yet practical
- Is detail-oriented and thorough
- Can meet deadlines and work under pressure
- Is familiar with purchasing
- Is familiar with computer applications
- Works well with numbers and statistics
- Is a perfectionist at the task level
- Has very good organization skills

Keep in mind that there is as much art as science to estimating, and therefore the need for seemingly dichotomous traits is essential. Throughout the estimating process, estimators must make judgment calls regarding techniques, pricing, and people, and they often put their reputations on the line. They are risk takers—calculated risk takers, but risk takers nonetheless. For this reason, senior or chief estimators are among the most respected and highest paid individuals in the industry.

Factors Impacting Project Cost

All projects are not the same. Even if you are in the business of building the exact same facility (such as a Wal-Mart store) over and over, the price of each project will differ. There are many specific factors that will always influence the pricing of the project, and the estimator must be able to discern the level of impact for each. Many of these factors call for the art of estimating, and the more experienced the estimator, the more accurate the "gut feel" for some of these impacts will be. Let's consider several of these factors and see just how they might influence the pricing of the project.

Project Size

Obviously, the larger the project, the more it is going to cost, simply because of the square footage involved. But the concept of "economy of scale" often comes into play with construction projects. The larger the project, the more opportunity there is to increase efficiencies around any particular activity. For example, if the cost to mobilize a project (bring in equipment, set it up, and prepare the area) for a particular trade such as masonry is $5000, then it would be more economical to set up to construct a 20,000 square foot building than it would be for a 4000 square foot building because the mobilization will cost the same either way. Economy of scale also applies to labor. If there is 900 square feet of floor tiles to lay, the first 100 square feet of the installation is going to cost more per unit than the last 100 square feet of the same operation or activity simply because repetition breeds efficiency and speed. So size often impacts the estimated cost of a project.

There is always more to any operation or installation than the work activity itself. There are always preparation, mobilization, and setup and always knockdown, cleanup, and demobilization. That's why a painter will quote you a higher price to paint the interior of your house if you want different colors in every room rather than one color for all walls. It may be exactly the same square footage, but every time you have to open up, close up, and clean up a new color, it takes time. You have to clean out the paint tray or paint sprayer, and clean or replace brushes and rollers, every time you start with a new color.

NOTE

Complexity of the Project

The complexity of the project and project details impacts productivity. So even if you are pricing a relatively simple material application such as a brick veneer or stucco finish, once the shape becomes anything but a box or the height goes beyond eight feet, for example, it will be more difficult to build. It will take greater skill and/or more time. Let me share with you some of the fundamental elements that estimators consider when pricing a project.

Shape of facility   The rule of thumb that I used to share with my clients was that every time you turn a corner, it is going to cost you more money. The facility can be exactly the same square footage, but if the shape moves from a square or rectangle and the number of corners increases, the price is going to go up. Shape impacts the price of all elements of the building: the ceiling, the roof, the doors, the windows, the staircases, and so on. A flat ceiling is easier to construct than a vaulted ceiling. A gable roof is easier to build than a hip roof. A rectangular window costs less than a circlehead window. A rectangular door costs less than an archtop door. And a straight stair costs a lot less than a winding stair. Shape clearly impacts cost.

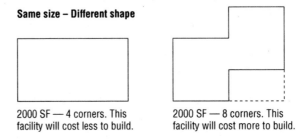

Same size – Different shape

2000 SF — 4 corners. This facility will cost less to build.

2000 SF — 8 corners. This facility will cost more to build.

Height of facility   Anything a worker cannot reach by standing on the ground will increase the cost of construction. Whenever you have to employ ladders, scaffolding, manlifts, and cranes, the price goes up. It takes additional time to set up, take down, and move this equipment around, and it also takes time to move manpower and materials up and down the equipment. The expected productivity by a craftsperson standing on the ground versus the expected productivity of the same craftsperson working on scaffolding is always less. For example, two carpenters experienced in drywall installation should place about 1700 square feet of wallboard in an eight-hour day. For walls and ceilings higher than 12 feet, the same crew would be able to place only 1445 to 1530 square feet of wallboard in a day. That's a decrease of 10 to 15 percent. Height makes a difference regardless of the building element.

Unique materials or applications   Most of us have tastes beyond our budgets. This is a common phenomenon in design and construction as well. The use of unique materials or unique applications of materials always adds to the construction costs. Knowing this will give the estimator a heads-up when he or she first reviews the plans and specs. The estimator can also count on the fact that a unique material is almost always going to require a longer *lead time* for delivery. If that delayed delivery is not anticipated by the management team in scheduling the work, the misstep can cause a delayed completion of the project overall and be very costly. Even a unique application of a common material will require special skill and take longer to install and therefore cost more money. Common ceramic tiles applied in a special geometric or artistic pattern, for instance, will always cost more to install than the same tiles installed in a standard pattern.

lead time

The amount of time it takes for a product or equipment to be delivered to the job site. Products that have a long delivery time are called long lead time items and require special planning considerations.

liquidated damages

A daily amount of money paid by the contractor to the owner for each day that the project fails to meet the completion date specified in the contract. Not all contracts contain a liquidated damages clause.

Real World Scenario

Red Flagging Long Lead Time Items

There was a project where the architect had specified a special Italian marble tile for the lobby of a high-rise office building. Unfortunately, the estimator on the job was somewhat inexperienced and did not red flag the material for early purchase, and instead waited to order the tile with all of the common or stock tiles being utilized. It turned out that that the lead time on the special marble tile was six months. There were only 90 days left in the contract for completion. The contractor made an attempt to talk the owner into a marble tile that was readily obtainable. The owner would not budge. To avoid a delayed opening of the project and having to pay *liquidated damages*, the contractor ended up installing a stock marble tile in the lobby temporarily so the facility could open on time. When the specified Italian tile finally arrived (approximately three months later), the contractor had to remove the stock tile and install the correct tile, all done during evening hours, resulting in overtime pay for the tile setters. The entire cost of installing the first tile and removing it was chalked up as a loss. (You will learn much more about liquidated damages in Chapter 7, "Contract Administration.")

This scenario illustrates the importance of the handoff of the project from the estimator to the project manager. Although the estimator picked up the added cost for the Italian tile in the estimate, he did not red flag the material when he passed the project on to the project manager. The team did not pick it up and the mistake was very costly—not just in dollars but also in the loss of goodwill because of the irritation and disappointment experienced by the owner.

Site Location

The location of the project impacts the ease of procurement and delivery of materials, labor, and equipment, and therefore affects the overall pricing of the project. Certain locations are simply more accessible than others for different reasons. For example, it is very difficult and very costly to get materials and equipment into a remote location such as the Alaskan pipeline. But at the same time, the logistics associated with getting materials delivered to a busy downtown metropolitan area such as San Francisco or New York can be just as difficult. Either way, the site location becomes a primary factor in preparing the estimate.

Location also impacts the availability and cost of labor. For example, when trying to construct a new facility in a small community, the contractor may run up against a shortage of skilled labor to perform the work. In a case like this, the contractor would have to import the needed labor from outside locations. When this occurs, the contractor usually has to provide housing and meals for the workers, adding to the costs of the overall project. If the estimator does not anticipate this added expense up front, there will be labor cost overruns. On the other hand, another location may have an abundance of skilled labor and the estimator can anticipate fairly competitive pricing in the area and estimate the job accordingly.

Pricing can also vary from city to city, even in the same state. For example, here in California where I live, the cost of installing 400 square feet of standard acoustic ceiling in San Bernardino is less than the price of the same work in San Francisco. According to R.S. Means, which is probably the largest publisher of construction cost information in the United States, the cost in San Bernardino would be approximately $990. But in San Francisco, the same ceiling would cost at least $1200, over 20 percent more. At the same time, according to Means, it would cost only $350 to install 400 square feet of standard acoustic ceiling in Farmville, Virginia. So you can see how important it is for the estimator to know about local costs in the area where the company will be building.

NOTE   In addition to providing location cost factors, R.S. Means publishes numerous annual construction cost guides and construction reference books. They are a great resource to novice and experienced estimators alike. You can access R.S. Means online at www.rsmeans.com.

Time of Construction

Time is one of the factors that every estimator must be very aware of when putting together the numbers for the project. There is always a time period between when a project bids and when the construction actually starts. There is also the time between when a project starts and when it is anticipated to end—sometimes several years. The estimator must be careful to anticipate fluctuations in prices and availability of labor during these stretches of time.

Time of year is another time factor that often comes into play when estimating project costs. Construction is often thought of as seasonal. However, the truth is that construction can take place any time of year, but certain considerations must be factored into the pricing. For example, if a contractor anticipates receiving the notice to proceed in mid-December, the estimator would factor certain cold weather preparations for the concrete work into the price. In addition to forming, placing, and finishing costs, the estimator would also have to consider the cost of heaters, special concrete blankets, and insulating materials to keep the concrete from freezing after it is placed. If the concrete pour were happening in July, none of these items would be included in the price.

There are other time factors that may not seem so obvious but must also be taken into consideration by the savvy estimator. For example, I was in the construction business in a part of the country where deer hunting was a very popular sport and most of the subcontractors in the area were avid hunters. I know it may seem very strange, but I would have to take "deer season" into account whenever estimating a project. It would take longer to complete the work during this time of year simply because many of the trades would not be as readily available, and this would definitely impact my price. Not only that, think of the challenge I faced trying to explain deer season delays to clients itching to move into their new home.

Quality of the Work

The quality of the project is defined by the standards set forth in the specifications. Quality clearly impacts project cost. The specifications stipulate what materials to use and equipment to install. There are grades of performance, durability, and aesthetics associated with every construction product. A project that specifies minimum standards for the products and equipment to be installed will cost less than a project that includes several high-end materials and installations. Obviously, marble or granite tiles are going to cost more than ceramic tiles. Stainless steel toilet partitions are going to cost more than painted metal partitions. Although both of them serve the same purpose, the degree of performance, durability, or appearance varies—the higher the quality standard, the higher the cost. An experienced estimator gets a good idea of just how much impact quality will have on the overall cost of the project after just a quick review of the plans and specs.

Market Conditions

Market conditions always have an impact on the estimate. The basic laws of supply and demand go to work here. In very tight markets where construction contracts are scarce, the cost of construction becomes very competitive and the estimates will reflect this condition. In an effort to keep good employees working, some contractors are even willing to take a job at cost with little or no profit on the project. However, when there is a lot of construction work going on, the market becomes very selective. General contractors and subcontractors alike become much pickier about which jobs they are willing to go after, and their pricing will reflect a more conservative approach to risk. The estimating team takes all of this into consideration when pricing the project.

Management Factors

Management factors are those considerations that once again have more to do with the art of estimating than the science of estimating. Management factors include such things as knowing that a particular owner or architect is more difficult to deal with than another, or sensing that you are going to have to watch things more carefully with an inexperienced subcontractor, or knowing that the owner is very slow at making decisions.

There are also some management factors that are much more predictable, such as dealing with a public project versus a private project. With a military project, for example, the paperwork and reporting required for standard contract administration tasks such as a submittal or an application for payment are at least twofold. All of that extra work takes extra time, and extra time means extra cost. Once again, an experienced estimator takes all of these factors into account before submitting a bid.

Types of Estimates

The amount of information available regarding the project will dictate the type of estimate that can be prepared. However, you must keep in mind that all estimates are not equal—the less information available, the less accurate the estimate. But sometimes the owner doesn't need a high level of accuracy. They simply need a rough idea about their building cost. At other times—for example, when preparing a competitive bid, or approaching a financial institution for a mortgage—accuracy is of vital importance. Let's take a quick look at the various types of estimates.

Conceptual Estimates

Conceptual estimates are often called ballpark estimates. Typically there are no drawings available at all. We use conceptual estimates when we are in the idea or concept stage of a project. Often an owner doesn't really know if their idea is economically feasible or not, and they don't want to start spending money on design until they know that the project is at least possible. An experienced estimator can help out in a situation like this by offering a rough order of magnitude (ROM) estimate. These estimates are based upon a cost per primary unit for the facility. For example, for hospitals, the primary unit of measure would be beds, and we would multiply the proposed number of beds by the appropriate unit cost. For a school, the calculation would be cost per pupil; for a highway, the estimate would be based on a cost per mile. Once the owner suggests how many primary units they would like to build, an estimator can whip out a rough order of magnitude estimate within minutes; however, the accuracy is limited.

Preliminary Estimates

If we have a preliminary set of drawings with overall dimensions, we can move to the next level of estimating. Preliminary estimates provide a somewhat higher level of accuracy and may be used to establish initial budgets and preliminary financing scenarios. However, these estimates should never be used to commit to a contract price. There are just too many factors that can influence the reliability of the numbers.

Although there are numerous preliminary estimate methodologies, the most common is probably the square foot method. In its simplest form, the estimator calculates the area of the floor plan and multiplies that number by a unit price. There are various levels of skill and detail that can be applied to the square foot estimating method, and the degree of accuracy increases with each step up, as will the time it takes to calculate the price.

Detailed Estimates

Whenever we have a complete set of plans and specs, we should do a detailed estimate. This is where we count every brick and stick, so to speak. Quantities and costs are calculated for every aspect of the project, and this is by far the most reliable estimate if the contractor is being asked to give a firm bid on a project. Detailed estimates are the most accurate. But keep in mind that as the accuracy increases, so does the time, effort, and skill required to complete the estimate. Although computerized estimating has reduced the time needed to compile project costs, it can still take two to three weeks and a team of estimators to put together a detailed estimate for a large, multi-story commercial building such as an office or retail complex. The estimators still have to put the bid packages together and spend time soliciting subcontractor and vendor pricing. Throughout the rest of this chapter, I will be talking about detailed estimates.

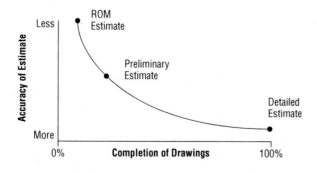

Understanding Project Costs

Before we can really get into the estimating process, it's important that we distinguish the types of costs that are included in the construction estimate. It takes a lot more than just materials and labor to build a project. There is a whole host of costs associated with construction that have nothing to do with the actual structure of the facility. For example, building permits, supervision, job trailers, portable toilets, scaffolding, freight charges, bonds, insurance, sales tax, and many other costs could be easily overlooked by an inexperienced estimator. If the estimator fails to recognize and include all costs in the project estimate, then the bid number will be off significantly. In making such a mistake, the estimator may indeed win the job by being the lowest bidder, but unfortunately will end up losing money on the project. These are hard lessons to learn but, as costly as they are, you rarely ever make the same mistake twice.

Direct Costs

Direct costs are those items that actually go into building the facility. An item is considered a direct cost if it can be linked to a specific item of work on a project. Direct costs make up the bulk of any construction estimate. The obvious direct costs associated with any project are:

- Materials
- Labor
- Equipment
- Subcontracts

Indirect Costs

Indirect costs are the expenses incurred in order to manage and deliver the materials, labor, equipment, and subcontracts employed on any given job. They are often referred to as job-specific overhead or general conditions. The list of indirect costs for any given project will vary but some of the common items include:

- Supervision
- Job trailer expense
- Temporary utilities
- Testing and inspections
- Job photographs
- Safety supplies

- Chemical toilets
- Security fencing and barricades
- Trash and debris removal
- Cleanup
- Bonds and insurance

Contractors are starting to direct their trash and debris to recycling centers rather than to the landfills. This operation takes a little more effort on the contractor's part and can actually be more expensive, but as the industry is slowly becoming more sensitive to environmental issues, recycling operations are showing up more and more in construction estimates.

NOTE

The Estimating Process

Accuracy and completeness are the fundamental objectives of the construction estimate. The ultimate goal is to have the estimated cost be greater than or equal to the actual cost of the project. When we do a construction estimate, we are concerned with three things:

- How many (quantities)
- How much (pricing)
- How long (productivity)

These three components make up the construction estimate and establish the management targets for the project team. You will discover that the estimate sets the parameters for the project budget and schedule and will be used throughout the construction process to monitor success. Now let's look at what it actually takes to put an estimate together.

Getting Started

Although an estimator can work alone in developing an estimate, the quality of an estimate improves when there is input from other members of the team. Fellow estimators, project managers, superintendents, subcontractors, material suppliers, and others can all add to the resource base when trying to make decisions during the estimating phase. The team works together to develop a unique strategy that might provide an edge in the bidding process. In preparation for the estimating task, the team becomes completely familiar with the requirements of the project by:

- Thoroughly reviewing the plans and specs

- Developing a list of questions and needed clarifications
- Attending the pre-bid meeting
- Visiting the project site

Reviewing the Plans and Specs

It is important to get a "big picture" perspective of the project before you get into the details of the work. Having an overall understanding of the difficulty of the construction will assist the estimator when making judgment calls that inevitably affect the accuracy of the estimate.

Ideally, the plans and specs are reviewed in detail before any estimating takes place. Among the first things to look for when making the initial review are any special conditions, clauses, or criteria that could adversely affect the project schedule or cause unusual risks to be taken. Such items should be highlighted during this process and red flagged for the project team when the job is passed from the estimator to the project manager. (Remember the earlier example regarding the imported Italian marble tile.) Many of these red flag clauses are found at the front end of the project manual in the Instructions to Bidders and Supplemental Conditions.

NOTE

One of the most costly red flag clauses commonly found in the project manual is a liquidated damages clause. Liquidated damages are a financial penalty applied to the contract resulting from a failure to meet a specific completion date for the project. For example, the Supplemental Conditions could stipulate that a penalty of $1000 to $10,000 a day be paid by the contractor to the owner for failing to meet a completion deadline. Liquidated damages pose a significant risk to the contractor and must be taken into account during the estimating process.

query list
A list of questions and needed clarifications compiled by an estimator as he or she reviews the plans and specs during the estimating process.

In addition to discovering red flag issues, the plan and spec review provides an opportunity for the estimator to uncover details that require clarification, or questions about the project that are not addressed in the contract documents. As the estimator thumbs through the drawings, he or she will prepare a *query list* in anticipation of the pre-bid meeting, site visit, or phone conference with the designer. The designer typically responds to each of the questions in writing. Those responses that result in a change to the original plans and specifications become official addendum to the contract.

Checklists are a common tool used to make sure that nothing gets left out or overlooked.

Pre-bid Meeting

Prior to bidding, it is common for the owner and/or designer to conduct a pre-bid meeting. This meeting often occurs at the project site and provides an opportunity for the bidding contractors to get many of their questions answered. It is very important that each of the bidding contractors sends a representative to this meeting. The estimator is often the representative sent, simply because he or she is the one most familiar with the project at this stage and has developed a query list after a thorough review of the plans and specs. Some projects require attendance at this meeting, and contractors who fail to attend are not allowed to bid.

Site Visit

No one should ever estimate a job without first visiting the job site. There are site conditions that just cannot be understood by merely looking at the plans and specs. Only by walking about will you get a good sense of the lay of the land, which will help you make the necessary judgment calls that ultimately affect your pricing. Even if the site visit is not part of the pre-bid meeting, it is your obligation to make every effort to mitigate risks associated with the bid. Visiting the site is one way in which you can mitigate those risks.

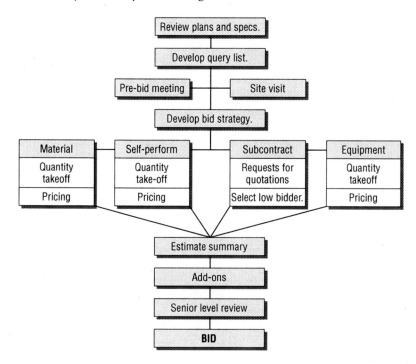

Estimators should consider the following when visiting the site:

- Distance from office
- Site conditions
- Site access
- Soil data

- Groundwater
- Security needs
- Traffic considerations
- Adjacent structures
- Possible contamination
- Water, electricity, and telephone service
- Obstructions
- Parking and storage
- Debris disposal
- Local weather patterns
- Local labor and subtrades
- Local regulations

How We Build the Estimate

You build an estimate in very much the same order that you build the actual facility. Generally, you start from the ground up and work through the 16 divisions of the CSI MasterFormat outline. (Refer back to Chapter 4, "The Construction Contract," for information about these divisions.) Each CSI division is broken down into detailed items of work. This format is one of the most common ways to organize the estimate. However you decide to organize the estimate, it is very important to stick with a consistent format. In this way, the estimate outline acts as a master checklist that should be consulted for every project to make sure that nothing gets left out of the estimate.

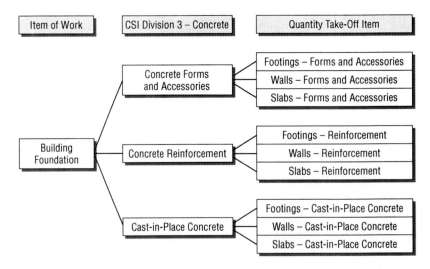

There are many computerized estimating programs on the market. Most of them build their estimates and their databases around the CSI 16-division format. Timberline and WinEst are two of the more common estimating software packages on the market. Many contractors develop their own estimating programs using basic spreadsheet software.

.... **NOTE** ....

Organizing the Work of the Estimate

Estimating the cost of a multistory office building or a high-tech manufacturing facility or a state-of-the-art concert hall is no easy job. It is a big job and takes a great deal of planning and organization. So how do you conquer this challenge? Well, the same way you eat an elephant—one bite at a time! Although the 16 divisions of the MasterFormat give us an overall outline to follow, there are literally thousands of activities and materials that must be considered before we can begin to price the project. As large as the task may seem, there actually is a logical method for organizing all of the work activities, materials, and labor associated with a project. Let's take a look at just how we eat this elephant!

Work Breakdown Structure

The primary organizational tool utilized by the construction estimator is the *work breakdown structure (WBS)*. The work breakdown structure establishes the basic building blocks of both the estimate and the schedule. (I will explain how it is applied to the schedule in Chapter 9, "Project Planning and Scheduling.")

The purpose of the work breakdown structure as it applies to the estimate is to organize and identify the work of the project by breaking each division of work into a separate *work package* or bid package. The work package identifies each step in the process of that work item. Work packages are usually assembled around the work activities typically performed by a single subcontractor or work group. Obviously, being familiar with construction materials and methods is pretty important here. One of the primary goals in creating a work package is to not overlook any of the steps needed to complete the work.

A sample work package looks something like this:

work breakdown structure (WBS)
A tool used by estimators to organize the work of a contract in a hierarchical fashion.

work package
Detailed items of work bundled together under a particular trade. Also called a bid package.

Work Package—Concrete Floor Slab

- Excavate the footings
- Install the edge forms
- Install under slab fill
- Install vapor barrier
- Install the reinforcing
- Place anchor bolts
- Place the concrete
- Finish the concrete
- Strip the form work

Once each step associated with a particular item of work is identified, it can be quantified and priced. But let me stop here and back up a minute to make sure that you remember how the work of the project is actually accomplished. The contractor has two options: to self-perform the work with his or her own forces or to subcontract the work to various trade contractors. The contractor will have to do all of the quantifying and pricing of each step of the work if he or she decides to self-perform a particular section of work. If the contractor decides to subcontract out some of the work, then the subcontractor will quantify and price the work and submit a bid to the general contractor. The greatest challenge either way is to make sure that nothing gets overlooked or left out of the estimate.

NOTE   **Sometimes the general contractor calculates his or her own quantities and estimates for subcontracted work even though the subcontractor will be submitting a bid. This is called a fair value estimate; it's done as a check to guard against inaccurate quantity surveying by the subcontractor and unreasonable pricing.**

Calculating Quantities

takeoff
A term commonly used in the construction industry to describe the process of measuring the plans to quantify materials, labor, and equipment.

Okay, now that we have assembled all of our work packages and identified all of the steps necessary to do the work, we can start doing our quantity *takeoff*. We must quantify all of our materials, labor, and general conditions before we can price any of the work. We need to calculate "how many" before we can calculate "how much." Once we determine the quantities, we can apply a price factor to the equation. Junior estimators often start off as *quantity surveyors*. The primary attributes of a good quantity surveyor are the ability to read and interpret plans, knowledge of common units of measure for construction materials and labor, and basic estimating mathematics.

quantity surveyors
Individuals who are responsible for counting up and calculating all of the quantities of materials, labor, and equipment necessary to build a construction project.

You will use algebra to measure ratio and proportion, plane geometry for lineal and area measurements, solid geometry for cubic measurements, and plane trigonometry for lineal, area, and cubic measurements. The following table shows some of the mathematical functions and their applications:

Mathematical Function	Measurement	Sample Estimating Application	Unit of Measure
Basic Math	Counting	To calculate the quantity of interior doors	Each
Algebra	Perimeter	To calculate the quantity of rebar in the footing	Lineal Feet

Mathematical Function	Measurement	Sample Estimating Application	Unit of Measure
Plane Geometry	Area	To calculate the quantity of stucco siding	Square Feet
Plane Geometry	Area	To calculate the quantity of carpet	Square Yard
Solid Geometry	Volume	To calculate the quantity of concrete in the footing	Cubic Yard

There are also a number of common estimating formulas that can be found in any estimating manual or text book. Here are a couple of samples:

Work Item	Common Formula	Sample Calculation
Standard Brick	6.67 bricks per square foot of wall area with 5% waste	1260 square feet × 6.67 = 8404 bricks 8404 bricks + 5% waste = 8824 bricks
Mortar for $3/8''$ joints	7.2 cubic feet per 100 square feet of wall area with 40% waste	1260 square feet ÷ 100 = 12.6 square feet 12.6 × 7.2 cubic feet = 90.72 cubic feet 90.72 + 40% waste = 127 cubic feet mortar

Quantifying Materials

Quantifying materials is the least risky of all the estimating activities. We are simply counting and calculating all of the parts and pieces that will go into the project. Quantity surveying represents more of the science of estimating. That's because we are working with known sizes and dimensions depicted in the drawings. If the plans are drawn correctly and include all of the information needed to do the takeoff, the estimator should be able to come up with very accurate quantities, assuming that he or she doesn't overlook anything and doesn't make mathematical errors. The estimator reviews the plans, the elevations, the sections, and the details, pulls the dimensions needed to make the appropriate calculations, and comes up with the lengths, areas, and volumes of work and material required for the project.

Probably the most difficult part of the quantity survey is making sure that the quantity is taken off in the proper unit of measure. The unit of measure for takeoff must be the same as the unit of measure for pricing. For example, concrete is priced by the cubic yard. The quantity surveyor must take off all concrete by the cubic foot (length × width × depth) and then convert to cubic yards to match the pricing unit. It takes a little time to learn all of the pricing units for the various materials and labor but this knowledge is an absolute necessity if you are an estimator.

In this typical quantity surveying exercise, you will estimate the cubic yards of concrete needed for this foundation. All inches are converted to decimals of a foot. Here are the steps:

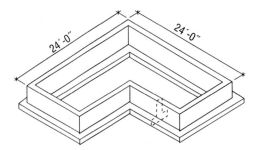 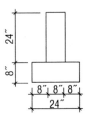

- ◆ Section area of foundation:

    Footing = 2.0 feet × .66 feet = 1.32 SF

    Wall = .66 feet × 2.0 feet = 1.32 SF

    Total section area = 1.32 SF + 1.32 SF = 2.64 SF

- ◆ Perimeter of building:

    24.0 feet + 24.0 feet + 24.0 feet + 24.0 feet = 96 feet

- ◆ Section area × perimeter = cubic feet

    2.64 SF × 96 feet = 253.44 CF

- ◆ Convert to cubic yards (unit of measure for concrete):

    253.44 CF ÷ 27 CF = 9.39 cubic yards

The answer is 9.39 cubic yards of concrete in foundation.

Quantifying Labor and Equipment

Quantifying labor and equipment is a little riskier. That's because we must deal with crew sizes and productivity rates. In other words, working with the human factors of construction is not quite the same as working with hard and fast dimensions on a set of drawings. Productivity is the amount of work that can be placed or installed in a specified unit of time. Productivity varies due to site conditions, weather, crew makeup, crew skill level, complexity of the project, and several other factors discussed earlier in the chapter.

This is where estimating moves way over on the art side of the equation. It's all about judgment. The individual estimator will determine the productivity for any given crew regarding any given item of work. Fortunately, productivity is something that is studied quite extensively in the construction industry, and there are databases and references available that can help the estimator make sensible judgments regarding labor and equipment quantity takeoffs. In the following, I show some average crew sizes and productivity rates for concrete work.

Item of Work	Crew and Equipment	Estimating Unit	Productivity Output
Forming Slab	3 carpenters 1 laborer 3 power tools	Lineal foot	600 lineal feet per day 75 lineal feet per hour
Reinforcing Slab	2 rodmen	Square feet	2700 square feet per day 338 square feet per hour
Placing Concrete	1 foreman 5 laborers 2 gas engine vibrators 1 concrete pump	Cubic yard	120 cubic yards per day 15 cubic yards per hour
Finishing Slab	1 concrete finisher 1 gas finishing machine	Square feet	625 square feet per day 78 square feet per hour

I've already referenced R.S. Means as a very valuable resource for construction estimating data. Another excellent source of information, especially regarding productivity, is *Walker's Building Estimator's Reference Book*. This handbook was originally published in 1915 and is updated every two years. If you are serious about construction estimating, Walker's is a must-have reference.

NOTE

Quantifying General Conditions

Also called job overhead, general conditions make up the indirect costs associated with any given project. Time, not productivity, is the normal unit of measure for general conditions. Therefore, the primary task of the estimator is to come up with a time estimate for the overall job duration. The estimator must make an educated guess as to how many days, weeks, months, or years the construction will take to complete. A sampling of general condition items and their respective units of measure are shown here.

General Condition Item	Common Unit of Measure
Supervision (salary)	Week
Job trailer (rent)	Month
Material storage trailers (rent)	Month
Temporary utilities (usage)	Month
Portable toilets (rent)	Month
Dumpsters (rent)	Month
Job photographs	Lump sum
On-site web cam	Lump sum
Job office supplies	Lump sum

Pricing the Work

Once all of our quantities are calculated, we are halfway there. Now all we have to do is plug in the unit cost for each item of material, labor, equipment, and general conditions in our estimate. You can see the price extensions displayed in Table 6.1. As an estimator, your primary concern is where the costs will come from and their reliability.

Sources of Information

Pricing information comes from a variety of sources. When it comes to materials, we can obviously get prices directly from our vendors and retail building suppliers. Or we can check the various construction cost guides such as R.S. Means. They list unit costs for every section of work for labor, material, and equipment. Many construction companies create their own cost databases based on historical performance. They track actual job costs from various projects over a number of years and come up with average unit prices for their self-performed work. If a company has an excellent cost reporting system in place, then this may be the best way to go. However, not all companies have such a system in place, and many rely on published cost data for their pricing.

There is one more alternative when it comes to pricing labor. Some estimators choose to use the productivity data from the various guides, but then calculate their own unit prices by using local wage rates in the formula. See the sidebar titled "Calculating Crew Unit Cost" for an example.

Table 6.1   Calculating the Estimate

Description of Work	Quan-tity	Mat. Unit Price	Total Mat.	Labor Unit Price	Total Labor	Equip. Unit Price	Total Equip.	Total Cost
Form slab	390 LF	$0.31	$121	$1.25	$484	$0.05	$20	$625
Reinforce slab	9500 SF	$0.18	$1710	$0.16	$1525	—	—	$3235
Place concrete	120 CY	$63	$7560	$11.15	$1338	$5.35	$642	$9540
Finish slab	9500 SF	—	—	$0.31	$2945	$0.06	$570	$3515
TOTAL SLAB CONCRETE			$9391		$6292		$1232	$16,915

Calculating Crew Unit Cost

According to *Walker's Building Estimator's Reference Book*, one tile setter with one helper can install approximately 90 square feet of mortar set, glazed wall tile in an eight-hour day. If I pay my tile setter $22 per hour and the helper $10 per hour, then my unit price for glazed wall tile labor will be $2.84 per square foot based on Walker's productivity rate and my wage scale. The unit price would vary as my wage rate varies.

$22 (tile setter) + $10 (laborer) = $32 per crew hour

Crew rate of $32 × 8 hour day = $256 per day

Crew can set 90 square feet of tile per day

$256 ÷ 90 = $2.84 per square foot for this particular crew

Obtaining Subcontractor and Vendor Bids

The final components of our estimate are subcontractor and vendor bids. Today, subcontractor and vendor bids make up the bulk of the construction estimate. While the estimating team is putting together their own pricing for self-performed work, they must also be gathering prices from subcontractors for the work they are not going to self-perform. The team must also be soliciting vendor pricing for all of the materials and equipment associated with the work. The management of this process is very important. If one of the trades needed to complete the project is not covered, there will be a big hole in the estimate, which will lead to a big problem on bid day. There are four steps to ensure that the solicitation of the subcontracted work and vendor pricing are complete and thorough:

- ◆ Solicit the bids.
- ◆ Receive the bids.
- ◆ Analyze the bids.
- ◆ Choose the bids.

Soliciting the Bids

After a complete review of the plans and specs, the estimator will create a list or chart representing all the work of the contract, showing which areas of work or trades will be self-performed, which will require subcontractor or vendor quotes, and which will require both. A sample sub/vendor list is shown in Table 6.2.

Table 6.2   Subcontractor-Vendor List

Div	Item Of Work	Self Perform	Sub	Vendor
2	Earthwork		X	
	Landscape		X	
	Paving		X	
	Landscaping	X	X	
3	Concrete Forming	X		
	Concrete Reinforcing	X		
	Concrete Placing	X	X	
	Concrete Finishing	X	X	
4	Masonry – CMU Block		X	X
	Masonry – Stone work		X	X
5	Metal Railings	X		X
6	Rough Carpentry	X		X
	Finish Carpentry	X	X	X
7	Roofing		X	
	Waterproofing	X		
8	Doors & Windows	X		X
	Skylights	X		X
9	Drywall		X	
	Painting		X	
	Tile		X	

Table 6.2   Subcontractor-Vendor List *(continued)*

Div	Item Of Work	Self Perform	Sub	Vendor
	Carpet		X	
10	Specialties		X	
14	Elevator		X	
15	Mechanical		X	
16	Electrical		X	

After it is determined which areas of work will require a price quote from a vendor or a subcontractor, a formal solicitation process gets under way. Although subcontractors and vendors watch the trade journals and construction news services for bid notices as closely as the general contractors do, most estimators choose to send out their own Requests for Quotation to a selected list of subcontractors and vendors with whom they have a past history. They usually send out requests to several companies representing the same trade.

It is important that these requests go out very early in the estimating process to give the subcontractors enough time to put together a price or notify you of their decision not to bid on the project. It is crucial that the estimator be aware of whom they can expect to receive quotes from on bid day. Trust me; you do not want to be left hanging on bid day waiting for an expected subcontractor quote that doesn't arrive. At the last minute, you will be left to guess what the estimated cost of the work in question might be. Estimators do everything they can to avoid this situation. And even though it takes a lot of time to solicit all of the bids, it is far better to play it safe than to be left standing without a trade covered by a reliable price.

NOTE

One of the most precious possessions of the estimator is their personal directory of subcontractor and vendor names, addresses, and phone numbers. It can take years to develop reliable relationships with a substantial list of steadfast trade contractors and material suppliers. When trying to win a job, this database can become one of the estimator's most powerful resources.

Receiving the Bids

The Request for Quotation includes all of the pertinent information relative to the project including project name and location, who the architect is, where the plans may be obtained, when the bid is due, and how the bid may be received by the contractor (by mail, phone, fax). Although some subcontractors and vendors send their initial quotes ahead of time, most bids are called in by phone on bid day—many at the last minute. I have already described to you the chaotic environment that ensues on a typical bid day in Chapter 3, "How We Get the Work."

Whether the bid is received ahead of time or at the last minute, it is very important that each one be recorded accurately and analyzed thoroughly to determine whether it covers all of the work detailed in the plans and specs for that particular section of work. Estimators typically use a standard telephone bid form as a checklist for vital information when they are receiving prices by phone.

Telephone Bid

Project: A.J. Coffee House   **Date:** July 18, 2004

Company: Wayne's House of Tile
Address: 432 Rocky Blvd., Rimrock, AZ 97660
Phone: 734-555-1212   **Fax:** 734-555-1212

Division of Work: FINISHES
Work Included: TILE

Scope:
Work includes all surface preparation, layout, mastic, tile, grout, and clean-up for kitchen area, storage area, customer area, and restrooms.

Exclusions:
Outside tile work

Quoted per plans and specs: YES
Acknowledged Addendum: No. 1 and No. 2
Includes Sales Tax: YES
Bond: YES

Analyzing the Bids

Although this is one of the more stressful tasks associated with the estimating process, especially when bids are arriving at the last minute, it is a crucial one. This is where we attempt to find any holes or overlap in our estimate. The estimator looks to make sure that every little detail associated with an item of work is covered in the bid. For example, with a painting bid, sometimes caulking is overlooked. The caulking must be covered somewhere. And if it is not part of the painting bid package, then where is it? Is it covered in the siding subcontractor's bid? Will it be done by the contractor's own forces? The estimating team must make sure that it is priced somewhere in the estimate.

scope sheet
Similar to a work package, a scope sheet describes the items of work to be performed under a particular trade heading. Often accompanies a subcontractor's bid or a Request for Quotation.

One of the tools that the estimator uses to assist this analysis is a *scope sheet*. These sheets go out with the Requests for Quotation and list all the items associated with that bid package, including any miscellaneous bits and pieces such as hardware, flashing, caulk, inserts, moldings, or trim. Some other common cost items checked during the bid analysis are:

- Sales tax
- Performance bond
- Shipping costs
- Delivery charges

Choosing the Bids

Once all of the bids have been received and analyzed, the estimator chooses which price to use. Under the traditional design-bid-build project delivery method, the low bid usually gets plugged into the estimate. However, it is always important that all bids be looked at as a group before choosing, because a situation may arise where one of the bids is actually too low. Yes, there is such a thing, and when you receive one, you should be very wary. A bid that appears to be significantly lower than the rest of the quotes should activate an immediate red flag to the estimator. When this occurs, a thorough review must take place. The estimator must determine whether the low quote is a result of an error or miscalculation on the subcontractor's part or if the subcontractor actually has come up with a legitimate price based upon a creative approach or strategic buying advantage. Making this determination is tricky business and if the estimator makes the wrong call, it could be quite costly. If the contractor uses the exceptionally low price in her bid, and then gets the job, she will expect the subcontractor to perform his work at the quoted price. However, if the subcontractor later discovers that he cannot actually do the work for the quoted price (because of an error or for some other reason), then the contractor is left with this huge gap between the low bidder's price and the next lowest bidder. The contractor will have to make up the difference.

Subcontractors have no contractual obligations to the contractor regarding their prices at the time of bidding. Subcontractor agreements are not executed until after the contractor has signed the contract for construction with the owner.

NOTE

Once all of the self-performed work has been quantified and priced and all of the appropriate subcontractor and vendor bids have been chosen, it is time to pull all the numbers together to prepare the final estimate.

Putting It All Together

It's time to compile all of our self-performed work and subcontracted work into one estimate summary. All of the subtotals calculated on the material takeoff sheets are transferred to the estimate summary sheet as well. The estimator must be very careful to accurately transfer all of the numbers. As you can see in Table 6.3, the estimate summary follows the CSI 16-division format discussed earlier in the chapter. However, a few very important numbers have been added down at the bottom. Once we calculate the cost of the project, we must also apply taxes, general overhead, and profit to come up with our final bid. These last few items are often referred to as project *add-ons*.

add-ons
A term commonly used in construction estimating to describe the taxes, overhead, and profit added to the estimate after all other costs have been calculated.

Taxes

We include two types of taxes in our construction estimate: sales tax and payroll taxes. That's why it is important to divide our summary into four columns: material, labor, equipment, and subcontracts. The subcontracted work and equipment bids will already have taxes included, but sales tax must be added to the material column and payroll taxes must be added to the labor column. We all know what sales taxes are, but you may not be as familiar with payroll taxes (also referred to as labor burden). Some of the payroll add-ons are not taxes at all but we merely refer to them as taxes to keep it simple.

When I was running my own construction company, employing approximately 14 to 20 people, it really surprised me to learn just how much "burden" labor really did put on the payroll. Sometimes this factor alone will cause a general contractor to subcontract work that otherwise they might self-perform. The percentage is significant. Those costs that I am classifying as payroll taxes include:

- Employer's portion of social security tax
- Workers' compensation
- Unemployment tax
- Employee benefits (health insurance, life insurance, vacation, paid holidays, and so on)

General Overhead

I've already mentioned job-specific overhead. These costs include such things as the job site office trailer, portable toilets, and job photographs. They are estimated item by item relative to a specific job. General overhead is a different story. Basically, general overhead represents the cost of doing business. These are expenses that would be incurred by the company whether they had a job to build or not, such as office expenses, executive salaries, and automobile insurance. General overhead is applied to the estimate as a percentage of total cost. This percentage will vary from company to company.

Profit

The goal for every project is to make a profit. Profit is what's left after all costs and expenses associated with the job have been paid. The estimate represents the contractor's best guess as to what those costs and expenses are going to be.

Profit is expressed as a percentage of the total estimated cost. Profit is rarely a fixed percentage in construction. The estimating team will make a determination as to how much that percentage should be for any given job. As previously

Table 6.3   Estimate Summary for Office Building

	Division of Work	Total Material	Total Labor	Total Equipment	Subcontracts	TOTAL
1	General Conditions	$112,400	$64,100	$1,040	0	$177,540
2	Site Work	$4,600	$3,500	$2,300	$176,800	$187,200
3	Concrete	$83,900	$54,340	$4,110	0	$142,350
4	Masonry	0	0	0	$46,300	$46,300
5	Metals	$5,100	$1,800	0	0	$6,900
6	Wood & Plastics	$243,500	$191,250	0	0	$434,750
7	Thermal & Moisture Protect	0	0	0	$86,000	$86,000
8	Doors & Windows	$43,970	$15,120	0	$1,775	$60,865
9	Finishes	0	0	0	$102,200	$102,200
10	Specialties	$7,950	$2,790	0	0	$10,740
11	Equipment	0	0	0	0	0
12	Furnishings	0	0	0	0	0
13	Special Construction	$1,345	$890	$950	0	$3,185
14	Conveying Systems	0	0	0	$45,000	$45,000
15	Mechanical	0	0	0	$210,000	$210,000
16	Electrical	0	0	0	$160,000	$160,000
	TOTALS	$502,765	$333,790	$8,400	$828,075	$1,673,030
	Sales Tax (7.5%)	$37,707	0	0	0	$37,707
	Payroll Tax (31%)	0	$103,475	0	0	$103,475
	SUBTOTAL	$540,472	$437,265	$8,400	$828,075	$1,814,212
	Overhead (6.5%)	–	–	–	–	$117,924
	SUBTOTAL	–	–	–	–	$1,932,136
	Profit (3.5%)	–	–	–	–	$67,625
	TOTAL ESTIMATE	–	–	–	–	$1,999,761

stated, when times are tight in construction and there is very little work to bid, profit margins may be quite small. On the other hand, when there is a lot of construction going on in a particular market and demand is high, profit margins will be adjusted upward. Either way, profit is an estimated number just like every other number in the bid.

It is highly unusual for the actual cost of the project to exactly match the estimated cost of the project. If we consider the 16 divisions of our estimate summary, and each of our add-ons, the most likely scenario will be that some divisions (and add-ons) will be over the individual division estimates, and some will be under the individual estimates. However, it's the final number that we are most concerned with. The goal is to have the actual overall cost of the project at the estimate or under.

Completing the Estimate

Once the estimate is complete, the contractor prepares and submits their bid and delivers it to the owner. (Remember Chapter 3?) The particular bid procedure will specify when and how the contractors will be notified as to whether they have been awarded the contract. Winning or losing depends upon the quality of the estimate—and of course, a little luck. High quality estimates display the same characteristics:

- ◆ Correct quantities
- ◆ Accurate labor hours
- ◆ Correct pricing
- ◆ Accurate calculations
- ◆ Completeness
- ◆ Proper overhead
- ◆ Proper profit

If the estimator was successful, he will gather together all of the documents and label or tag them as "original bid documents." It is very important that there is a clear paper trail detailing exactly how the final bid was compiled. Eventually a clean set of drawings and specs will be issued to the builder to formally execute the contract. The estimator will want to check these documents against the original bid documents to make sure nothing has changed. All of the calculations, price quotes, subcontractor bids, and any other pertinent documentation that could track the estimate logic will be organized and bundled into a package that will be passed on to the project manager charged with running the job. And although the estimator's primary job is complete once the bid is finished, he will provide support to the project team as the job moves forward, often clarifying information and pricing change orders.

If the estimator was unsuccessful, he will gather all of the bidding documents (plans and specs) and return them for deposit refunds. All of the paperwork associated with the estimate will be filed for possible future reference.

Remember, It's All a Game

Bidding is a competition, and just as in any other competitive sport, there's emotion involved. Sometimes you win and sometimes you lose. When you win, you feel really good. Winning a contract is a *big* deal! Getting jobs for your firm is what keeps the business going, and it is no small achievement. Some companies actually instigate a formal celebratory event each time a project is won, such as ringing a bell or sounding a horn. Other companies, such as my own, would simply execute high fives around the room and go out to dinner. But either way, it is definitely a time for celebration.

On the other hand, when you lose a job after all that work, you feel really bad. You go over and over in your head what you could have done differently. You check your calculations, you review the subcontractor bids, and you consider your add-ons. However, it is usually to no avail. As hard as you try, you will probably never figure out why someone else won and you lost. Every company is different, with different personnel, project approach, overhead, and logic, and no two estimates will ever be the same. And the truth is that no one will know the final outcome until the job is complete and the last numbers are added up. Only then can one declare the estimate a winner or a loser.

Terms to Know

add-ons	scope sheet
lead time	takeoff
liquidated damages	work breakdown structure (WBS)
quantity surveyors	work packages
query list	

Review Questions

1. What is a construction estimate?

2. Name the four primary categories of costs in the construction estimate.

3. How are construction estimates typically organized?

4. What type of estimate would we probably do if we were meeting with a client for the first time and they wanted to get a rough idea about their project cost?

5. Identify the four preparation steps taken to start the estimating process.

6. What are general conditions?

7. What unit of measure is typically employed for pricing general conditions?

8. What is a scope sheet?

9. Identify at least four characteristics exhibited in a quality estimate.

10. When will we know the true accuracy of our estimate?

Chapter 7

Contract Administration

Contract administration is all about managing the business details and relationships. When you consider all of the General Conditions, Supplemental Conditions, and specifications associated with the contract, you can understand what a challenge this is. Every statement and every clause in the contract sets forth rules, regulations, and procedures for every aspect of the construction process. Nothing goes forward without some paperwork leading the way: written requests for information, change orders, submittal logs, shop drawings, pay requests, lien waivers, progress reports, and on and on. Staying on top of it all is a huge task and a critical one.

It is virtually impossible for one person to accomplish the job; support from the main office and the job site is required. Although one person may be the contract administrator, it takes the efforts of the entire project team to accomplish the task. From the notice to proceed to the Certificate of Completion, every notification, clarification, correction, approval, request, change, letter, e-mail, phone call, and administrative transaction must be tracked. Without proper attention to the contract details, the whole job could end up in one big lawsuit. No matter how good your concrete finishers or carpenters might be, you can't really fulfill the requirements of the project without strong contract administration.

Starting Off Right

By now, you are well aware that the owner of the project really sets the stage for how the construction game is going to be played. The owner establishes the project program (along with the architect), decides which project delivery method to use, and selects a contract form. Each of these decisions has an influence on how the players relate to one another in general terms. However, once everyone—architect, contractor, subcontractors, and vendors—is on board for the project, it is time to flesh out the details about how the team is going to work together for the duration of the project. It is very important that the owner take a leadership role in directing the team and make sure that everyone gets started off on the right foot. Virtually all construction projects start with a formal preconstruction meeting led by the owner.

Preconstruction Conference

The purpose of this initial meeting is to establish the rules by which the game is to be played and to clarify the lines of authority and communication. It is critically important that the owner's representatives, the architect, the primary engineers, and the contractor's project manager and supervisory staff be present at this first meeting. It is important to have the major subcontractors and vendors attend as well. There may even be some outside agencies that should be called in, especially if they have a substantial influence on the project, which they often do. Public utility personnel, fire marshals, and highway department representatives are some of the more common public agency players brought in on the initial discussions.

The agenda for this meeting usually covers all of the items listed in the General Conditions and Supplemental Conditions of the contract (think back to Chapter 4, "The Construction Contract") but in much greater detail. This initial preconstruction meeting is an opportunity for the parties to be introduced and primary relationships to be established. The agenda covers the fundamental administrative and coordination issues associated with the construction project. A number of common discussion items are listed next:

- Introductions and Accountabilities
- Mobilization and Site Logistics
    - Site access
    - Temporary utilities
    - Temporary facilities
    - Site security
    - Traffic and pedestrian issues

- ◆ Construction Coordination Issues
  - ◆ Subcontracts
  - ◆ Submittals
  - ◆ Shop drawings
  - ◆ Requests for information
- ◆ Schedule Issues
  - ◆ Notice to Proceed
  - ◆ Sequence of work
  - ◆ Work hours
  - ◆ Liquidated damages
- ◆ Payment Issues
  - ◆ Schedules of Value
  - ◆ Applications for Payment
- ◆ Change Orders and Extra Work
- ◆ Dispute Issues
  - ◆ Claims
  - ◆ Alternative Dispute Resolution
- ◆ Completion Procedures
  - ◆ Substantial Completion
  - ◆ Final Inspection
  - ◆ Final Payment

The Contract Administration Function

Contract administration has to do with the management of the details and information presented in the General and Supplemental Conditions of the contract and at the preconstruction meeting. Sometimes this role is handled by an individual identified as a contract administrator and sometimes the function is handled by numerous individuals associated with the project team. For example, applications for payment are often handled by a contract administrator back at the main office, but requests for information and submittals are handled by field engineers located on the job site.

The need for a clear and accurate paper trail in construction is paramount, and the individuals charged with the contract administration duties must be particularly dedicated to the chore if the job is to move along smoothly. Poor performance here can be devastating. For example, inaccurate payment applications or delayed information attainment will cause havoc with the entire construction process. The work flow will suffer and affect both the schedule and the budget. That of course puts the entire project at risk. So, you can see how important the contract administration function is to the overall project success even though it has very little to do with the actual bricks and sticks of building. You will get an even better sense of how these administrative and organizational issues impact the job in Chapter 8, "Construction Operations and Job Site Management."

NOTE

Keeping up with all of the paperwork and red tape of the contract is a real challenge, and it cannot be taken lightly. Poor contract administration procedures are one of the main reasons that projects get into trouble. And if the project should go to court, the party with the most organized managerial procedures will win the majority of the time. The contractor must train all of his management personnel in good administrative practices.

Setting the Tone

Partnering
A team-building technique, calling upon the parties to the construction contract to establish a common set of project goals and objectives and develop a mutually acceptable protocol for communication and conflict resolution through a formal agreement.

The tone expressed by the owner and their representatives at the initial preconstruction meeting will set the tone for the entire project. I cannot stress enough how very important it is for this meeting to be conducted in a spirit of trust, cooperation, and fairness. Any hints of heavy-handedness on the part of the owner or the architect will only cause distrust and apprehension on the part of the workforce. This is not the way to start off the job. Owners who understand the importance of setting a positive tone up front sometimes employ a team-building technique called *partnering*. Partnering has been used successfully to build cooperative relationships between the owner, the design team, and the construction team on numerous projects of every size and type, resulting in improved communication, speedier decision making, fewer change orders, improved quality, shorter schedules, lower costs, fewer disputes, less litigation, and higher satisfaction all around. Let me give you a brief synopsis of what partnering is and how it works.

Partnering

The concept of partnering is not new, but it really didn't start showing up in the construction arena until the Army Corps of Engineers embraced it in 1988 on a project in Alabama. Then in January 1991, the Associated General Contractors of America (AGC) took hold of the Corps of Engineers' concepts and started promoting the technique on a regular basis.

The reality of the traditional owner-designer-contractor relationship is this: the environment can often turn antagonistic and adversarial. The intent of partnering is to gather together all stakeholders—owner, contractor, designers, subcontractors, and material suppliers—early in the project, to establish a mutually acceptable protocol for communication and conflict resolution through a formal agreement. The goal of partnering is to create a win-win situation for all involved.

The partnering process itself starts with a few intensive planning meetings before the construction ever gets started. Led by a qualified facilitator, the team first develops a mission statement for the project. Then they knock out a charter identifying specific goals and objectives for the project. They continue by developing an effective communication system, a reliable method for monitoring and evaluating the system, and finally, an effective conflict resolution system. Once this structure is in place, all members of the team confirm their commitment by signing a formal agreement.

The key to partnering is to embrace it as a process, not just a one- or two-day event. It is an everyday practice that needs to be maintained and monitored throughout the duration of the project. For the partnering agreement to have meaning and merit, the leadership of the team must be steadfast in their commitment to the process. AGC defines seven essential elements of partnering for it to be successful. These are:

- Commitment to partnering by the top management of every organization involved in the project

- Equity in considering all stakeholders' interests to create shared goals and commitment by all stakeholders

- Trust among all parties through personal relationships and open communication, with mutual sharing and understanding of each party's risks and goals

- A partnering charter developed jointly by all parties that identifies specific mutual goals and objectives

- Implementation of mutual goals and a mechanism for problem solving

- Continuous evaluation based on the goals to ensure that the plan is proceeding as intended and all stakeholders are carrying their share of responsibilities

- Timely resolution of all disputes at the lowest level possible during the project

I will be the first to tell you that carrying a complex project from start to finish, while working with a wide array of personalities and diverse agendas, is no easy task. However, the proper implementation of partnering and other team-building efforts before the work begins can help in a big way. Several studies have shown that partnered projects outperform non-partnered projects in practically every category tested. Obviously, partnering is one way to set a tone that really works.

NOTE   To learn more about partnering in construction, I recommend checking out *Partnering: Changing Attitudes in Construction* (Associated General Contractors of America, 1995) or *Partnering Manual for Design and Construction* by William C. Ronco and Jean S. Ronco (McGraw-Hill, 1996).

Who's on First?

In any game, not only do you need to know what the rules are, but you also need to know who is playing what position. As stated earlier, construction presents new challenges every day, and as a construction manager, you must be prepared to take on these challenges. Well, you can't do that all by yourself. You must depend on your team. And you can't depend on your team unless you know who they are and how to get hold of them, fast.

The very first task in contract administration is to create a contact list for every single person associated with the project. That includes the owner of the project, the project architect, the project manager, the superintendent, the field engineer, each subcontractor, vendor, and material supplier, the lumberyard foreman—even the driver of the mobile lunch van. This list becomes the lifeline for the project; the communication chain is an integral part of the management plan. The contact list must contain all of the information needed to reach each person at any time, day or night. Office, cell, home, and fax numbers must be listed along with e-mail addresses and mailing addresses. I have found that it is also a good idea to list secretary and assistant phone numbers as well.

Many issues come up on a project that require a fast response from exactly the right person in order to keep the work flowing. Solving problems doesn't happen in a vacuum, and you can't have too many contact numbers or too many people on your team. In addition to the contact list, it is important to know the specific accountabilities for the primary players on the list. Therefore, it is wise to also create a responsibility matrix as a quick reference for everyone on the project team. A sample responsibility matrix is illustrated in Table 7.1.

NOTE   One of the things that new field engineers get nervous about when they first go to work on the job site is their inexperience in construction. All of a sudden, they go from working summers cleaning up construction debris for their father's home-building business to being smack dab in the middle of a multi-million-dollar high-rise project somewhere. And on top of that, now they are actually accountable for something important. My advice to new recruits is always the same. "No one expects you to know everything there is to know about construction, but they do expect you to know where to go to get the information you need."

Table 7.1   Sample Responsibility Matrix

OWNER REPS Peabody Industrial	ARCHITECT Keller & Hendricks	UTILITIES Various	SUBCONTRACTORS Various
President Tom Peabody (805)768-0674 (O) (805)768-5220 (C)	Project Architect Sandra Keller (805)891-1723 (O) (805)891-4590 (C)	SO-CAL Electric Co. Diane Eppersen (805)768-0674 (O) (805)768-5220 (C)	Brian Hap Electric Brian Hap (805)617-8944 (O) (805)617-9332 (C)
Clerk of the Works Bob Stevens (805)768-0098 (O) (805)768-5411 (C)	Project Manager Ron Michaels (805)891-2234 (O) (805)891-1144 (C)	Cal State Gas Wayne Koppel (805)268-0554 (O) (805)268-1772 (C)	Thompson Mechanical Kyle Gibbons (805)459-9008 (O) (805)469-4571 (C)
Resident Manager Steve Bosco (805)768-1134 (O) (805)768-7604 (C)	Design Administrator George White (805)891-8278 (O) (805)891-7306 (C)	Beaumont City Water/Sewer John Dirk (805)445-0974 (O) (805)445-0610 (C)	Vander Excavation Mike Shepard (805)768-3331 (O) (805)768-8200 (C)

The one sure thing about construction is that problems are going to arise every single day on the job site. Regardless of your position on the team, you must be able to respond quickly when the problems arise. In construction management, you don't need to have all of the answers, but you do need to know where to find them. So probably the most valuable tool in your tool belt is the telephone. The second is the contact list and responsibility matrix that you create for the project, and the third is your own personal "special resource" list created over time. (See the following sidebar titled "Help Is Just a Phone Call Away.")

Coordinating Construction Details

You've probably heard the expression, "The devil's in the details." That couldn't be truer than it is in construction. The amount of information that must be processed on a construction project is tremendous. It is probably one of the biggest and most arduous challenges of the job and one of the primary contract administration functions.

There are literally thousands of bits of information and approvals pertaining to the construction that must be checked and rechecked, clarified, and confirmed. Just think for a minute about the details that you would have to consider if you were to build a new home. Even though you already have decided upon the house design and have the plans in hand, there are still numerous decisions and approvals that you would have to make. (Those of you who have already built a home will know exactly what I am talking about!) For example, you would have to decide on and approve the color of the siding, color of the trim, color of the front door, door hardware style and finish, garage door style, type of garage door opener, type of windows, type of glass in the windows, roof shingle color, color of the gutters and downspouts, exterior lighting styles and finish, and so on. And we haven't even moved to the interior of the house yet, where we would have to approve dozens of details regarding each room and its features. Then, of course, there are all of the technical approvals associated with the heating, air conditioning, electrical, plumbing, and other equipment. Do you get my drift? Multiply this process about 100 to 1000 times and you will get a sense of what it takes to manage and coordinate all of the approvals and information associated with the details of construction.

Real World Scenario

Help Is Just a Phone Call Away

Some of the most valuable resources that I had when working as a construction manager were vendors and manufacturers of products. Many problems that arise on a project stem from not knowing exactly how a material or product is going to react to various conditions.

For example, one time we were trying to install a synthetic concrete topping compound to about 20,000 square feet of an existing manufacturing plant floor. Having never used the product before, we read the installation instructions very carefully and proceeded to apply the material exactly as stipulated. Well, it wasn't working. Even though we had scarified the floor, as directed, to give the product better "sticking" power, it would still just chip right off. We contacted the architect, the product manufacturer, and the owner. No one had a clue as to why it wasn't working.

Finally I called a friend of mine, Charlie, who was a sales rep for another manufacturer (not of the product that I was using). Charlie was an expert when it came to anything to do with concrete and concrete products. As soon as I told him what I was trying to do, and the product I was using, and what was happening, he immediately explained that the old concrete floor had probably been cleaned numerous times with a particular cleaning solution and it had penetrated deep into the concrete. Therefore, I needed to spray the floor with a household vinegar and water solution before the topping compound would stick.

Sure enough, Charlie's suggestion fixed the problem. Thank goodness for Charlie and thank goodness for my "special" contact list! Charlie knew more about concrete problems than any person I had ever met in construction, and I knew that he would always help me out when I ran up against a problem I couldn't solve. He always said, "All you need to do is ask." It is a lesson that I learned early on in my career.

Spend time developing relationships with people who know more than you do and learn from them. There were a number of great people on my "special" contact list and they helped me solve tough problems more than once in my career as a construction manager.

This is no easy task. Keeping things straight is a real challenge, and it is vital that this job be handled in the most expeditious way to keep the work moving along smoothly. For that reason, there are two key process tools that are used to track all of the inquiries, decisions, and approvals that occur during the construction process. They are requests for information (RFIs) and submittals.

Requests for Information (RFI)

Getting questions answered fast is one of the biggest challenges of the construction process. I know that this may seem like a very simple thing, but believe me—it is no simple thing! In construction there is a formal document used for asking questions called the *request for information* or RFI. There is also a formal procedure for processing and keeping up with these forms. It is critical that every single inquiry and every single response be tracked and documented. There *must* be a clear and accurate paper trail to reference and confirm all correspondence related to requests for information, especially if there is a dispute over specific directives.

RFIs primarily stem from questions regarding the details of the design. They often originate from a craftsperson or subcontractor needing information or clarification from the designer to keep working. Most general contractors develop their own RFI forms and require their subcontractors to use the same form. This way, the information is consistent. A sample RFI is shown next.

Request for information (RFI)
A written request for clarification regarding the details presented in the plans or specifications. The requests are usually made by subcontractors through the general contractor to the architect.

ABC Construction Company
REQUEST FOR INFORMATION

Project: Spinnaker's Restaurant   **Date:** May 14, 2004
RFI No. 042

Required Response Date: May 20, 2004

To: Tracy Doud   **From:** A.L. Jackson
Doud & McDylan Architects   ABC Construction
1650 First Street, Suite 2A   1400 Elm Grove
San Piatra, CA 96744   Carpenter, CA 83347
(701) 667-9871   (509) 711-8223

Subject: Grout color in men's & women's restrooms

Description of Request: The finish schedule shown on sheet #A-17 indicates that the grout color for the men's and women's restrooms is to be "Buff #032." The specifications call for all tile grout to be "Charcoal #016" throughout. The tile setters will be starting tile work on May 25, 2004. Please advise regarding correct grout color.

Support Documents Attached: Drawings A-17, Spec Section 09310

REPLY: The grout in the men's and women's restrooms is to be Charcoal #016 as indicated in the specifications. Please correct the finish schedule to reflect this change.

Signed: Tracy M. Doud   **Date:** May 17, 2004
Doud & McDylan Architects

Many times, an RFI is of an urgent nature—meaning that the subcontractor needs the answer now! Unfortunately, the RFI process is cumbersome and slow and a real source of frustration for everyone involved. There are instances where some minor piece of information ends up holding up a major portion of work. The job can be delayed and even stopped because of a failure to expedite RFIs. Real schedule and budget issues with serious consequences can result if the process isn't managed properly.

Some projects require few RFIs, as few as 10 or 15. And some projects are an RFI nightmare, requiring hundreds or even thousands of clarifications, corrections, or directions. It is usually the charge of an entry-level field engineer to keep up with the communications, track their progress, and coordinate the results with the subcontractors and field personnel as required. Written records or RFI logs will be kept on the job site. Many field offices make use of electronic tracking systems, although there are still instances where the old file cabinet houses the record. Either way, as tedious as the job may sound, it is a critical contract administration function, and if you work in construction management, you will indeed get a turn at processing RFIs. Of this you can be certain!

Good RFI tracking methods have saved more than one contractor in a claims dispute, and poor tracking has sunk many a contractor as well. Some RFIs result in extra work and changes in the contract cost, but we'll talk about this later in the chapter. When an RFI does result in a price adjustment, the process can take even longer because the estimators have to get involved.

Submittals

submittals
Data, samples, details, colors, and product literature required by the terms of the contract to be presented to the architect by the contractor for approval prior to ordering and installation.

Submittals are similar to RFIs but are processed with a different purpose in mind. Submittals contain information concerning products and equipment that are to be used in the building of the project. Submittals provide a means by which the architect and owner can confirm the intent of the design. The architect checks for conformance with the plans and specs and confirms dimensions, colors, texture, sheen, pattern, details, and installation procedures. As a general rule, everything that will be installed in the facility requires a submittal.

mock-up
Physical models or small samples constructed to allow the architect and owner to review the appearance and function of materials, colors, textures, and other aesthetic features before incorporating them into the actual project.

Although many submittals consist of a simple catalog description, diagram, or data sheet, others are quite substantial. For example, if a building is to have brick as an exterior finish, a *mock-up* of the wall must be constructed for the architect's approval. Sometimes the contractor has to build several mock-ups with various colors and textures before they develop one that satisfies the designer and the owner.

The submittal process requires the same tenacity as the RFI process and must be managed as competently. It is a big chore and the project team must stay on top of the process or it will get away from them in a hurry.

Shop Drawings

There are many items associated with construction that cannot be ordered out of a product catalog or off the shelf. Many items have to be fabricated in a shop or manufactured specifically for the job. In these instances, a special type of submittal called a *shop drawing* is required. Shop drawings include details, dimensions, and configurations of the item to be fabricated. Shop drawings are typically prepared by a subcontractor or a vendor and then submitted to the general contractor for review. The general contractor sends them off to the architect for a final approval. The drawing moves back down the chain, eventually reaching the subcontractor or vendor, authorizing fabrication to begin. Steel rebar bends, steel beams, ornamental handrails, trusses, and architectural woodwork are all examples of construction products that require shop drawings.

Shop drawings require extra time to process, and this effort must be managed in a timely fashion. As a matter of fact, they are so important that they often show up on the construction schedule as a work item.

shop drawing

A supplemental drawing to the plans and specifications that details fabrication methods, materials, and models of a product or installation associated with the project.

The Information Flow

RFIs, submittals, and shop drawings must all be routed up and down a similar approval chain. That approval chain is illustrated next. As with any associative process, the actions (or inactions) of one party clearly impact the actions of another. A bottleneck at any one of the stops along the way will most likely mean a delay in the work progress.

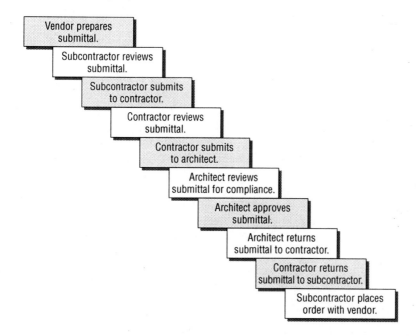

Bottlenecks in the RFI, submittal, and shop drawing process are the scourge of construction management. Trying to stay on top of the flow of information up and down the chain is a huge challenge but a manageable one. The ability to expedite the process will increase the overall reliability of both the schedule and the budget. That's why good contract administration is so important.

Nothing is more frustrating to the contractor than having to deal with paperwork that slows work progress. The temptation to bypass an approval or a change order is high. But whenever contractors decide to go forward without proper authorization, as they sometimes do, they are taking a risk that could backfire on them. On the other hand, if work is held up while they wait for authorization, the consequences could be even worse. It is a constant struggle between trying to maintain the schedule while dealing with administrative requirements that can drive you crazy. However, it is exactly the kind of struggle that the team has to face throughout the construction process.

Very recently, I was told by a large national contractor that they would no longer take on small school district projects because the owners were simply unable to manage the pace of the jobs and respond to RFIs in a timely fashion. This lack of management capability and decision-making expediency placed too high a risk on the contractor, and the contractor was no longer willing to take on that risk.

NOTE   In situations where an owner lacks the management experience and expertise to handle their own construction process, a professional construction management firm can be hired as an agent of the owner. The agency CM firm works with the general contractor on the owner's behalf. This arrangement mitigates risks for both the owner and the contractor.

Getting Paid

One of the most important contract administration functions from the contractor's perspective is getting paid on time. This doesn't just happen automatically. There is a formal payment request process involved that must be followed to the letter; otherwise, the payment request may be kicked back to the contractor, delaying receipt of the payment by a whole billing cycle. Missing even one payment cycle can cause severe cash flow problems, especially for smaller contractors or subcontractors, and can even jeopardize the solvency of a company.

Many construction projects are very, very large and represent millions and even hundreds of millions of dollars under a single contract with one general contractor. For this reason, the perception is that all of this money is collected month after month and just sits around somewhere in a special contractor account, adding to the company coffers—right? Wrong. The reality is that the money is just passing through the company accounts—coming in one end, and going out the other. On a monthly basis, there is actually little or no revenue being retained during construction. The payments made by the owner to the contractor are being passed directly on to the subcontractors doing the work, and to the vendors and suppliers providing the material on a monthly basis. Furthermore, the contractor gets paid only for work already completed. So in truth, most contractors are, in essence, fronting money to the owners, covering as much as 30 to 60 days of bills and expenses for work completed before receiving even one payment from the owner. This point is illustrated in the following graphic:

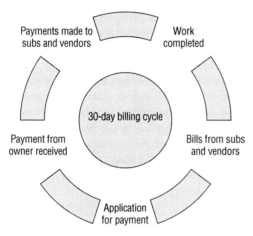

I hope you can see how very critical it is for payment requests to be handled correctly. Sloppy administrative work here means big trouble, especially on those multi-million-dollar jobs. The superintendent and project team have enough to worry about just keeping the work going. They sure don't need to be worrying about delayed payments or cash flow. Let's take a little closer look at exactly how the payment request process works.

Payment Request Process

Requests for payment are made by the contractor, to the owner via the architect, on a monthly basis. The project manager or contract administrator is usually responsible for compiling the request. The payment request is due by a certain day each month, usually at the end of the month (for example, the 25th day of each month). That means that the project manager must determine a cutoff date (probably the 20th of each month) by which he or she must receive all bills from subcontractors and vendors, and payroll data for self-performed work, in order to meet the submittal deadline.

After the payment request is submitted, the architect reviews the application and either recommends it for payment by the owner or sends it back to the contractor for revisions. You do not want a payment request returned. Even the simplest revision can result in a missed payment, and not many contractors can absorb the financial hit. However, if everything goes well, the contractor should receive payment by the 10th of the following month if the pay request is submitted by the end of the current month. Unfortunately, this is not always the case, and some owners are notoriously late with their payments. Consistently late payments not only put a financial strain on the contractor, but also put a real strain on the contractor/owner relationship.

Once the payment is received from the owner, the contractor is obligated to promptly pay their subcontractors and vendors. Many subcontractors run relatively small operations and cannot afford to wait longer than just a few days before receiving payment. In instances where the owner's payment to the contractor is delayed, it is important that the contractor go ahead and pay their subcontractors and vendors anyway. Delaying payments to smaller subcontractors can add a significant burden to an already stretched payroll and end up damaging this very important working relationship.

NOTE — Owners who are slow payers get the attention of the construction community. Word gets around, and a slow-paying or cantankerous owner should not be surprised when there are few bidders on their future projects. This can be a real problem for owners because fewer bids usually mean less competition, and sometimes less competition results in higher bids. Not a good thing for an owner with a strict budget.

The official payment request requires the assemblage of three specific documents: the schedule of values, the pay request continuation sheet, and the application for payment. Each of these documents is described next.

Schedule of Values

The first step in the progress payment process is to complete a document called a *schedule of values*. This schedule represents the project budget derived from the original project estimate. (You will learn more about the project budget in Chapter 10, "Monitoring Project Performance.") The schedule of values is typically organized by the 16 divisions of the CSI MasterFormat. Each line item on the schedule represents a complete dollar amount, including overhead and profit, for each section of work. The schedule of values is one of the administrative submittals that must be approved by the architect very early on, before construction actually begins. The schedule provides the benchmark measure for each payment throughout the project duration. Every payment will be a reflection of the percentage complete for each section of work shown on the schedule. A sample schedule of values is shown below.

schedule of values
A budget template established early on in the project against which progress payments are measured. The schedule summarizes the total project cost by the various divisions of work.

ABC Construction Company
1400 Elm Grove
Carpenter, CA 83347

Schedule of Values
Spinnaker's Restaurant

March 17, 2004

Line Item	Description	Contract Value*	% of Total
1	General Conditions	$175,550	9.08
2	Site Work	$196,000	10.14
3	Concrete	$137,000	7.08
4	Masonry	$16,500	0.85
5	Metals	$5,500	0.28
6	Carpentry	$427,000	22.09
7	Thermal & Moisture Protection	$76,400	3.95
8	Doors, Windows, Glass	$58,600	3.04
9	Finishes	$154,000	7.97
10	Specialties	$49,500	2.56
11	Equipment	$106,000	5.48
12	Furnishings	$126,000	6.53
13	Special Construction	$0	0.00
14	Conveying Systems	$0	0.00
15	Mechanical Systems	$243,000	12.57
16	Electrical Systems	$162,000	8.38
	TOTAL CONTRACT AMOUNT	$1,933,050	100.00

* Includes overhead and profit

Pay Request Continuation Sheet

This form is simply a continuation of the schedule of values, tracking previous payments and change orders as well as identifying the current payment due. The American Institute of Architects publishes a standard continuation sheet (AIA Form G703) as part of their application for payment form described in the next section. An updated continuation sheet must accompany the application for payment form each month. The form below is similar to the AIA G703 document.

ABC Construction Company
1400 Elm Grove
Carpenter, CA 83347

Continuation Sheet
Spinnaker's Restaurant

Date: June 1, 2004
Billing Period: 05/01/04 – 05/31/04
Payment Request: No. 5

A LINE ITEM	B DESCRIPTION	C CONTRACT VALUE	D PREVIOUS COMPLETION	E COMPLETE THIS MONTH	F (D + E) COMPLETE TO DATE	G (F/C) PERCENT COMPLETE	H (C – F) CONTRACT BALANCE
1	General Conditions	$175,550	104,500	13,600	118,100	67.27%	$57,450
2	Site Work	$196,000	196,000	0	196,000	100.00%	$0
3	Concrete	$137,000	137,000	0	137,000	100.00%	$0
4	Masonry	$16,500	9,800	5,500	15,300	92.73%	$1,200
5	Metals	$5,500	1,700	2,100	3,800	69.09%	$1,700
6	Carpentry	$427,000	207,500	67,550	275,050	64.41%	$151,950
7	Thermal & Moisture Protection	$76,400	33,600	11,500	45,100	59.03%	$31,300
8	Doors, Windows, Glass	$58,600	47,800	2,250	50,050	85.41%	$8,550
9	Finishes	$154,000	0	0	0	0.00%	$154,000
10	Specialties	$49,500	0	0	0	0.00%	$49,500
11	Equipment	$106,000	39,400	9,500	48,900	46.13%	$57,100
12	Furnishings	$126,000	0	0	0	0.00%	$126,000
13	Special Construction	$0	0	0	0	0.00%	$0
14	Conveying Systems	$0	0	0	0	0.00%	$0
15	Mechanical Systems	$243,000	109,000	31,600	140,600	57.86%	$102,400
16	Electrical Systems	$162,000	54,900	27,700	82,600	50.98%	$79,400
	CURRENT TOTALS	$1,933,050	941,200	171,300	1,112,500	57.55%	$820,550

Application for Payment

The application for payment is the final document needed to process a payment request. This form summarizes the actual payment amounts and provides the official approvals required before the payment can be released. The American Institute of Architects also publishes a standard application for payment form called an "Application and Certificate for Payment" (AIA Form G702). This standard form is commonly used across the industry, although some projects may provide their own customized form. A document similar to the AIA Form G702 is shown below.

ABC Construction Company
1400 Elm Grove
Carpenter, CA 83347

Application and Certificate for Payment

Project: Spinnaker's Restaurant	**Billing Period:** 05/01/04 – 05/31/04
Application Date: June 1, 2004	**Payment Request:** No. 5

Contractor's Application for Payment:
Application is made for payment as shown below, in connection with the Contract Continuation Sheet attached.

1.	Original Contract Sum	$1,933,050
2.	Net Change by Change Orders	$0
3.	Contract Sum To Date (1 + 2)	$1,933,050
4.	Total Completed to Date (Column F)	$1,112,500
5.	Retainage: 5% of Completed Work	$55,625
6.	Total Earned Less Retainage (4 – 5)	$1,056,875
7.	Less Previous Payments (Column D)	$941,200
8.	**Current Payment Due**	**$115,675**
9.	Balance to Finish, Including Retainage (3 – 6)	$876,175

CHANGE ORDER SUMMARY:	Additions	Subtractions
Total Changes Approved in Previous Month	$0	$0
Total Approved This Month	$0	$0
Totals	$0	$0
NET CHANGES by Change Order:	**$0.00**	

The undersigned Contractor certifies that to the best of the Contractor's knowledge, the work covered by the Application for Payment has been completed in accordance with the Contract Documents.

CONTRACTOR:
By: _____ Date: _____

ARCHITECT'S CERTIFICATE FOR PAYMENT:
In accordance with the Contract Documents, based on on-site observations and the data composing this application, the Architect certifies to the Owner that to the best of the Architect's knowledge, the Work has progressed as indicated, the quality of the Work is in accordance with the Contract Documents, and the Contractor is entitled to payment of the AMOUNT CERTIFIED.

AMOUNT CERTIFIED: $ 115,675

ARCHITECT:
By: _____ Date: _____

retainage
A certain percentage of money owed to the contractor for work progress that is held back by the owner to encourage completion of the project.

You will notice a line item on the application for payment identified as *retainage*. Retainage is an amount of money that is commonly withheld from each payment as an incentive for the contractor to complete the project, including all of the final paperwork and submittals at the end of the job. The retainage amount is typically calculated as 10 percent of the contract payments for the duration of the job. Release of the retainage is tied to substantial completion, which you learned about back in Chapter 5, "Project Stages." Once substantial completion is achieved, the entire amount of retainage is paid to the contractor.

NOTE

It is a common practice for the general contractor to impose retainage on their subcontractors as well. Once again, though, consideration is often given to the smaller contractors, especially the ones who complete their work very early on in the construction. It seems quite unfair to withhold 10 percent of a subcontractor's money for the entire duration of the project when their work was completed in the first 30 days or so. Most general contractors try to work with their subcontractors as best they can to see to it that they receive all of their money upon completion of their work.

Final Payment

I told you in Chapter 5 that the job startup and job closeout are two of the most difficult stages to manage. I want to discuss the final payment as a separate issue because, administratively, it is indeed a real challenge. Once the job starts closing down and the punch list work is complete, and the trades start pulling off the job one after another, it is really hard to stay focused. Like everyone else, the project team wants to move on to the next job. As a matter of fact, several members of the team have probably already been reassigned to the next job. However, the few remaining folks (probably the superintendent and a field engineer), along with contract administration support from the main office, still have plenty of work to do. The job is not complete until all of the paperwork and final submittals have been delivered to the architect. Only then is the final payment released. The typical contract documentation needed to wrap up the job includes:

◆ As-built drawings
◆ Operation and maintenance manuals
◆ Product and equipment warranties
◆ Test reports
◆ Surplus materials
◆ Permits
◆ Lien waivers

These final little details usually leave a lasting impression. In other words, no matter how well the rest of the job went, the owner has a tendency to remember only the latest event. If it goes smoothly and is completed in a timely fashion, the owner will remember how efficient and expeditious you were. However, if you drag this process out in an agonizingly delinquent fashion, they will only remember that. When I was running my construction firm, I regularly reminded my project teams that they always had to start strong and finish strong. No matter what happens in the middle, it is the first impression and the last impression that establish your reputation.

Schedule Issues

Remember the three-legged stool mentioned back in Chapter 2 ("What Is Construction Management?")—time, cost, and quality? You already know that these three factors are at the heart of every project. However, on most projects, one of these factors shows up as more important than the other two. Time is often the one. You've heard the expression "Time is money," right? Well, I'm sure you understand by now that when time becomes an issue in construction, it can mean *a lot of money*!

There are many scenarios where the construction schedule becomes the all-important issue in the process. For example, school projects must be completed by August or September, when the facility opens for the new academic year. There is typically little to no flexibility in these schedules, period. The work must be done! The completion dates are critical and school buses will be arriving with children whether the contractor is ready or not. Another example is the opening of a new retail facility. Often these projects are designed around a pro forma that calculates a particular return on investment tied to the date when the operation opens for business. In some instances, even a single day's delay can cost the owner a significant amount of revenue. So it is pretty easy to see why an owner might want to try to influence the contractor's performance relative to time of completion for their project, and they often do.

Stick or Carrot?

There are two basic philosophical approaches that the owner can take in an attempt to influence contractor performance. They can threaten with a stick or they can coax with a carrot—and, believe it or not, there are actually standard procedures for both actions in construction. The construction manager must be fully aware of how each works and plan accordingly. The stick approach calls for liquidated damages to be imposed if the contractor does not meet the completion date. The carrot approach gets more creative, providing performance incentives for work completed in advance of the completion date, or for other criteria deemed important by the owner. Let's take a look at each of these techniques.

Liquidated Damages

Liquidated damages are an amount of money that is assessed to the contractor for a failure to meet a specified contract completion date. The theory behind this mechanism is that the payments would mitigate the losses that the owner would experience if the project is not completed on time. It is unlawful for them to be instigated in an amount in excess of actual damages to the owner.

The specific amount can be as little as a few hundred dollars a day, or as much as several thousand dollars a day. When an owner opts to utilize this technique, it is presented in the contract documents right up front so the bidding contractors are well aware of it. For example, the liquidated damages clause may state that the contractor must pay $1000 per day in damages to the owner for each calendar day that the project is late.

Although liquidated damages cannot be legally used as a penalty, they sure show up that way for the contractor under the gun. This is not a position that contractors want to be in if they can avoid it. Liquidated damages are a risk that must be considered and managed just like any other risk in construction. But in most cases where a liquidated damages clause is imposed, the entire project management scheme will be designed around the avoidance of this action kicking in.

NOTE When bidding on a job with liquidated damages, the estimating team tries to figure out how many days the project could possibly run over completion deadline. Based on past experience and a little research regarding the current industry conditions, they try to anticipate delivery delays, labor interruptions, weather conditions, and anything else that might cause a delay in the schedule. They make their best guess, multiply the number of days by the penalty, and add this amount to their bid, thus hedging their bets. This is a tricky thing to do, because the contractor must also remain competitive.

Project Incentives

I don't know about you, but incentives have a tendency to motivate me more than techniques that I might perceive as penalties. And by nature, contractors really like a good challenge and love a good game. That's why they are in the business in the first place. So if you want to influence positive behavior, why not come up with some positive incentives? Interestingly enough, the industry is starting to do just that.

One of the more common approaches is to reward contractors with a certain financial benefit if they complete the job before the dedicated completion date—sort of like reverse liquidated damages. For example, a contractor might receive $500 per day for each day substantial completion is achieved ahead of the project completion date. Some contracts contain both clauses: a liquidated damages clause and an incentive clause. Furthermore, this same concept could be developed to create incentives around any number of factors, such as safety, workmanship, quality, or value engineering. And what really makes this concept powerful is that it has the potential to affect the performance of the entire project team, not just the superintendent or project manager. When you've got the whole team committed to superior performance, you really have the potential for extraordinary results.

Making Changes

It is extremely rare to find a project that is built exactly as it was originally designed without any changes. It is virtually impossible to present every detail needed to construct a complex (or even simple) project in a standard set of plans and specifications. There are always errors or omissions in the documents that are discovered during the construction process. But remember, the contractor bid on the job per the plans and specs. Therefore, when the deficiencies are noticed, the contractor is entitled to extra compensation for correcting the errors or completing the missing details. Managing the many changes on a project is another one of the primary contract administration functions. The mechanism used to instigate these changes is called a change order, and there is a standard procedure for processing them. (Change orders were first discussed back in Chapter 4.) Change orders either add work to the contract or, in some cases, delete work from the contract, but either way the contract will be changed. Let's take a look at how this important process is handled.

Change Order Process

As a rule, owners don't like change orders very much; change orders often spawn many of the disputes that arise on a project. Therefore, it's important to handle the process correctly to avoid disagreements or discrepancies associated with these changes down the road. The change order process is one of the key issues discussed at the preconstruction meeting. Mishandling or misuse of this process can result in all kinds of costly disputes, and the construction team must be vigilant in administering the process correctly.

The main rule in construction is to *never* execute the extra work or change without first receiving a written order to do so by the architect or the owner. A verbal approval is not enough. I don't care if the project is as simple as a little storage building. The best way to ensure that you will be properly compensated for the extra work is to have a written change order in hand, signed by the proper authority. This can be harder to manage than you think. Remember, the building trades people are on site to get the job done. They are not inclined to sit around and wait while the owner makes up his or her mind. The temptation is very strong to just go ahead with the fix on a verbal cue from the architect because you want to keep the work going. Change orders take time to process, and whenever you decide to proceed without one in hand, the contractor is taking a chance that they may not get paid for doing the extra work. Therefore, as the construction manager, you must insist that none of your workers or subcontractors proceed with a change in the work until the change order has been properly authorized.

A change order may be instigated by the architect or by the contractor. Once the deficiency is discovered, an estimate is computed to determine what the cost of the change will be. These estimates may require a simple computation that can be handled on site, or they may need to be sent to the main office where the estimator can perform the quantity takeoff and pricing necessary to come up with the price for the change. The estimate total, including overhead and profit, is presented in a standard change order form that gets submitted to the architect. Some change orders also require that additional time be added to the contract. This request is made right along with the request for extra compensation. The architect presents the change order to the owner and a decision is made to authorize the change. The change order document is then rerouted back to the contractor and the contractor orders the workforce to proceed with the work.

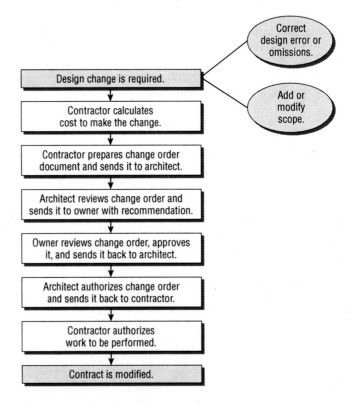

Every change order changes the contract amount and becomes a binding, legal document. Sometimes the change increases the contract total and sometimes the change actually reduces the amount. For example, an owner may choose to change a room full of floor tile to carpet. Carpet is usually less expensive than tile, and therefore the result would be a reduction in the contract amount. The contractor would go ahead and calculate the cost and process a change order accordingly.

Changes in Scope

Scope changes are some of the easiest change orders to process because they are normally instigated by the owner. Examples may range from upgrading the floor covering in the lobby to a request for more cabinets in the kitchen to adding more square footage to the whole facility.

This type of change typically starts with a request from the owner or architect for a cost estimate of the new work. The estimator comes up with a price based on the sketches and specifications provided. There may be some negotiation involved, but generally the owner simply decides whether they want to go forward with the additional work. If they do, a change order is processed and the work is added to the contract. Depending on the size and complexity of the change, there may be a time extension associated with these change orders as well.

Time Extensions

There are occasions when the contractor is compelled to request a time extension to the contract. Time extensions are processed just like any other change order but are often more difficult to get approved. There are many reasons why a time extension might be appropriate:

- Delays resulting from severe weather
- Delays caused by slow responses to RFIs
- Delays caused by slow processing of submittals or shop drawings
- Delays caused by delinquent deliveries
- Delays caused by labor strikes
- Delays caused by slow permit processing
- Delays caused by the architect (poor quality contract documents, work interference)
- Delays caused by the owner (slow decision making, work interference)
- Delays caused by outside protests (political groups, environmental groups, others)

Time extension change orders may consist of a simple request for extra time or they may be more complex and include a request for cost reimbursement associated with the extra time. Simple time extension requests are relatively easy to process. For example, severe weather (especially unexpected) often results in a time extension change order with little or no objection from the owner, as long as the bad weather days are properly documented and the owner has some schedule flexibility. On the other hand, the time extensions that include additional costs are usually quite difficult to negotiate and unfortunately often end up as disputed items at the end of the project. For example, it can be hard to prove that the owner or architect interfered with construction operations and therefore delayed work progress, resulting in extra costs to the contractor and creating a need for extra time. But it is very important that the construction manager be alert to circumstances where delays beyond his or her control result in extra costs, especially if liquidated damages are at stake. Once again, this is a situation where having strong contract administration skills and the right paperwork make all the difference.

I told you there was a lot more to this construction management job than just bricks and sticks!

NOTE   Police officers, firefighters, and pilots are often exposed to something called "awareness training." This training teaches a supersensitivity to circumstances that may pose a danger in a given situation. When I was running my construction business, I actually created a type of awareness training for my project managers and site personnel. A lot of it focused on job site safety, but it also addressed risk points relative to the conditions of the contract, including change orders.

When Things Go Wrong

As hard as we may try to prevent it, the likelihood is high that there will be disagreements among the parties associated with the construction contract. As it turns out, construction is one of the most litigious industries out there. That is one of the reasons that alternative project delivery methods such as at-risk CM and design-build have become so popular—there tends to be less litigation with those methods.

claim
An issue that occurs during construction and remains unresolved after the job is complete.

As you might imagine, most of the disagreements that arise in construction have to do with money. When one of these disagreements reaches an impasse and cannot be resolved through the standard change order process during construction, the contractor must file a *claim* after the job is complete. The rules regarding the submission of a claim are spelled out in the General Conditions of the contract. There is a specified time during which the contractor must inform the architect and owner of his or her intentions to file the claim. Construction claims typically result from one of the following causes:

- Disagreements regarding the terms of the contract
- Defective or deficient contract documents
- Denied and unresolved change orders
- Denied time extensions resulting from delays beyond the contractor's control
- Differing site conditions that resulted in extra cost to the contractor

The owner or architect must formally respond to the contractor's claim. If they reject the contractor's claim for additional compensation, the matter becomes a formal contract dispute. Some form of dispute resolution must be implemented; most construction contracts today call for methods other than traditional litigation.

Dispute Resolution

Earlier in this chapter, I indicated how important it is for the owner to kick off the construction project with a positive tone of trust and collaboration. I made reference to a formal management and communication technique called partnering. The whole premise behind partnering is to avoid the need for time-consuming and expensive dispute resolution at the end of the project. The idea behind partnering is to resolve issues along the way as they occur. Whether we employ partnering or not, once we get to the end of the project and are left with unresolved issues, we must find a way to resolve them. There are actually several options available to us short of going through the full litigation process. Let's consider a few of these options.

Mediation

In mediation, an impartial third party (the mediator) facilitates the negotiation between the disputing parties. Sometimes it just takes a new set of eyes and ears in the room to be able to move the disagreement to a settlement. The objective is to assist the parties in coming to a mutually acceptable agreement. Obviously, this methodology is going to be less time consuming and less expensive than going to court. There are no attorneys involved, and the basis of resolution is still negotiation between the parties who are most familiar with the matter at hand.

Minitrial

Minitrials are one step up from a mediation in terms of the amount of time and cost invested. A minitrial is conducted as an informal private process that combines aspects of both mediation and litigation. As in mediation, a neutral outside advisor is engaged; as in litigation, an attorney is employed to represent each of the parties. The unique element in the process is that an executive from each of the firms involved in the dispute is brought into the mix.

Basically, the attorneys are charged with making an abbreviated case for each argument to the executives of the firms. In the best scenario, the executives are expected to come to a settlement after seeing all of the exhibits and hearing the evidence. If they can do that, fine; everyone shakes hands and goes home. If they are unable to come to an agreement, the third-party neutral advisor may offer an opinion upon which the parties may or may not settle. The outcome of a minitrial is nonbinding and therefore the dispute could still end up in litigation, although every effort should be made to avoid that.

Arbitration

The use of binding arbitration in lieu of litigation is often stipulated in the General Conditions of the contract for construction. Arbitration is a more formal process and is generally more costly and time consuming than either a mediation or a minitrial, but it is less expensive than litigation. (Having participated in three arbitration cases, I can tell you that they are *very* costly and *very* time consuming indeed.) Although the arbitration method employs a neutral third party to preside over the proceedings, everything else about the process is quite similar to a traditional trial. Each party is represented by an attorney, witnesses are called, and exhibits and evidence are presented. The preparation involved can take months, and the hearings themselves can go on for days. In the end, the arbitrator makes a ruling and the decision is final. Although the process is indeed less demanding than a full-blown trial, it is still an arduous exercise, and my recommendation would be to do whatever is necessary to settle the dispute before it ever gets to arbitration.

It's All about the Relationships

It has been my experience that anything the contractor can do to avoid legal action and settle disagreements before they become disputes should be the first line of action. That's why the contract administration function is so important. Although there will always be differences in the interpretation of the contract documents, adherence to the protocol spelled out in the General Conditions and the rules set forth in the preconstruction meeting will at least explicate the argument for the contractor.

One of the most important management tasks associated with construction is the management of good relations with the owner, the architects, the subcontractors, the vendors, and all other vested parties associated with the project. I cannot stress enough how vital it is to maintain clear and direct lines of communication with everyone on the team. Communication is the key to any relationship, and construction is no different. As a matter of fact, construction may call for extraordinary measures of communication, given the level of detail that must be coordinated.

Every project has its share of problems; they cannot be avoided. However, if the parties can establish a firm trust through open communication and a cooperative attitude, many difficulties can be immediately defused. Otherwise, disagreements can escalate to a crisis level and end up being addressed in an arbitration hearing. However, I believe that architecture, engineering, and construction management education is beginning to shed much more light on the relationship side of our industry, which should result in a much less adversarial environment in the future. Although we still have a way to go, progress is definitely being made.

Terms to Know

claim

mock-up

partnering

request for information

retainage

schedule of values

shop drawing

submittals

Review Questions

1. What is partnering?

2. How does the contractor receive clarification from the architect regarding details of the design?

3. What is the purpose of a submittal?

4. What is a shop drawing?

5. What is the name of the document that establishes the template for measuring work progress as it relates to requests for payment?

6. What is the name of the document that formally and officially authorizes a payment to the contractor?

7. What are liquidated damages?

8. What is retainage?

9. Identify two instances when a change order might need to be initiated.

10. Name three alternatives to traditional litigation for resolving construction contract disputes.

Chapter 8

Construction Operations and Job Site Management

Construction operations is where the action is! This is where the ideas presented on paper by the designers become the reality of a new facility—a new office building or hospital—or some magnificent bridge or highway.

What may appear as absolute chaos at first glance—with all kinds of people running around, delivery trucks coming and going, and lots of noise and banging and dirt and dust flying—is actually a well-orchestrated effort typically directed by one person, the superintendent, with support from an on-site project team.

After setting up the temporary field office, the superintendent sets out to organize the job site in a systematic, logical fashion so that it provides the greatest efficiency for getting the work done as quickly and as safely as possible. The superintendent must figure out the best way to manage, control, and coordinate all of the subcontractors, labor, materials, tools, equipment, deliveries, inspections, noise, dust, security, safety, quality, cleanup, and even visitors to the site—all the while trying to keep the project within budget and on schedule.

In this chapter, you will learn that there is a lot more to construction operations than labor and materials. When you get done reading this chapter, you might have a whole new understanding of the word "super" as it applies to superintendent!

Building the Project

Construction operations are the actual work that it takes to build the project. This includes laying out the foundation, placing the concrete, laying the block, setting the steel, framing the walls, installing the roof, installing the electrical, running the plumbing, and every other construction activity needed to complete the facility. It is these activities that most clearly define construction from a practical standpoint. An owner needs a facility and the contractor puts together a package of materials, labor, and equipment to construct that facility. As the construction moves forward, the ultimate goal is to keep the project on schedule, within budget, and of high quality. In order to do this, the on-site construction management team must concern itself with several issues:

- Subcontractor coordination
- Material and equipment deliveries
- Productivity
- Coordination with outside agencies
- Job site safety
- Quality control

How well each of these issues is handled determines how successful the team will be at controlling the project schedule and costs. Let me explain how each of these items can impact the overall project goals.

Subcontractor Coordination

You may have heard the expression "Jack of all trades, master of none" to describe an individual craftsman who, while capable of performing a number of trade skills, is not quite talented enough to be considered an expert in any one of them. A "Jack of all trades" may work perfectly well for a handyman operation, but the skills needed to construct complex facilities today require an expertise that can only be classified as "mastery." For this reason, most construction firms subcontract the bulk of the construction work on their projects to various specialty trade contractors. In other words, they hire experts to perform the work—plumbers do plumbing, electricians do electrical, carpenters do framing, and painters do painting. This way, the work is done much more efficiently and expertly, increasing project quality, decreasing project cost, and reducing contractor risk.

However, as the construction manager, you must keep in mind that each of these subcontractors is an independent operator and each of them typically has several projects that he or she must attend to in addition to yours. This is where subcontractor coordination gets a little tricky. Just because your schedule requires the subcontractor on a specific date doesn't necessarily mean that he or she will be available.

It's very important to develop reliable and realistic schedules when planning the work, especially when it comes to subcontractor coordination. Nothing frustrates subcontractors more than being called to a job before it is ready for them. There is often interdependency between the various divisions of work. With most trades, certain items of work must be completed before they are able to proceed with their work. Sometimes the general contractor tries to keep things moving along by bringing in a subcontractor before the preceding subcontractor is 100 percent complete. For example, a trim carpenter may be brought in to install wood baseboard before all of the floor tile work is completed. This means that you are going to have two different subcontractors trying to work in the same space; more than likely, one of them is going to be holding up the work of the other. This does nothing to aid progress; instead, it totally frustrates the process.

Project scheduling is covered in depth in Chapter 9, "Project Planning and Scheduling."

NOTE

Proper scheduling, preparation, and planning are the keys to successful subcontractor coordination. And successful subcontractor coordination is at the heart of successful construction management. The construction manager must have a keen sense of work sequencing and project planning in order to organize the schedule in such a way that the subcontractors can perform their work in the most efficient manner possible. When I was in business and scheduling subcontractors on a regular basis, there were three fundamental axioms that I tried to remember:

◆ Resist bringing subcontractors onto the job until you are 100 percent ready for them.

◆ Once you bring them onto the job, make sure that they have everything they need to proceed.

◆ Pay all subs promptly upon completion of their work.

Coordination Meetings

Open and honest communication goes a long way in helping coordinate all of the subcontractors involved in building any type of facility. One of the strategies used to improve coordination efforts is the weekly subcontractor meeting. The primary focus of these meetings is to review work progress, update changes in the schedule, discuss potential interface conflicts, share information regarding equipment and personnel requirements, address any discrepancies in the plans and specs, and clarify any procedural questions. It is important that all appropriate subcontractors be encouraged to attend each of these meetings so that everyone hears the same information. The superintendent should direct the meetings and facilitate the group's interaction to best serve both the project and each individual subcontractor.

Material and Equipment Deliveries

will-call

A will-call acts as a verbal confirmation of an order that has been placed prior to the date it is actually due for delivery. The will-call, generally made by the superintendent, occurs just before the scheduled delivery date.

Scheduling and coordinating material deliveries can be as tricky as scheduling subcontractors. There are literally hundreds, if not thousands, of materials and pieces of equipment that get incorporated into a construction project. Many of these items originate by way of a purchase order issued through the main office by estimators or contract administrators. However, once the order is placed, the tracking and delivery of those orders must be handled by the field personnel on the job site, because they are the ones most familiar with the day-to-day operations. The goal is to make sure that the material is on site when it is needed and preferably not before. And although an order may be scheduled for delivery days or even weeks in advance, the final *will-call* order and delivery confirmation should be left up to the job superintendent.

Once the product or piece of equipment arrives at the job site, it is very important to make sure that someone is there to receive the order and direct the driver to place the material as close to the work site as possible. Whoever receives the merchandise should thoroughly inspect it and make sure that it is correct as ordered and free from defects or damage. If the material passes inspection, the on-site representative can sign off and log in the delivery. If the order is not as it should be, the delivery should be refused and sent back to the supplier immediately. Proper inspection at the time of delivery will prevent the problem of arguing with suppliers later.

The worst-case scenario is when the proper inspections have not been made and the product error or defect is discovered as you are ready to install the material. Obviously this is way too late in the process, and a lot of costly time and energy will be wasted because of poor material management.

Productivity

Productivity is all about expectations. When the estimators put together the price for the project, they based their labor calculations on an expected output of work per unit of time. In most instances, the productivity rates are calculated from past performance and historical databases. In order to meet the cost and schedule goals for the project, the productivity goals must also be met. That means that the Construction Manager must keep a close watch on productivity and do everything he or she can to optimize the conditions that contribute to enhanced productivity.

Whenever a job is taking longer than expected, the construction manager must step in and take a look at exactly what is going on that might be interfering with the productivity for that task. There are many factors that can negatively influence the flow of work. Here are just a few that commonly cause lower productivity regardless of the trade involved:

- Crowded work spaces
- Poor coordination of work activities

- Poor supervision or lack of supervision
- Inexperienced or poorly trained workforce
- Not having the proper tools and equipment
- Adverse weather conditions
- Confusing plans and specs
- Changes in the work plan
- Inefficient job site layout

The construction manager's objective is to see to it that the job conditions support maximum productivity. The ability to organize the job site and schedule the workforce in the most efficient manner possible is critical to meeting productivity goals. It takes keen planning, excellent organization skills, and effective communication to pull this off.

Real World Scenario

When to Will-Call

Will-calls are a mechanism developed to allow the contractor to tentatively schedule deliveries while still maintaining flexibility should an unexpected circumstance thwart the plan. Concrete is one of the material deliveries that works best when placed as a will-call. There are so many things that can go wrong in preparing for a concrete pour that it would really be ludicrous to try to pinpoint the exact date, time, and quantity too far in advance. For example, the night before the pour, it might rain, or the forming subcontractor might not complete on time, or the inspector may not pass the rebar layout.

And yet at the same time, it is very important to get on the concrete supplier's delivery schedule in advance of your need. So, for example, if I am planning to pour concrete on Friday, I would typically call the concrete company on the preceding Monday morning to inform them of my intentions. This way, I am tentatively scheduled for a delivery but under no obligation to take it unless my superintendent confirms it. I would give the supplier the estimated number of cubic yards needed but remind him that my job superintendent will confirm the quantity and the order with a will-call late Thursday afternoon. If we aren't ready for the pour, the superintendent informs the supplier that the delivery is a "no go" and the supplier will bump us off the list. If we are ready, the super calls Thursday evening, confirming the exact number of cubic yards needed and the exact time she wants to start receiving concrete trucks on the job site. Sometimes it really does take right up to the last minute to determine whether a delivery is needed or not, so contractors and suppliers are accustomed to this "will-call" dance.

I told you it was tricky business trying to schedule and arrange material deliveries for construction!

Coordination with Local Agents

Way back in Chapter 1 ("The Construction Industry"), I talked about a number of secondary players in the construction game that have a great influence over the process. One of the major challenges associated with managing construction operations is coordinating building activities with these agencies.

For example, the building department that issues the building permit for the project is one of the agencies that you have to work with throughout the process. There are several building inspections that must be scheduled as the work progresses. For instance, referring to the example given in the previous section, the contractor can't pour concrete unless the building inspector approves the excavation, the formwork, and the reinforcing.

Some of these agencies are more responsive to scheduling needs than others. Building inspectors generally try to be responsive within a few days of a request for their services. They realize that the contractors and subcontractors are depending on them to be quick in their response so the project can move forward. However, other agencies are not so predictable. In my own experience, I have been delayed by weeks and even months on a project waiting for a public utility to respond to an inspection request, authorization, or approval. When this happens, there really isn't a lot that you can do other than try to schedule around them and keep the pressure on the agency to respond as quickly as they can. Some of the agencies that you have to deal with throughout the construction process are:

◆ Building and zoning departments

◆ Planning commissions

◆ Independent testing agencies

◆ Utility companies (electric, telephone, water, sewer, and natural gas)

◆ Fire marshals

Although these agencies have no contractual agreement with you, the architect, or the owner, they do have a lot of power. The reality is that they can literally bring your job to a standstill. Coordinating inspections and agency approvals is one of the most critical components of managing construction operations. If someone is not on top of this task right from the beginning, the consequences can be disastrous and there will be very little that you can do about it. You've heard the expression "You can't fight city hall," right? Well, not only can you not fight them, but it's also very hard to move them any faster than they are willing to go.

Job Site Safety

Although poorly managed subcontractor coordination, low productivity, or delayed material deliveries can result in cost overruns and scheduling fiascoes, serious job site accidents can prove catastrophic in terms of loss of life and personal injury.

Construction sites are noisy, dirty, and dusty places to work, and the likelihood of being struck or crushed, or injured in some other way by falling materials, moving equipment, or hazardous materials is quite high. It is very important that the construction manager make every effort to prevent such accidents from happening and protect all workers and the public from these potential hazards. Job site safety must be the number one priority when it comes to managing construction operations.

Safety management will be addressed as a separate issue in Chapter 11 ("Managing Quality and Safety"). For now, to give you a sense of the kinds of details associated with safety planning, here are some ways to help ensure a safe work environment:

◆ A fully equipped first-aid kit should be on site at all times.

◆ "No Trespassing" signs should be posted and maintained around the site for the duration of construction.

◆ Emergency phone numbers for ambulance, fire, haz-mat, police, and hospital should be posted at every telephone.

◆ A list of hazardous materials used on the project should be readily available.

◆ Hard hats, safety glasses, hearing protection, and other personal safety equipment must be worn by all workers and visitors.

◆ Trash and debris must be removed from the construction site on a regular basis.

◆ All heavy equipment and job vehicles must have backing-up alarm signals.

◆ All open excavations must be properly protected by barricades and security tape.

◆ Flagmen, wearing orange safety vests, should be used for traffic control as needed.

◆ Fire extinguishers and required fire equipment should be certified and maintained.

◆ Safety meetings should be held on a regular basis with all subcontractors and workers.

◆ Power tools should be inspected regularly for defects or unsafe conditions.

◆ Only qualified personnel should be allowed to operate cranes, forklifts, and other equipment requiring special training.

◆ Scaffolding should always be erected correctly and inspected to ensure that it is in good condition.

◆ Trench shoring should be used to support walls and faces of excavations exceeding five feet.

Quality Control

Of all the construction management responsibilities associated with operations, quality control has the greatest influence on long-term project success. Poor work performance and quality not only impact the immediate schedule and budget but can also contribute to additional damage and liability down the road, resulting in even higher losses.

The best way to control quality during construction is to develop a comprehensive plan to avoid defects, deficiencies, and problems from the start. However, getting the work done right the first time is no easy task. With so many different companies and people working on the project, and so many different materials, products, and equipment to keep track of, it can be a real challenge.

In Chapter 11, I go into much more detail about this very important aspect of construction operations. For now, keep in mind that it is critical that the superintendent and entire on-site management team pursue quality control from the outset of the project. They should, at a minimum:

- Be fully aware of the quality standards specified for the project.
- Understand the quality of workmanship expected to be performed on the project.
- Be able to recognize and reconcile actual performance with the quality expectations.
- Establish and implement a quality control plan that ensures that expectations are being met.

If the team is able to meet these qualifications, then the odds of a negative impact to the project as a result of poor quality, customer callbacks, or defective work are minimized.

Construction Impacts

In addition to the more obvious management tasks such as coordinating subcontractors and tracking material deliveries, there are some management issues that arise from the construction activity itself. For example, construction can create a lot of noise and stir up a lot of dirt and dust; depending on where your building site is located, controlling these aspects can become a major management challenge.

Not every project encounters the same construction impact issues. It all depends on the particular project location, project owner, weather conditions, proximity to other activities, and so on. Obviously, projects that are out in the middle of nowhere are less burdened with some of these issues. But if your project is smack dab in the middle of an urban area, you'd better be ready for a possible onslaught of issues, crises, and complaints—some of which can be quite controversial, and all of which you, as a construction manager, are responsible for controlling. Let's consider a few of these issues.

Noise Control

Construction is inherently a noisy business—the sound of tools and equipment running, big trucks moving about the site, and the clanging of steel on steel are expected. But noise is becoming a bigger and bigger problem, especially on sites that are close to schools, neighborhoods, and other work environments, and contractors are being challenged more than ever to find ways to mitigate the noise.

Owners will often communicate their restrictions regarding noise in the supplemental conditions to the contract, and the project manager can plan accordingly right from the start. For example, today it is not uncommon to find clauses in the contract restricting work hours to starting later in the day or prohibiting the use of radios on the work site.

However, sometimes the extent of the noise effects are not known until the project has already started. Under these circumstances, the contractor is usually confronted with a statement something like, "I knew it would be noisy but I didn't know it would be *this* noisy!" In these instances, the contractor must be willing to take reasonable steps to mitigate the nuisance and satisfy the wishes of his or her client or an unhappy neighbor. But sometimes these steps can add significant expense to the job and an agreement must be reached between the owner and the contractor as to who shall bear the brunt of the mitigation costs.

Real World Scenario

Intolerable Noise Impacts

I know of a recent job in downtown Sacramento where the architect and contractor had to literally redesign the foundation system on a building because of the noise factor. The original foundation on this high-rise building was designed (and bid) as a pile foundation. A pile foundation consists of tall concrete, wood, or steel columns driven deeply into the ground to support the structure of the building. These piles are driven into the ground by a very large hammer called a pile driver and it is quite a noisy operation. Sacramento is the capital of California and this new office complex was downtown in the heart of the governmental hub. The noise caused by the pile driving was so disturbing to the surrounding work environment that the project was temporarily halted while the foundation system could be redesigned from a pile foundation to a spread foundation, therefore eliminating the need for the pile driver. Although the owner picked up the tab on this one, it delayed the job nonetheless and caused a significant amount of wasted time and energy.

Dust and Mud Control

Everybody knows that construction is a dirty business. Once we clear the building site and start laying out the foundation, we are into the dirt. There's no way around it. However, once that dirt gets stirred up or rained upon, we have dust or mud—both of which can become site management challenges.

The supplemental conditions to the contract usually address the issue of dust control. Contractors are required to use whatever means are necessary to control dust on a daily basis. I'm sure you have seen water trucks sprinkling dusty building sites or access roads on a construction project. This is a common practice that is repeated numerous times per day and is typically anticipated as an overhead expense item by experienced estimators.

However, mud control is not usually addressed in the contract documents and it can become a management headache in a hurry. Mud can cause all kinds of problems on the construction site. First, mud makes it very difficult to move vehicles in and out of the job site, which can slow down operations significantly. In an effort to keep things moving along, the contractor will often spend extra money to bring in gravel and temporary road-base material just to keep expensive equipment, trucks, and trailers from getting stuck.

Second, mud makes things look very dirty. For example, a freshly poured concrete slab, or a newly laid brick wall, or attractive wood siding will appear distressed and blemished once mud gets tracked or smeared onto it. And even though the contractor will take steps to protect these surfaces by covering them with plastic film or tarps, it's almost impossible not to track or smear the mud. The mud must be removed and the surfaces cleaned, and unfortunately, this extra work is often not anticipated, adding extra cost and slowing the project down.

NOTE

The fact that construction is naturally noisy and naturally dirty doesn't keep the public from complaining about the noise and the dust. Owners and contractors alike must be aware that these complaints can pose serious risks to project efficiencies, progress, and cost. The industry is quite able to ease these nuisances but I'm not sure that the public at large understands that the costs associated with the mitigation are ultimately passed on to the consumer. It is just one more reason why construction management has become such a high-demand profession. Building is no longer just about putting together a package of materials, equipment, and labor. All of the risks associated with the construction must be anticipated and managed while still maintaining strict budgetary targets, on-time project delivery, and high quality.

But the problems associated with controlling dust and mud can go even further than that. Sometimes they can impact much more than operations on the site itself. Let me explain with another real-life scenario.

Keep My Streets Clean!

Many years ago, I was managing a residential development project in Virginia. In addition to being in charge of building approximately 20 new homes, I was responsible for building all of the new streets, water, sewer, and utilities needed for the community. Everything was going quite well until spring when the rains started. Although all of my streets were graded with the initial road base (gravel) down, we had not yet paved the streets; we still had a number of construction activities going on with the building of the homes and we did not want to risk damaging any new pavement. During this rainy season, the gravel on our roads allowed us to continue moving in and out of the site. However, as the trucks were moving in and out of the site, they were picking up a significant amount of mud on their tires. Still, as long as they were able to keep moving, I was not concerned—until one afternoon when I got a visit from the town manager.

The town manager presented me with a stop work notice and basically read me the riot act, threatening severe fines for getting *his* streets dirty. Once the trucks left my site, they were apparently dropping and smearing mud all over the clean (paved) streets of the town and the manager was not happy. Well, I was in a real pickle. I couldn't prevent the rain or the mud and I couldn't very well put the project on hold waiting for it to dry up. Fortunately, the town manager was willing to consider a proposal I presented that would eliminate the tracking of mud on his streets and allow me to continue working.

I had to start by sending a crew of workers to sweep up and clean all of the mud on the streets that could be traced back to my site. This took several days. I had argued that the next rain would just wash the mud away, but I think the manager just wanted to assert his authority. I learned a long time ago *not* to argue with the people who basically hold the future of your project in their hands by their power to shut you down, right or wrong! It is much better to apologetically acknowledge their concerns and do everything you can to mitigate the situation.

I then built a temporary tire-washing station (concrete slab, floor drain, and high-pressure water hoses) at the entrance/exit of my building site. There we would wash the tires of every pickup truck, delivery truck, and concrete truck leaving the job site before it entered the public street. I also stationed two laborers at the site entrance full time to sweep the street clean of any mud or debris that still dropped from the truck tires. Keep in mind that none of these remedies was figured into my initial estimate because the severity of the problem was never anticipated. The developer and I split the cost of this lesson learned.

Continues

This went on for most of the spring until I was able to complete my own street paving, thereby eliminating the encounters with the mud. The town manager and I actually became pretty good friends, and at the grand opening of the project, he readily acknowledged the quality of the construction and the professionalism of the construction team.

Apparently I am not the only contractor who has been blindsided by the muddy street problem. I have since visited several building sites that post signs warning subcontractors that they will be fined by the contractor for tracking any dirt or mud onto the public streets. These contractors have decided to shift the risk of the potential penalty to the subcontractors working on the project. By the way, in most of these instances, I noticed that the subcontractors opted to park off site and carry their tools and equipment in by hand or on dollies—inefficient, yes, but probably less risky.

Environmental Protections

Today, the need for some type of environmental protections during construction is a given. In many instances, the contractor is well aware of the special care that must be taken regarding some of these environmental issues. For example, soil erosion is always a concern during construction and the measures needed to control that erosion should not come as a surprise to any contractor. However, sometimes an environmental issue does show up as a surprise, and that's when construction managers become concerned. They did not anticipate making special provisions, and their project budgets and schedules will be at risk without some concession from the owner. I have listed just a few of the possible environmental issues that may arise during construction.

Soil erosion   Erosion is always a consideration on a newly graded construction site. Once we disturb the natural vegetation of the building area, we are at risk of causing unwanted damage on or off the site from excessive water runoff. The contractor is responsible for coming up with an erosion-control plan that will be instituted at the beginning of the project and maintained throughout the duration of the construction. This plan includes temporary installations such as silt fences, filter fabrics, and straw bale barriers intended to hold soil in place. Poor management here on the part of the contractor can result in significant fines and even lawsuits, both of which can and should be avoided.

Endangered species protection   While it doesn't happen often, your project may be in a location where you have to contend with an endangered species. Maybe you have heard stories about some little frog, bird, or rodent holding up progress on a construction site and thought at first that the story was somewhat humorous. But if the incident happens on your job, you will soon learn that it is no laughing matter.

The discovery of an endangered species on the building site usually shuts down construction operations while proper authorities evaluate the situation and decide what to do. In a very recent incident, an endangered beetle was discovered during excavation on a $40 million college dormitory project and the foundation work was completely halted for two months. In the end, the foundation was redesigned and reconfigured to avoid altogether the area the beetles inhabited.

The key, as far as the contractor is concerned, is whether or not the owner was aware of the problem and if they disclosed the information ahead of time. Most of these discoveries come as a complete surprise to everyone and the ramifications are usually borne by the owner.

However, that doesn't mean that the contractor is off the hook. Unexpected delays can throw a real monkey wrench into the project plan even if the builder isn't liable. Any number of problems can arise while waiting for the issue to be resolved. For example:

◆ Foundations that were scheduled for fall now must be dug in the middle of winter (think snow).

◆ Your low-bid subcontractor who was available to start work this month has been forced to take another job that will have him tied up for a year.

◆ Interest rates that were reasonable at the start of the project are now set to rise before project completion.

As I said, it's no laughing matter.

Protected vegetation   There are projects that require the contractor to protect and maintain certain natural vegetation that exists on the building site. For example, when grading the site, there may be certain trees that need to be protected and saved, and it is the contractor's job to see to it that they are not harmed throughout the construction process. The builder will place physical barriers such as fences around the trees or other vegetation and flag them with security tape to alert all workers of the challenge. And it is indeed a challenge. Whenever such a request is made, it will invariably slow down production and cause some consternation among the equipment operators, especially if they were unaware of the requirement when they bid on the job.

Wetlands protection   Wetlands protection has become a major environmental concern in our country, and construction (or development) is often in the middle of the controversy. Whenever a contractor prepares to build in an area close to natural wetlands, he or she must adhere to a number of federally mandated regulations. I include just a few here (taken from the National Park Service's *Procedural Manual 77-1: Wetland Protection*) to give you an idea of the impact these measures would have on productivity, budget, and schedule.

◆ The contractor must install and maintain adequate erosion and siltation controls during construction.

◆ Construction activity cannot adversely affect the natural water flow and circulation, or negatively impact water level fluctuations.

◆ Water quality must be maintained. The contractor must prevent or control spills of fuels, lubricants, or other contaminants from entering the waterway or wetland.

◆ The contractor should avoid the use of heavy equipment in wetland areas. If heavy equipment is used, steps must be taken to minimize any disruption to the soil or vegetation.

None of these actions, other than erosion control, are standard operating procedures in construction.

Historical or cultural artifacts   Another unique circumstance that can shut down your job site in a hurry is when you stumble across historical or cultural artifacts while moving dirt or excavating at the site. For example, the discovery of pottery shards or arrowheads may indicate a significant archeological find and the contractor must stop operations long enough to notify the architect and owner so they can verify the situation.

Another surprise along these lines is the unearthing of bones of any kind on a job site. If this happens, the contractor must stop construction and contact the owner immediately regarding the discovery. Work in the area of the find usually cannot resume until an investigation is done to ascertain the source and significance of the remains. These are clearly not the types of occurrences that you want to happen on your job, but if they do, you must keep things moving as best you can while making every effort to work with the owner and the appropriate authorities until the situation is resolved.

Keep in mind that the typical construction worker is constantly encouraged to complete his or her work in the shortest time needed, getting on and off the job site as soon as possible. Anything that slows down this process becomes a frustration to workers, however noble the cause might be. But when workers are performing these extra steps required for environmental protection, it is very important that the superintendent pay close attention as this work is being done. A slip-up resulting in damage to a tree root, an endangered species, or a historical artifact could end up costing a whole lot more time and money than the actual measures taken to protect them in the first place.

Cleanup and Trash Removal

With all of the high-risk operations associated with construction, site cleanup and trash removal might not seem like very important issues, but they are. To begin with, a clean site is a safe site. The cleanliness of the building site also reflects upon the image of the contractor. Many observers believe that a neat and clean building area is indicative of how the rest of the contractor's business is conducted.

back charge
An amount of money charged against a subcontractor for work that the general contractor performed because the subcontractor failed to do so.

However, it is not an easy job to maintain a clean working environment. One of the greatest challenges to the contractor is in trying to get subcontractors to be responsible for the removal of their own debris. You would think that this would be a slam dunk, but actually it is a universal frustration among general contractors—so much so that most subcontracts now have a clause in them threatening *back charges* against any subcontractors who fail to clean up after themselves. Even with this threatened penalty, many subcontractors still resist cleaning up their work area, claiming that their bids are already too low to make a decent profit. Having to spend dollars to clean up the job site just adds to the predicament. On the other hand, some are just lazy, plain and simple.

My method for managing cleanup and debris removal was to hire special crews to systematically go through the job site on four-wheelers with small dump trailers at the same time every day and pick up the trash or cajole subcontractors into picking up their own trash and throwing it into the trailers. I usually hired young people who needed part-time work after school and especially enjoyed driving these vehicles around the site. We even gave them a special nickname—the junkyard dogs! I found that if I could make it easy for the subcontractors to pitch in on the cleanup by bringing the trailer right up to their work area, I had a better chance of getting them to cooperate. Although I had to spend a little more money to make this system work, I found that it was much better than issuing back charges. In my experience, back charges were really only good at causing hard feelings, so unless a subcontractor was blatantly disrespectful regarding my request for cooperation, I didn't apply them. I also never hired that subcontractor again.

Opportunities for Recycling

Construction results in a lot of trash. Every year, thousands of pounds of construction debris must be removed from the construction site. In fact, you might be astounded to learn that approximately 25 to 45 percent of all waste in North America comes from the construction and development process, according to the Construction Materials Recycling Association (CMRA). You can learn more about the CMRA by visiting their website at `http://www.cdrecycling.org`.

Trying to estimate and predict exactly how much waste is going to be generated on any given project has become a futile effort for many contractors. Cleanup and trash-removal operations consistently run over budget and cause great frustration among estimators, construction managers, and superintendents alike.

However, as more and more contractors view this problem as the serious issue that it is, new ways are being found to work with recycling companies to reduce expensive hauling costs and disposal fees. Almost everything that comes out of the construction site is recyclable—concrete, block, drywall, metals, wood, plastics, and cardboard. In 2003, the W.G. Clark Construction Company recycled 75 percent of its job site waste on a Communications Center project located in Renton, Washington. The company ended up saving approximately 20 percent of its estimated cleanup and trash removal cost by instigating this practice alone. Several other companies have followed suit, and recycling has become a priority on many job sites.

Construction cleanup, debris removal, and trash removal present a very tough management challenge. However, new incentives are being created every day and new opportunities are emerging for the construction industry to finally conquer this burden.

There's More to It Than Meets the Eye

From a distance, construction just looks like a bunch of workers and materials hustling and bustling about the building site. Having to pay so much attention to noise, dust, mud, spotted frogs, and trash removal was probably not what you had in mind when you first considered construction management as a career. But this is all part of the process, and the construction manger is really charged with creating and maintaining a job site environment in which people can perform their duties at the highest and most efficient level possible. Not an easy task, but definitely a challenging one.

Now that you have a better sense of what the contractor is actually up against while trying to manage the construction operations, let's take a closer look at exactly how he or she actually accomplishes this task. The best place to start is by taking a good look at the one individual primarily responsible for pulling off this whole challenge: the superintendent.

The Superintendent

As you learned in Chapter 5, "Project Stages," the superintendent represents the company leadership in the field and is responsible for the oversight of all construction operations. More than any other person on the construction management team, this individual is responsible for getting the project built on time and within budget. He or she is responsible for organizing the job site and managing the construction on a daily basis.

First and foremost, the superintendent must be very knowledgeable about construction. But he or she must also be organized and able to lead a diverse workforce. It is the superintendent's job to work with and get things done through other people—primarily subcontractors. At the same time, the superintendent must be able to win their respect and gain their confidence and cooperation.

The superintendent and the project manager continually monitor project progress through a number of field reports and observations. Every day on the job site, the schedule and budget targets are either met or missed. Whenever it appears that the schedule or budget goals are in jeopardy, the two work together to make adjustments to get the project back on track. (I will discuss project controls in Chapter 10, "Monitoring Project Performance.")

Initially, there are three things that the superintendent must do before the construction work can begin. He or she must:

◆ Set up the field office.

◆ Organize the job site.

◆ Establish the work hours.

Once these things are done, the rest of the on-site team joins the superintendent and goes to work managing the construction operations through a number of subcontractor trade foremen. Depending on the project size, the team typically consists of an assistant superintendent and at least one field engineer, as shown next.

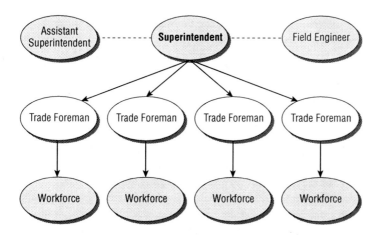

Setting Up the Field Office

Think of the field office as the command center of construction operations. From this space, the superintendent directs all of the activities needed to get the project built. The office itself is a temporary facility. In most cases, the field office is a portable trailer on wheels, similar to a mobile home except that the interior is very utilitarian. In other words, do not expect to see a living room and kitchen in the job trailer. However, just because the spaces are utilitarian doesn't mean that they are necessarily small.

Some projects require only a single trailer to accommodate a small on-site project team of three to five individuals. Other projects may be so large that they require on-site office facilities for as many as 30 or 40 people. In these instances, the field office may comprise four to eight double-wide trailers all connected together. These projects may take several years to complete.

Each field office is fully equipped with every kind of office supply and equipment needed to carry on business from the building site. Computers, telephones, fax machines, copiers, drafting tables, and plotters are all available to the project team as they go about overseeing the construction and managing the project budget and schedule.

Temporary Utilities

Our temporary command center can't function without proper utilities—water, electricity, heat, air conditioning, and telephone. These utilities are required as soon as the project team arrives on the site, and will be needed for the duration of the project. The construction work itself, of course, depends on having these services; all of the various power tools and equipment needed to cut, drill, saw, and weld operate on electricity. A mix-up in the coordination of temporary utilities can actually delay the launch of construction and put a damper on the whole startup operation. For example, having no electricity means bringing in a bunch of portable generators, which are noisy, smelly (gasoline or diesel), and expensive.

Once the site is equipped with the temporary power that it needs to operate tools and equipment, an agreement must be reached between the superintendent and the numerous subcontractors working on the job site. There is a cost associated with these utilities. Even though the contractor may bear the burden of having them brought to the site, he or she may expect the subcontractors to pay their fair share to use the utilities. On the other hand, sometimes the paperwork associated with tracking the use of the power and water is simply not worth the effort, and it is cheaper for the contractor to just pay for all of the utility bills.

dry shacks
These facilities may be constructed on site or brought in as modular units equipped with tables and storage lockers. They provide a dry place for workers to eat their lunch and change their clothes. Union agreements often require that the contractor provide a dry shack on site.

Once construction is well underway, there is the possibility that the construction activities can actually operate using the permanent power sources brought in to serve the new construction. The cost of these utilities may now be billed to the owner instead of the contractor, and the superintendent must make sure that all parties are in agreement regaining these charges.

Portable Facilities

There are a number of portable facilities that support the field office and construction operations. The contractor needs to provide secure tool storage, *dry shacks*, and temporary toilets that are available to all workers on the job site. The placement of each of these facilities is important to the overall efficiency of operations. It is not uncommon for some subcontractors to request that they be allowed to bring their own storage trailers on site to accommodate their special tools, parts, products, and equipment. These extra facilities must also be taken into consideration when developing the overall site logistics plan. (Site logistics planning is discussed in the next section of this chapter.)

In addition to these primary facilities, the contractor is also responsible for providing:

◆ Clean drinking water with paper cups

◆ Clean washing water and paper towels

◆ Trash receptacles and dumpsters

Organizing the Job Site

After setting up the field office, the next challenge faced by the superintendent is organizing the job site for the greatest efficiency and safety. Some construction sites are way out in the middle of nowhere; others may be right in the middle of a major urban area. Either way, the superintendent must have a strategy for directing and organizing all of the materials, manpower, and equipment that will be congregating on the site on a daily basis and moving in and out of the construction area throughout the duration of the project. Every aspect of getting the job done must be considered when trying to prepare the site for construction operations. Decisions about where to place everything from the portable toilets to the dumpsters can make a big difference in how smoothly the job runs.

Site logistics, also called project staging, are crucial to the overall efficiency and coordination of the work. In addition to laying out the most efficient placement of the field office and portable facilities mentioned above, the *site logistics plan* should also take into account a number of other factors, such as:

◆ Material storage and handling

◆ Job site security

◆ Site access

◆ Employee parking

◆ Traffic control

◆ Pedestrian safety

◆ Crane location

◆ Miscellaneous facilities

site logistics plan
A layout plan identifying the placement of all temporary facilities needed during the construction stage of the project, such as the office trailer, storage, security fencing, dumpsters, and portable toilets.

Although it may seem silly to think that the location of the dumpster, the storage trailer, or the tool shed has any bearing whatsoever on project productivity and profitability, studies have shown that job site layout contributes appreciably to the bottom line. The following graphic illustrates what a typical site logistics plan might look like.

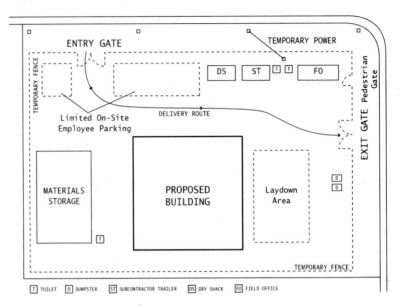

| | TOILET | D DUMPSTER | ST SUBCONTRACTOR TRAILER | DS DRY SHACK | FO FIELD OFFICE |

Let's take a closer look at some of the factors that must be considered when planning job site layout.

Material Storage and Handling

Earlier in the chapter, I discussed the importance of trying to schedule material deliveries as close to the actual date of installation of that material as possible. However, sometimes you need to bring materials on site before they are ready to be installed. When this happens, you must make sure that they are properly stored and taken care of.

On most large jobs, the superintendent brings in several trailers for use as storage facilities. These trailers can be used to store tools, equipment, materials, or even spare parts for generators, tractors, and power tools. Sometimes subcontractors will bring in their own storage trailer. This is especially true of mechanical and electrical subcontractors. They generally have large pieces of expensive equipment, ductwork, or piping that must be protected from the elements, vandalism, and theft.

In addition to trailers, it is common for the superintendent to designate a specific area on site where materials can be stored until they are utilized on the job. This area is often fenced off separately with a locked gate. It's not unusual to assign a field engineer to receive deliveries and manage the inventory coming in and out of this area. In addition to a fenced storage area, the job might require

laydown area

A designated area on the building site where large orders can be stored and sorted in an organized manner so that the parts can be easily identified for use on the project.

a *laydown area* where very large orders such as structural steel beams, girders, columns, and angles can be sorted for easy identification. Sometimes these two areas are combined into one.

When storing materials, it's important to know that some materials are more susceptible to damage and deterioration than others. For example, certain products can be ruined by mud or snow during extreme weather. Or in hot weather, lumber can dry out and warp. Care must be taken to make sure these materials are properly cared for and always stored on skids or pallets; some should be covered at all times.

When it comes to material handling and storage, little things can make a big difference. For example, you should always make sure that delivered materials are unloaded and stacked with the materials to be used first on top of the pile. Otherwise you will have to spend time moving all of the stuff on top to get to the needed material on the bottom. You never want to handle material more times than you have to. With a little planning, you can minimize the effort.

NOTE

Job Site Security

Building sites have always appeared as curiosities worthy of a little exploration. Most of us, at least in our youth, have been tempted to hop the fence in the late afternoon to climb the piles of dirt, play around the big tractors, and run in and out of some partially completed structure as if it were a jungle gym placed there just for our pleasure. However, the construction site poses a number of hazards, and it is the obligation of the contractor to secure the premises, protecting the public from the inherent dangers associated with construction operations.

Although public safety is the primary reason for securing the job site, it is also important to protect the installation, materials, tools, and equipment from vandalism and theft. There are several means by which to do this. The most common methods are:

- Perimeter fencing
- Guard dogs
- Private security patrols
- Electronic alarm systems
- Night watchmen

These measures enable you to protect the construction project from the people around it—and vice versa. For example, fencing both keeps unauthorized people from entering the work area and protects authorized workers and visitors from hazards that occur within the perimeter of the site. An open excavation, for instance, is clearly hazardous to the safety of workers on the job; it should be fenced off and marked with warning devices such as barricades, security tape, and traffic cones to alert workers to the risks associated with an open pit.

Although some security arrangements may be required by the contract (perimeter fencing, for example), it is really up to the superintendent to decide what measures should be taken to best protect the public and the interests of the contractor and owner.

Because most job site thefts occur during times when no workers are on site, it is best to avoid scheduling material deliveries just prior to weekends or holidays.

Site Access

On some construction sites, access is really not much of a big deal. You might be in a remote area with very little traffic and nothing around you. On other sites, access can become a major issue. This is especially true in highly congested areas. For example, daily traffic may have one entrance and delivery traffic may need to be routed to another entrance. The hours of access may also be restricted. Of course, this impacts your work hours, all of your deliveries, and your ability to move equipment onto and off the site as needed. All of these details must be considered when developing the site logistics plan.

Employee Parking

Employee parking is another staging plan issue that must be addressed. As with site access, parking on some sites is not much of a problem, especially when there is plenty of room and employee parking can be managed on site. On smaller sites, parking can be a big problem—and a costly one, too. On some downtown projects, for example, parking must be arranged with a local parking garage and tools and equipment be moved in and out of the site on golf carts or dollies. In this instance, the superintendent must try to negotiate blocks of parking spaces at reasonable costs or suffer the consequences of his or her daily workforce depending on random luck to find parking in the area. That's not exactly the best way to create a happy work environment for your troops.

Traffic Control

Traffic control and pedestrian safety tie right into the site access and parking issues. The traffic associated with the construction process can add a significant burden to heavily traveled streets and highways. The posting of flag men and women to direct traffic around the construction site is a common occurrence. This effort adds to the project cost and in heavily congested areas can impact productivity significantly. Because heavy traffic adds a significant risk when it comes to job site safety, this is one aspect of site logistics that cannot be overlooked or neglected.

Pedestrian Safety

Pedestrian traffic must also be taken into consideration when creating the site logistics plan. This is especially true when the building site is located in a downtown metropolitan area. You have all seen covered sidewalks at the edge of busy building sites. These protected walkways are designed and built to protect pedestrians from falling debris as well as from the dust and noise of the construction. Although these temporary structures seem simple in their design, they actually add thousands of dollars to the project budget. However, public safety is not the only use for these wood-framed structures. Some municipalities permit them to be used as public display areas for street art and other community outreach purposes. When this is the case, the contractor can end up saving a little money by not having to paint the structure.

Crane Location and Miscellaneous Facilities

Many construction jobs require the use of a crane on site to lift and move very heavy objects about the site. These cranes may require a fixed location on site or be mobile. Where to locate the crane on the building site is a very important decision. There are several factors that need to be considered. For example, height restrictions, required horizontal reach, and maximum loads influence which type of crane is needed. However, unless the crane is mobile, once it is in place, you are not going to want to move it until you are done with it. It is therefore important to place it correctly the first time. Of course, not all building sites require a crane; some may instead require other types of lifting equipment. If this is the case, it is always a good idea to know exactly what you are going to need ahead of time so you can properly plan for its use on the job site, even if you don't have to decide on a fixed location.

There are many other miscellaneous facilities, amenities, and equipment needs that should be considered when developing the site logistics plan. A few of these are tool sheds, dumpsters, vending machines, water hydrants, and portable generators.

Establishing Work Hours

Setting work hours is another responsibility associated with construction operations and job site management that the superintendent must attend to. The standard 8-to-4 routine is not always the norm in the construction industry. Adjusting work hours to accommodate the task at hand or to accommodate special conditions happens all the time. For example, working in the middle of the night is a common occurrence in highway construction or commercial remodeling that requires working after hours. Most of us have encountered the late-night road crew constructing a new section of a busy highway.

The superintendent must consider the demands of the project as well as the demands on his or her work force in establishing the working hours. There are times when different trades may need to be scheduled to work on different shifts to keep them from getting in each other's way, and other times when all of them must work weekends to get the project back on schedule.

Contractors generally like to start their workday very early, especially during the summer when the temperatures can rise to triple digits in some parts of the country. It is not uncommon for some crews to start the day as early as 5 or 6 o'clock in the morning. But sometimes the superintendent must adjust hours to better serve the overall project goals. For example, as you learned earlier in the chapter, when noise is an issue, the superintendent may be required to restrict the work hours by starting later in the day to accommodate those neighbors who may still be sleeping at 7:00 A.M. In these instances, the crews may not be allowed to start work until as late as 8 o'clock in the morning.

Late starts in construction are not a simple matter. Sometimes they can actually interfere with certain construction operations and the consequences can be costly. For example, concrete is a fickle material and reacts differently to different temperatures and atmospheric conditions throughout the day. Under cooler temperature conditions, the later in the day that concrete is placed, the more likely that it will require a longer period of time to set up before it is ready for finishing. And unfortunately, it's not as if the crew can just walk away and do something else while they wait. They must stay with the concrete and continually watch it and test it the whole time it is setting. During certain months of the year, it is not uncommon to find the concrete crews still working under lights at 11 o'clock at night trying to finish concrete that was poured at 9 o'clock in the morning. If you have ever been involved in finishing one of these delayed pours, you know how exhausting and frustrating it can be—especially when you know that if you had been able to pour at 5 or 6 o'clock in the morning, you could have gone home hours ago.

NOTE

Even the workweek may be adjusted to better serve the project and the crews. For example, whenever I had a project that required a one-way travel time of more than one and a half hours, I would schedule the crews to work ten hours per day, but only four days per week. This way the crews could enjoy a three-day weekend every week to make up for the three hours that they had to spend each day traveling back and forth to and from the job. It helped tremendously with morale and actually gave the management staff a relatively quiet time every Friday to catch up on paperwork and reports.

Documenting Construction Activity

With all the action happening on the construction site, you would think that paperwork would be the least of your worries. Unfortunately, paperwork is a crucial factor when it comes to job site management—and it is probably the hardest part of the whole job. After all, when you are in the middle of a concrete pour, the last thing you want to do is sit down and record the exact times the trucks arrived and what the temperature was that day. However, this is exactly the type of information that must be tracked and recorded.

It is extremely important that the construction activity be documented throughout the entire duration of the project. There is so much happening and so many conversations going on that unless someone is keeping track of it all, something is bound to be miscommunicated or fall through the cracks.

Obviously, the superintendent must be very knowledgeable when it comes to construction methods and techniques. But he or she must also be a stickler for detail when it comes to the paperwork. Good record keeping is a must and all information should be:

♦ Accurate

♦ Objective

♦ Complete

♦ Legible

♦ Timely

♦ Retrievable

There are many different mechanisms used to track and record all of the activities that occur on the job site. In addition to the administrative requirements of construction, much of the information collected and documented throughout the construction process is used to analyze project performance and make management decisions. Let's take a look at some of these mechanisms now.

Project Meetings

Throughout the construction process, a number of meetings take place at the job site. Sometimes these meetings are scheduled at regular intervals, such as weekly, biweekly, or monthly. At other times, they are called as special meetings to address a specific issue or problem.

The purpose of these meetings is to discuss construction progress and provide a forum in which the major project participants (architects, engineers, contractors, subcontractors, and owner representatives) can discuss their concerns. The meetings are usually somewhat formal in nature with a written agenda.

Meeting minutes should always be recorded at these events. It is common practice to bring in a field engineer or secretary to record these minutes. Every discussion and decision made must be documented. These minutes should become a part of the formal record pertaining to the project and be distributed to all appropriate parties in a timely fashion. Any discrepancies found in the minutes should be communicated within a limited time frame—ten days, for example— to avoid misunderstandings later. Any corrections or clarifications to the minutes should be duly recorded and distributed.

Although this formality may seem quite tedious to the seasoned superintendent when there are so many other practical things that may need his or her attention, discipline here protects the contractor's interests throughout the construction process, and may help to avoid some sticky conflicts down the road.

NOTE

I always made a practice of using new field engineers to record the minutes at progress meetings. This way they were able to hear firsthand the kinds of issues and concerns that owners, architects, engineers, and subcontractors brought to the table on a regular basis. It turned out to be one of the best training venues that I could provide on the job site.

Logs, Diaries, and Daily Field Reports

One of the best ways to keep up with all of the day-to-day activities that go on at the job site is by tracking them in some type of a standard log or by recording them in project diaries.

Logs

Logs are used to track a number of regular activities occurring on the job site. Some of the more common logs are:

◆ Phone logs for tracking phone calls, both incoming and outgoing. They usually record the date and time of the call, the participants in the call, and the purpose of the call.

◆ Transmittal logs track the dates and addressees of all transmittals as well as the actual information being transmitted, such as shop drawings, product cut sheets, samples, or some other submittal.

◆ Delivery logs help keep up with all of the material and equipment deliveries that are made to the site. The log contains the date of the delivery and the material received, and notes any problems with the order and the actions taken.

◆ RFI logs track all requests for information submitted to the project participants and their responses. The date the RFI was sent and the date that the response was received are also noted in the log.

Diaries

Every member of the project team, but especially the superintendent, should be encouraged to keep a project diary. This tracking tool can take the form of a simple spiral notebook or something more elaborate, such as a day planner or electronic organizer. The diary is used to track all of the day's events in a summarized fashion and in the individual's own words. Diaries are used to note daily work activities, conversations, observations, and any other information worth recording. It is important that each member of the team keeps his or her own diary, because different people will have different interactions and conversations throughout the day. The diaries provide a reliable historic record and can become very important when disagreements or discrepancies arise on the job. Handwritten diaries are often permissible in the courts as evidence of actual events and conversations. Electronic entries are sometimes viewed as less credible.

Daily Field Reports

In addition to the informal project diaries, most construction companies require that a more formal record be kept. These field reports are intended to simplify the capture of some fundamental information needed to track job progress and confirm that various project requirements are being met. For example, a notation indicating that an inspector was on site and approved a footing excavation would verify that required quality checks are being conducted. The reports are usually written on preprinted standard forms that contain consistent information. They are relatively easy to fill out and must be filed with the superintendent's signature and date marking it as an official document. The types of information recorded are:

- The name of the individual making the report
- The date, project name, and location
- A brief description of the day's activities
- The temperature and general weather conditions
- The contractor's own work forces on the job
- The subcontractors' personnel on the job site
- Materials or equipment delivered
- Equipment used on the job
- Visitors to the job site
- Other notable events

Daily reports are often summarized into weekly or monthly reports that are distributed to upper management within the company. These reports make up some of the data used to analyze project performance and make adjustments to the overall project plan.

Labor Records

If the popular adage "time is money" holds true, then labor represents the greatest risk to the construction schedule and budget—and indeed it does. Keeping accurate labor records is one of the most important functions of construction managers in the field. The data that they collect by way of time cards is extremely valuable to the construction company. The time cards provide the payroll clerk with all of the information needed to calculate wages and distribute paychecks—pretty important, especially if you are one of the workers expecting a check. In addition, time cards provide the fundamental information needed by the construction manager to track and monitor productivity and labor expenditures.

Employee Name	Trade Class	RT/OT	Cost Codes				Rate	Total Hours	Gross Amount
			3.010	3.020	3.120	3.801			
Stevens, Pete	Concrete Finisher	RT			2	6	$27.00	8	$216.00
		OT							
Platt, Debbie	Labor	RT	2	2	4		$18.00	8	$144.00
		OT							
Doud, A.J.	Carpenter	RT		5	3		$24.00	8	$192.00
		OT							
Michaels, Ron	Labor	RT		2	3	3	$18.00	8	$144.00
		OT							
Alvarez, Manny	Rodman	RT	4	2	1	1	$29.00	8	$232.00
		OT							

On large projects, time cards are usually filled out by supervisory personnel for each trade or labor group working on the job. If it is a small job, the individual workers record their hours on a weekly time card. In either instance, once the cards are completed, they should be reviewed and checked by the superintendent for accuracy before being sent to the payroll clerk.

The information gathered from the time cards is used to create a weekly labor report, typically prepared by the superintendent or assistant superintendent. The report tracks labor hours and dollars spent on various aspects of the work. Labor is categorized and tracked by cost codes, which I will explain in much greater detail in Chapter 10. But for right now, it's sufficient that you understand how the report is used and why it is so important. The purpose of the report is to summarize cumulative labor costs and compare them with budgeted labor costs. This information helps the management team keep the project on target for meeting its cost and schedule goals.

Visual Records

You've heard the expression "A picture is worth a thousand words." This is certainly the case in construction. There are many reasons for visually recording work progress on the job site. Progress photos help document construction methods, highlight and capture problem areas, and supplement written reports. For example, some contractors are using videotape and still photos to record the location of wires and pipes in walls in lieu of sketching them on the as-built drawings. This way, everyone has a record of where these items are after the walls are covered with drywall. This can be very helpful, especially if you decide to remodel the space down the road. With digital photography, you can literally take hundreds of photos on your project site and easily archive them electronically for record and historical reference.

Web Cameras

Web cams are websites that host images or live video streams from remote digital cameras. This technology is utilized in a variety of ways, but has become quite popular in construction and is now readily available on many job sites. These cameras literally provide 24-hour access to the building site by any member of the project team who is authorized. The opportunity now exists to sit in an office hundreds of miles away and attend an on-site meeting where a specific construction problem is being discussed. You can see the work as it is being performed in real time. Although web cams should never be used as an excuse for not visiting the job site in person, they are definitely useful for keeping an eye on things between visits.

In addition to providing real-time access to the job site, web cameras have become an amazing tool for teaching construction management in the classroom. Streaming video creates the opportunity to take your students on a virtual field trip.

NOTE

Correspondence

Every day, numerous communications are generated among the project participants. E-mails, letters, and faxes fly back and forth among the architects, engineers, owner reps, building officials, subcontractors, material suppliers, testing organizations, government agencies, and community groups. All of the correspondence must be filed and recorded throughout the duration of the project. The types of documents that must be saved include:

transmittal
A tracking document that serves as a cover notification to any communication, submittal, or shop drawing being transmitted among the project participants.

- Submittals
- Payment requests
- Punch lists
- Change orders
- *Transmittals*
- Requests for information
- Letters
- E-mails
- Faxes
- Miscellaneous items

Today most of these documents are created and stored electronically. It should go without saying that these records should be backed up on a regular basis. Handwritten documents are usually filed in three-ring binders. Although this may seem like a lot of work, it takes only one major claim or lawsuit to justify the effort.

Paperwork and record-keeping are not the only non-construction related activities that the superintendent and on-site construction management team must contend with. They must also handle a number of public relations issues.

Public Relations

Every construction project requires some level of public relations work to be managed by the superintendent. Because he or she is the frontline representative for the company, it is important that good relations be established and maintained throughout the duration of the construction. Although most superintendents will probably tell you that they would rather deal strictly with construction issues, they understand that they must sometimes contend with owner relations, employee issues, subcontractor conflicts, company image, and publicity.

Owner Relations

I cannot stress enough how very important it is to maintain positive, cooperative relations with the project owner and his or her representatives. This requires a high level of communication. Making the extra effort to make sure that the owner is in the loop when it comes to project progress is vital.

Although most formal communications must be routed through the architect, I have found that it is very beneficial for the project manager to pick up the phone and check in with the owner (or the owner's job site representatives) on a weekly basis. The superintendent is really the first line of communication on the job site, but most owners really appreciate the extra consideration. You would be amazed at how often a potentially serious conflict can be defused with just a simple phone call. Whatever action can be taken to catch and discuss problems while they are still small is always in the contractor's best interest.

One of the ways that the construction industry has increased overall owner involvement in the construction process is through a variety of collaborative software programs. These programs establish intranet sites that allow the owner to take part in the numerous discussions between the designers and contractors as they work out the details of the construction. This helps eliminate problems when someone gets left out of the communication loop. Most large contractors now use some type of collaborative software to integrate all of their project management systems. Web cameras are often linked to these intranet sites, which allows the owner and other authorized parties to watch the work as it is being performed.

NOTE   Check out Autodesk Buzzsaw under the Products link at the Autodesk website (http://usa.autodesk.com). Buzzsaw is an example of a collaborative software program that is on the market. This product is designed to improve construction management processes and enhance project tracking and control.

Employee Relations

There are a number of employee issues that must be addressed by the superintendent as he or she goes about managing the construction operations. Some of them warrant strict policies and procedures, such as sexual harassment and drug and alcohol use, while others are dealt with only as issues arise, such as personality conflicts among individual project team members. Let's take a look at some of the more serious problems.

Racial and Sexual Harassment

Harassment is a serious issue and should not be tolerated in any work environment. The company leadership must send a very strong message regarding specific anti-harassment policies. All managers and superintendents should be trained to recognize and stop all forms of racial and sexual harassment, and be required to communicate a zero-tolerance for harassment philosophy to the workforce on site. Failure to do so can end up being very costly to the contractor and destroy company morale in a hurry.

Even seemingly harmless actions such as graffiti-writing can no longer be viewed as naive expressions. A company can now be held liable for failing to curb such immature behavior when it contains racial or sexual innuendo. For example, in January 2000, a $1.3 million settlement was reached between the U.S. Equal Employment Opportunity Commission (EEOC) and a large construction company based in New Jersey that performs work throughout the United States. The lawsuit arose from complaints received by the EEOC regarding racial and sexual harassment at a specific construction project in Illinois. The harassment included racist and sexist graffiti in portable toilets on the job site.

The attorney prosecuting the case made this statement upon notification of the award: "This case ought to serve as a lesson to the construction industry at large. Racial and sexual harassment, including racial and sexual graffiti, is no more acceptable at construction sites than at other places of business. It's illegal, and construction industry employers who permit it may be looking at costly litigation." The attorney went on to say that "the case was important because it challenged a persistent problem in the construction industry, harassment in the form of graffiti."

Obviously, there are more blatant expressions of harassment than graffiti, but this example shows just how serious the issue is. No matter what your views are regarding the credibility or fairness of harassment claims and awards, there is no doubt that the stakes in permitting questionable behavior are getting very high. A workforce left unchecked when it comes to any kind of irresponsible and harassing behavior is a liability.

Drug and Alcohol Policy

Construction is a dangerous business. The use of drugs and alcohol cannot be tolerated on the job site. It is critical that every construction company have a written policy regarding substance abuse. The policy must be posted and clearly visible on the job, and the superintendent must uphold the requirements of the policy to the letter. The superintendent is responsible for making it crystal clear to every subcontractor and every worker on site exactly what that policy is, and what the consequences of violating it are. (This very important issue will be addressed in further detail in Chapter 11.)

Subcontractor Relations

It would probably be a miracle if your construction project completed without experiencing at least one conflict among subcontractors, or a subcontractor and a vendor, or even among your own management team. But part of the job of a superintendent is to referee conflicts and do whatever can be done to defuse tensions and maintain high morale among all members of the project team. This is not always an easy task, but it is a crucial one. The project's success depends on it.

Most conflicts on the job site arise out of misunderstandings and scheduling snafus, both of which can be avoided. Good communication networks and conscientious planning efforts help prevent most of the serious conflicts that can arise among co-workers. Getting projects built on time and within budget is hard enough when everyone gets along and enjoys what they are doing every day. Trying to accomplish this task when people are fighting and complaining just makes it that much more difficult. The best superintendents possess at least as much leadership ability as they do construction knowledge.

Company Image and Publicity

Although it may not seem as if publicity should be considered a part of construction operations or job site management, the truth is that your construction project itself is one of the biggest advertising tools that you have. The problem with this notion is that the publicity could end up being a good thing or a bad thing. For example, if your project is a high-profile, greatly appreciated facility, viewed as contributing to the overall betterment of the community, that is a good thing. On the other hand, if the project ends up in the middle of some political or social controversy where picketers are standing outside your entrance gate every morning, that can be a bad thing. Either way, the issue must be managed both at the job site level and at the corporate level. The key is not to let the publicity interfere with the actual work of getting the project built in as timely a manner as possible.

To start, it always helps to be perceived as a good neighbor. Keeping the job site clean, limiting the noise, and controlling the dust all adds to your company's image as a responsible contractor. Making the effort to keep nearby residents and businesses informed about your activities—especially those that will cause inconveniences, such as late-night concrete pours or temporary traffic detours—will help maintain harmony and save you a lot of headaches.

There are numerous ways in which to make an impression while constructing your project and doing your job. As stated earlier, nothing speaks louder than the quality of your work and the conduct of your people. However, there are a couple of simple additional things that you may want to consider.

Signage

Job signage is one of the easiest ways to advertise your company and bring attention to your construction abilities. Most construction contracts require that the contractor fabricate and install a large construction sign at a prominent location on site that announces the project name, the project architect, engineers, general contractor, major subcontractors, and major financier.

There are other types of signage that are commonly displayed on construction sites. There are signs painted on company vehicles and company equipment, and logos pasted on company hardhats. Many contractors fly large banners at the top of their high-rise buildings under construction or on top of their cranes high in the air to advertise their company name. I recently visited a rather prominent developer/builder on the East Coast and I was surprised to witness three superintendents all arguing over which one was going to get to fly the largest of the company banners on his job. Apparently all three projects were high visibility and each superintendent wanted to make sure that the community was aware of exactly who was responsible for bringing these new facilities to the area.

Dealing with the Media

When you work on high-profile projects, it is not uncommon to encounter the press. Sometimes they may even show up on your job site unannounced. The superintendent must make sure that they are never allowed to wander around the construction site unescorted. First, it is dangerous, and second, you need to be fully aware of what they are photographing with their cameras and who they are talking to.

Some projects actually warrant a full-time public relations person to handle all media requests. However, if you do have the opportunity to be interviewed by the press or for television, make sure that you are equipped with accurate information and the authority to speak. It is always a good idea to discuss publicity issues with the owner up front. You don't want to do anything that might damage your relationship, and it is very easy to slip up and say something you should not have said. The possibility of your words being misconstrued is always a risk.

On the other hand, under the right conditions, free press can end up being a boon for your marketing plan. For example, I had a client back in the early 1990s who was remodeling a unique historic home. The local newspaper decided to do an article on the project (because of its historical significance) and interviewed me at length on the job site. A photo of me inside the house and a lengthy article ended up on the front page of the real estate section in the Sunday edition of the paper. That little interview ended up being worth about $15,000 of free publicity for me. The phone started ringing off the hook from all over the state. Apparently there were a lot of people who were interested in remodeling their historic homes!

NOTE   It may surprise you to learn that both the National Association of Homebuilders and the Associated General Contractors conduct workshops teaching contractors how to deal with the media and do live interviews. I took the course myself years ago and can tell you that it was very professional and improved my public interviewing skills tremendously. Once again, you can clearly see that there is a lot more to this construction business than bricks, sticks, hammers, and nails!

Terms to Know

back charges	site logistics plan
dry shacks	transmittals
laydown area	will-call

Review Questions

1. Identify at least three issues that the superintendent must be concerned with when trying to manage construction operations.

2. When scheduling subcontractors for the job, there are three fundamental rules that you should try to follow. What are they?

3. What does it mean to order something on will-call?

4. Identify at least three factors that can negatively impact construction productivity.

5. Identify at least three environmental issues that might interfere with the project schedule and cause unexpected delays on the job.

6. What is a laydown area?

7. What types of information should be shown on a site logistics plan? Name at least four items.

8. Why is it important for the job superintendent and the other members of the on-site team to keep project diaries?

9. Why is it important to accurately report hours and cost codes on time cards?

10. Identify the way in which the construction industry has increased overall owner involvement in the construction process.

Chapter 9

Project Planning and Scheduling

Trying to take on a construction project without a well-thought-out plan is like trying to drive to an unknown location without a map. Without a plan, there is no way to coordinate your workforce, no way to schedule deliveries, no way to track progress, and no way to make adjustments when you do get off track. As a matter of fact, you won't even know that you are off track unless you have a plan. And given what is at stake if the project should stray off course, it would be ludicrous to think you could manage the construction of a multi-million dollar facility, or even the construction of someone's home, without a plan. The primary tool associated with project planning is the schedule.

In the introduction to Chapter 6, "Estimating Project Costs," I said that there are always two questions asked by a client considering an investment in construction: "How much?" and "How long?" You learned in Chapter 6 that estimating addresses the "How much?" question. Scheduling addresses "How long?"

Planning and scheduling concern two interrelated elements of construction management: strategy and time. Every construction project presents a new set of circumstances and conditions. The project team must come together at the start of the job and hammer out the details associated with both of these elements before the first shovel of dirt is turned on the project.

It's All about Time!

We've all heard the expression "Time is money." When it comes to managing a construction project, that statement is especially true.

Let's look at it from the owner's perspective. Manufacturers, or industrial facilities, or service facilities do not make their money by constructing buildings. They make their money by making and selling widgets or providing their services. As long as their new facility is under construction, it is a liability. The facility becomes an asset to them only when it is completed and can function as it was intended. So completing a project on time is a *big* deal. However, completing a project on time does not happen by accident. It takes a great deal of effort and planning. You have already learned in previous chapters that there are many factors that can interfere and delay the work. A good plan and a reliable schedule will help you prepare and avoid some of those factors that can derail your project.

Trying to plan, assign durations, and schedule every little activity associated with building a project that is going to take one, two, or even ten years is an awesome task. But it is exactly what you are challenged to do as a construction manager. You must break the project down into manageable activities linked to increments of time that can be monitored and adjusted as the project schedule moves along.

How long will the project take to complete? Just as with cost estimating, no one really knows until the project is all done. But as a construction professional, your job is to make your best educated guess based on the experience of your project team and using the planning and scheduling tools available. Let's take a look at some of those tools now.

Types of Schedules

network diagram

A common type of construction schedule, also called the critical path method (CPM), that depicts a continuous chain of activities showing both activity durations and the relationship of the activities. There are two types of network diagrams: activity-on-arrow (AOA) and activity-on-node (AON).

Although several different types of schedules are used in the construction industry, the two most common types are bar charts and *network diagrams*. Which type a construction manager uses depends on a number of factors, some company-related and some project-related.

- ◆ Size of the company
- ◆ Volume of work
- ◆ Type of construction
- ◆ Project size
- ◆ Project complexity
- ◆ Computer capability
- ◆ Contract requirements

For some projects, a simple bar chart is all that is needed, because the project is straightforward with a limited number of activities and systems. Complex projects require the more sophisticated scheduling techniques made possible by network diagrams. Most contractors employ both types of schedules and apply them to best suit the scheduling needs presented.

NOTE

You will encounter a whole menagerie of scheduling techniques and formats in the construction industry. Although most large construction companies today use some type of computerized network scheduling program, some smaller operations, especially in the residential market, still depend on hand-drawn bar charts.

Bar Charts

You are probably pretty familiar with bar charts already. The big advantage to bar chart schedules is that they are very easy to understand and follow. That's because they can relate activities, and their durations, to calendar days. You can easily see and understand when an activity will begin and when it will end. The biggest disadvantage to bar charts is that they do not show the interrelationships among the activities. For example, bar charts are not very good at showing the impact that a delay in one activity might have on another activity, or on the overall duration of the project. These impacts can be shown only in a network diagram. For complex projects, it is critical to be able to assess these relationships.

Activities	1	2	3	4	5	6	7	8	9	10	11	12	13	14	15	16	17	18	19	20	21	22	23	24
Layout	█																							
Sitework & excavation		█	█	█	█																			
Foundations				█																				
Structure					█	█	█																	
Roof								█																
Walls								█	█															
Exterior doors & windows											█	█												
Interior partitions														█	█									
Finishes																█	█	█	█	█				
Plumbing								█	█								█	█						
HVAC																	█	█						
Electrical				█	█	█											█	█						
Closeout																							█	█

NOTE

Bar charts provide visual clarity. They are very good schedules for presenting the project timeline to the owner, end user groups, or the public. Such charts are easily understood and do a good job of identifying when things start and when things end, which is what an owner is most interested in. Owners don't particularly care about the relationships between activities—they are primarily concerned with when the job will be done.

Network Diagrams

Many activities in construction are dependent upon other activities in construction. For example, you can't hang wallpaper until the drywall is in place, and you can't install drywall until the walls are framed, and you can't frame walls until the floor system is in place, and you can't install the floor system until the foundation is in place. I could continue with this string of activities but I think you get my point. Not only are the activities often dependent upon one another but many activities also overlap or run parallel to one another. For instance, electricians can be pulling wire on the inside of the building at the same time the masons are installing the brick veneer on the outside of the building. Network diagrams give us a structural tool that combines activity relationships and activity durations to best determine the right schedule for the project. Although bar charts are very easy to understand, they don't really provide the level of sophistication needed to evaluate and examine the relationships between activities as well as the network diagram.

The network diagram method of scheduling, also referred to as the critical path method (CPM), is the most common type of schedule used in the commercial, civil, and industrial construction industry today. (I'll discuss the critical path later in the chapter.) Although there are plenty of projects that can be managed from a bar chart schedule, the more complex jobs require the more sophisticated method.

precedence diagram

A graphic presentation of a schedule depicting project activities on a node with an arrow that depicts the dependencies that exist between the activities.

There are two techniques used to develop a network diagram. The first is called the activity-on-arrow (AOA) method because activities are noted on the arrow as shown next. The second technique is called the activity-on-node (AON) method because the activity is notated on the node, also shown next. The activity-on-node technique, also called *precedence diagramming*, is the method of choice for most of the industry. Therefore, my focus throughout the chapter will be on precedence diagramming as shown in the second illustration.

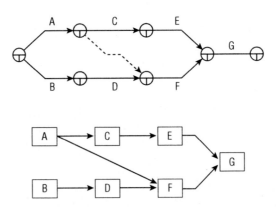

How We Use Schedules

Schedules serve a number of purposes in the construction industry. How the schedule is to be used will determine the complexity and level of detail that it contains. Because it is a communication and management tool, it's important that the information being conveyed is understandable and appropriate for its intended purpose.

Detailed schedules   As the name implies, detailed schedules break major work activities down into smaller tasks so the schedule can be analyzed in greater detail. For example, foundations would be broken down into formwork, reinforcing, and cast-in-place concrete. These categories would be broken down even further in the schedule. Detailed schedules are often used at the field office level to discuss the finer points of a work activity. They are often pinned up on the office wall with highlighting and red lines all over them as details of the job are discussed.

Summary schedules   Summary schedules group activities under broader headings such as mobilization, sitework, foundation, and rough framing. These schedules are most often used for management reports and presentations where it is important to convey the overall plan and status of the work but not necessarily all of the details of that plan.

Mini-schedules   Basically, a mini-schedule is any portion of a summary or detailed schedule broken down into even finer detail. Sometimes a particular division or area of work requires more scrutiny regarding the various activities needed to accomplish the work—such as the mechanical division, which includes plumbing and heating, ventilation, and air conditioning (HVAC).

Short-interval schedules   *Short-interval schedules*, also called look-ahead schedules, are developed by superintendents and trade foremen to coordinate activities and manage the work flow over a relatively short period of time, usually two- to four-week intervals. They are often hand-drawn and are distributed to the specific trades involved. Although they originate from the larger detailed schedules intended for management, the look-ahead schedule really acts like an individual work plan for the work crews on site.

Special-purpose schedules   Not all schedules used in construction are used to organize and sequence work. Some schedules are used to keep track of activities that support the work, such as delivery schedules, submittal schedules, and inspection schedules. However, some of these activities should also be integrated into the detailed schedule to make sure that their impact is not overlooked in the overall plan. I'll explain more about the importance of an integrated schedule later in this chapter.

Now that you have an idea about how schedules are used, let's take a look at how we create one.

Building the Schedule

One of the great things about being on the team that develops the project schedule is that you really get to think through the project before it is ever built. Similar to the estimating process, scheduling forces you to consider details and elements of the job long before you ever encounter them on the job site.

You'll get to think about all of the materials, labor, subcontractors, and equipment that it will take to complete the project. You'll also get to consider all of the factors that influence the efficient use of those resources. You'll have a chance to ponder and discuss the circumstances that could slow down the process and cause the project to be delayed. You'll have an opportunity to develop the strategy that will carry the project to a successful completion.

It's a lot of work to mentally process all of this information, but this is what it takes to put together a construction schedule. It also takes experience and a good knowledge of the construction process so that you can identify and sequence all of the activities needed to complete the job. In addition, you'll have to perform a few scheduling calculations.

Because most construction projects are scheduled using network diagrams, I am going to focus my discussion on how to build a precedence diagram schedule. There are three fundamental stages to this process:

- Planning stage
- Sequencing stage
- Scheduling stage

Let me walk you through these three stages.

Planning Stage

Planning is at the heart of creating the schedule. This is where the construction manager identifies all of the activities needed to build the project. An activity is a task, function, or decision that has a time commitment, or duration, associated with it. Activities provide the fundamental building blocks of the schedule.

Although novice builders can usually come up with an activity list, the more experienced you are, the easier time you have of it and the less likely it is that you will overlook any of the steps needed to get from A to Z—or in construction terms, from mobilization to project closeout.

When developing an activity list, it is important to consider the purpose of the schedule and who will use it. The number of activities and the level of detail needed in the schedule will vary from job to job. The more complex the project, the more detailed the activity list will be. The detail level should correlate with the control level desired. The goal is to have enough activities and just the right amount of detail so that you can effectively monitor and manage the work flow (see Table 9.1).

Table 9.1   Level of Detail

Activity Detail: Adequate	Activity Detail: Too Much

Frame Floor System	Frame Floor System
	    –Install sill plates.
	    –Install rim joists.
	    –Install floor joists.
	    –Install blocking.
	    –Install subfloor.

Frame Wall System	Frame Wall System
	    –Install bottom plates.
	    –Install studs.
	    –Install headers.
	    –Install top plates.

Frame Roof System	Frame Roof System
	    –Install roof trusses.
	    –Install bracing.
	    –Install roof sheathing.

Using the Work Breakdown Structure

So what is the best way to make sure that we have identified all of the activities needed to manage the project effectively? Back in Chapter 6, I introduced you to the concept of the work breakdown structure, or WBS. If you recall, the purpose of the WBS is to organize and identify the work of the project by breaking each division into separate work packages, assembled around the work activities typically performed by a single trade subcontractor or work group. When estimating, we use the WBS to develop bid packages for pricing purposes. When scheduling, we use the WBS to help develop our activity list. For example, when estimating a work package for roofing, you would include three activities:

- Install building felt.
- Install roof flashing.
- Install roof shingles.

Each of these activities would be performed by a roofing subcontractor. However, the construction manager has to be careful not to let any required work activity slip through the cracks. This roofing work package is an excellent example, because there is one more activity that must be performed by the roofer but is typically included in the plumber's work package. That item is the plumbing vent flashing, commonly called a vent boot. The vent boot (special flashing configuration) is installed after the building felt but prior to the shingles.

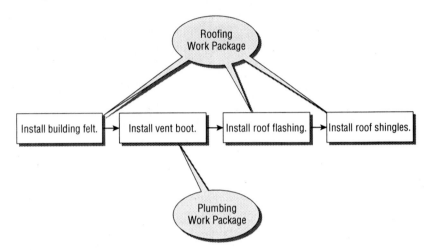

This unique circumstance requires a special schedule consideration because the rest of the plumbing package will most likely not be performed until later in the schedule. So, although the WBS is very helpful when it comes to identifying activities for the schedule, you must be aware that trade contractors (or parts of their packages) may appear more than once in the schedule if they perform more than one activity or if they perform work at different stages of the project.

Interface issues among trades is just one of the factors that can make the activity-listing task kind of tricky. That's why it is so important to engage team members with experience in the scheduling development process whenever possible. The ultimate goal of the construction manager is to make sure that there are no overlaps and no holes in their activity list and overall work plan.

Types of Activities

There are a thousand steps to getting from mobilization to project closeout, and although all of the steps have a time frame associated with them, they don't all have to do with the actual building of the structure. Some have to do with supporting the building of the structure, such as submitting light fixture orders or securing the building permit. There are three types of activities that must be planned and included in the schedule: production, procurement, and administrative. Most schedules include all three types of activities.

Production activities   These activities identify tasks that are associated with the physical building of the project, such as pour concrete foundation, erect structural steel, or hang acoustic ceiling. For further clarification, sometimes these activities have to be identified with their location. For example, in a multistory office building, an activity might read "Hang first floor acoustic ceiling."

Some production activities don't actually require any physical effort but they do take time. For example, concrete requires a certain amount of time to cure. Although there is no physical activity associated with the curing of concrete, the activity needs to be identified in the schedule because there is a time requirement associated with it.

Procurement activities   These activities are primarily associated with obtaining materials and equipment for the project. They can be some of the most crucial activities in the schedule, and if not properly considered, can cause major delays on the project. For example, steel is often a long lead item (you learned about long lead items back in Chapter 6). If the steel delivery activity is not accurately displayed in the schedule and the ordering of the material comes later in the project than it should have, the project will suffer dire consequences. That's why it is so very important that several experienced members of the project team be involved in creating the activity list.

Administrative activities   These activities are mostly associated with contract administration tasks such as permitting, submittals, inspections, and testing. All of these activities can eat up a lot of time and are probably some of the most unpredictable activities on the schedule. Permit processing, for example, is really out of the contractor's hands. Therefore, he or she has very little control over the activity. Although the contractor knows that the activity must occur and when it must happen, the duration of this activity is often a hopeful guess. It's the same thing with submittals. Sometimes a color or sample submittal is rejected initially by the architect and the contractor has to resubmit it for approval. So predicting time on these types of activities can be pretty nerve-wracking, especially when the scheduling of the actual construction work depends on accurate time estimates.

Although a number of these types of activities should be integrated into the detailed schedule, sometimes they are assembled into a special schedule, as indicated earlier in this chapter.

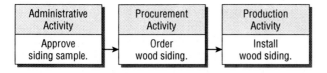

Sequencing Stage

network logic
The order in which activities are sequenced in the network diagram relative to their interdependent relationships.

Once you have identified all of the activities that need to be performed on your project, it is time to develop the sequencing of those activities, or *network logic*. In other words, in what order must these activities occur and which ones can occur simultaneously? This is where we begin to consider and define the relationships among the various activities. As stated earlier, the activity-on-node, or precedence diagramming technique is the most commonly used method in the industry and this is the technique that I will describe.

Developing the Precedence Diagram

A network diagram is nothing more than a work plan. Although the work plan should flow without interruption, it must be understood that the order in which the work occurs is somewhat flexible. In other words, different contractors will take a different approach to sequencing the work. For example, the coordination of interior trim work with painting can be handled in a couple of different ways. Some contractors will insist upon installing all interior trim first, tape it off, and then paint the walls. Others will insist that the walls should be painted first, then installation of the trim, and come back in and do touch-up painting. Both sequences will work. The construction manager, along with the project team, will decide the best path to move the project from start to finish. The great thing about this process is that it gives the project team an opportunity to brainstorm the plan together and organize the job before it goes to the field. The important thing is that once the plan is in place, the team actually uses it!

In the activity-on-node precedence diagram, each node identifies an individual activity and is assigned an activity number. For example:

You will notice that the activity numbering is done in intervals of 10. (You can use any spacing interval you choose.) There is a good reason for doing it this way. If activities need to be added later, you have at least 10 opportunities to plug them in between nodes without having to adjust the numbering of the whole network. The numbering system is particularly helpful for monitoring purposes and when using a computer for your scheduling needs.

Relationships Among Activities

All network diagrams have a beginning and an end, and they are intended to flow continuously. Except for the first and last activity in the network, each step has some activities that must come before it and some activities that must come after it. In order to figure out the network logic, there are three basic questions that you must ask regarding each individual activity:

- Which activities must be completed before this activity can begin?
- Which activities can be started once this activity is completed?
- Which activities can be going on at the same time as this activity?

Once you have figured out the sequencing logic, you can start to plot the network. This can be a messy endeavor. It usually takes several tries before the team can get it just the way they want it. Once again, this is where experience really comes in handy. The following diagrams illustrate some of the sequencing patterns that start to emerge once the activities are evaluated.

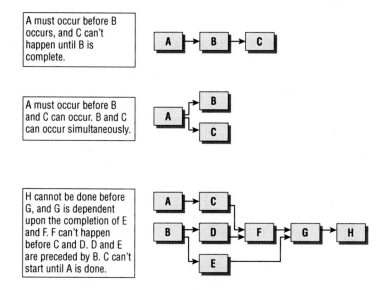

The invention of the Post-it note was a boon for construction scheduling. Post-it notes are often used to work out a network's logic on a wall, large piece of paper, or white board. Each activity is written on a sticky note and then placed in the proper sequence. On a complex project, it can take a lot of shuffling the notes around to get it right!

NOTE

Scheduling Stage

Now that all of the activities are identified and all of the sequencing is figured out, it is time to assign durations to each activity. After all, we don't really have a useable schedule until time is factored into the equation. Although you already considered productivity as a factor of the estimate when you calculated unit costs, scheduling requires a different kind of estimate. Unit costs are applied to quantities of work and deal with "how much?" Schedules deal with "how long" and reflect the efficiency with which you coordinate and utilize the resources needed to perform the work. You must accurately predict, to the best of your ability, how many days, weeks, months, or years it will take to complete the project. There are several tools available to you for making this prediction. You start by estimating how long it will take to perform each individual activity in the schedule.

Determining Activity Durations

In determining activity durations, the cost estimate is a good place to start, but most construction managers and superintendents will rely on their experience and information obtained from their subcontractors when calculating durations for specific activities. But keep in mind that predicting durations is not an exact science. Even if you have been successful in identifying all of the steps needed to complete the job, and figured out the best way to sequence the activities, you may still miss the mark if you miscalculate the time it takes to complete the individual tasks.

When trying to establish activity durations, the project team must assess all factors that may potentially impact the time needed to complete any one of the activities. As you learned back in Chapter 6, there are several activities in construction that are impacted by the weather. For example, it takes a lot longer to finish concrete in the winter than it does in the summer. On the other hand, installing interior trim is virtually unaffected by the weather or the time of year. There are some basic rules to follow when trying to determine activity durations:

- Try to evaluate each activity as an independent operation.
- Consult with experienced tradesmen to get their time estimates regarding specific activities.
- Initially, assume a standard crew size and makeup for the activity.
- Adjust production rates to fit the specific job conditions.
- Use a standard eight-hour day as your unit of measure.

Once you come up with how long you think each activity will take, it is time to start putting all of this information together to create the schedule network and use it to determine the overall project duration.

How Long Will This Job Take?

At first glance, it may seem quite easy to come up with the overall project duration by adding up all of the individual activity durations. Ah, but remember: not all activities require that all preceding activities be complete before they can begin. Many activities can be going on simultaneously. As a matter of fact, one of the goals of the construction manager is to maximize the workday output by coming up with ways to have multiple crews working on multiple activities without interfering with one another.

So if we don't just add up the individual durations, how do we figure out how long the project will take to build? This is where the activity-on-node concept comes into play. By using the activity-on-node precedence diagramming method, you are able to determine:

◆ How long it will take to complete the project—the overall schedule length

◆ What activity times must absolutely stay on track in order to meet the planned schedule

◆ What activity times have some leeway and flexibility in them without jeopardizing the schedule

One of the reasons that the activity-on-node precedence diagram works so well in construction is because it allows us to calculate the *critical path*. The critical path is the continuous chain of activities with the longest overall duration—or, more simply, the critical path is the project duration. Any delay in any activity along the critical path results in a delay in the overall project. If you are a construction manager or superintendent trying to meet your schedule targets, then it is pretty important for you to know which activities will impact the outcome most significantly so you can focus your attention there.

critical path

The longest path through a network diagram schedule and includes those activities that have zero days of float. The critical path determines the overall project duration.

Schedule Calculations

Now it's time for the fun part of scheduling. It's time to do some calculations. By knowing each activity's individual duration and by using some standard critical path calculations, you can determine the early start, early finish, late start, and late finish of each activity. Not only that but you can also determine exactly how much *float* or slack you have in the noncritical activity times. Let me explain what each of these terms mean.

float

The amount of leeway available to start or complete an individual schedule activity before it affects the planned project completion.

Early start (ES) This is the earliest possible time that an activity can start according to the relationships appointed to the activity.

Early finish (EF) This is the earliest time that an activity can finish given its allocated duration.

Late finish (LF) This is the latest time that an activity can finish without delaying the project's completion as planned.

Late start (LS) This is the latest time that an activity can start without delaying the project's completion as planned.

Float (F) The amount of time an activity's start can be delayed before it impacts the project's completion as planned. Float also allows an activity to exceed its planned duration without becoming critical if its completion remains within its total float allowance.

Each of these concepts, along with the individual activity durations, is used to complete the schedule calculations. It all starts with the activity node. When you create the network, each node represents an individual activity, and all of the information listed above plus duration is labeled on the node as shown below:

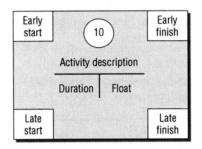

Let's presume that you have listed all of the activities to complete a small project. You have come up with the proper sequencing and figured out how long each activity is going to take. Table 9.2 lists all of your project information. (For illustration purposes, I am using letters to designate activities instead of descriptions and numbers.)

Now you can use the information in the table to create a network diagram and do the critical path calculations. Once the network is drawn, you basically have to perform three computations; a *forward pass*, a *backward pass*, and a float calculation.

Forward pass The forward pass determines the early start date, early finish date, and overall project duration.

Backward pass The backward pass determines the late start date and the late finish date.

Float calculations Float for individual activities can be determined after the backward pass calculations are complete.

forward pass
A scheduling technique used to calculate an activity's early start and early finish. The forward pass must be completed before the project duration can be determined.

backward pass
A scheduling technique used to calculate an activity's late start and late finish.

Table 9.2   Activity List

Activity	Dependent on Activity	Estimated Duration
A	—	1 day
B	A	3 days
C	A	2 days
D	A	4 days
E	B, C	2 days

Table 9.2   Activity List *(continued)*

Activity	Dependent on Activity	Estimated Duration
F	C	5 days
G	E	3 days
H	E, F	6 days
I	D	3 days
J	G, H, I	3 days

There are some simple formulas and some basic rules to follow when making these calculations:

Early start + duration = early finish   The forward pass calculations start at the beginning of the diagram at the first node and proceed forward to the end of the network. The first activity always has an early start time of "0," so the first activity's early finish will always be equal to its duration.

The early finish of the last activity in the network equals the total project duration. Whenever a node has more than one activity preceding it, the highest early finish number must pass forward as the early start number on the node.

Late finish – duration = late start   The backward pass calculations cannot be done until the forward pass is complete and the project duration is known. Backward pass calculations start at the end of the diagram and work backward to the beginning of the network. To start the pass, the late finish for the last activity is the same as the early finish for that activity. Whenever a node has more than one successor activity, the lowest late start number must pass backward as the late finish number on the node.

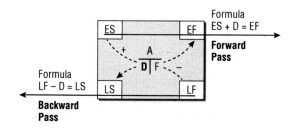

Float = late finish – early finish or late start – early start   Float cannot be calculated until you complete the backward pass. It makes no difference which formula you use to calculate float. The important thing to know is that those activities with no float make up the critical path.

The following network diagram, created from the information in Table 9.2, illustrates a completed forward pass and backward pass, along with float calculations. The critical path is highlighted with a heavy black line and the activities are circled. The results of these calculations are also shown after the diagram.

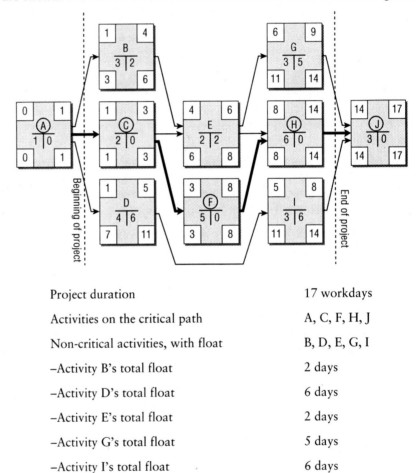

Project duration	17 workdays
Activities on the critical path	A, C, F, H, J
Non-critical activities, with float	B, D, E, G, I
–Activity B's total float	2 days
–Activity D's total float	6 days
–Activity E's total float	2 days
–Activity G's total float	5 days
–Activity I's total float	6 days

Keep in mind that each number in the diagram represents a workday, not a calendar day. The construction manager must convert the number of workdays to calendar days when communicating the schedule to the owner or subcontractors.

NOTE   The critical path can change throughout the duration of a project. Activities that possessed a lot of slack at the beginning of the project can become critical if they are delayed too much and exceed their total float. This is why it is very important to monitor and track all activities in the network, not just the critical ones.

It can take several years to become really proficient at creating network diagrams and CPM schedules. But I'm sure you can see what a powerful tool they can be for managing the construction schedule. Fortunately there are several computer programs available that can create the networks and do all of the calculations for you, but you still have to come up with the activities, the sequencing, and the durations. These scheduling skills and abilities are fundamental to construction management.

There are several popular construction scheduling software programs on the market today. They include Primavera Project Planner (P3), Primavera SureTrak Project Manager, and Microsoft Project. Sometimes the contract will actually require the contractor to use a particular software program because it corresponds to the system that the owner already uses internally. When this happens, the contractor is obliged to buy, learn, and use the new software.

NOTE

Once we have created the schedule, it's time to actually put it to work. Let's take a look at how we use it to direct the construction operations and keep the project team updated regarding planned activities and job progress.

Communicating and Updating the Schedule

The schedule is one of the most powerful management tools that we have. It allows us to communicate the overall game plan for accomplishing the project goals to the owner, the subcontractors, the vendors, and our entire project team. But that doesn't mean that we can just sit back and watch the work unfold precisely as we had predicted. No, it's a lot messier than that. Both you and I know that most things in life don't always go the way we had planned. There is a lot of tweaking that takes place on that schedule before you ever get to a finished project.

Lots of things can go astray—deliveries can be delayed, the plumbers or electricians or carpet layers may not show up when they are supposed to, and your crews won't always accomplish what you had hoped they would in a workday. The schedule is not some fixed, rigid document that gets created and doesn't ever change. It is a dynamic tool, and every activity's duration on the schedule is tracked and monitored with adjustments being made all along the way. Therefore, the schedule must be updated to reflect these adjustments on a regular basis.

These frequent updates must be communicated to the affected parties in the most efficient manner possible. Although you can always find a working version of the schedule pasted somewhere on the office trailer wall (remember the one with all the red lines and highlighting on it), it would be almost impossible to keep up with all of the changes manually. As previously mentioned, most construction companies use computerized scheduling software and anyone working as part of the on-site construction management team will be familiar with this software. With a few keystrokes, a field engineer or assistant superintendent can input all of those red-lined or highlighted changes and adjust activity starts, activity finishes, and activity durations. Once these modifications are entered, the computer automatically adjusts the overall schedule and recalculates the critical path if need be. The updated schedule can then be electronically transferred to the senior management back at the main office as well as the subcontractors, vendors, designers, and owners. The updates can occur as often as every other week, but in most instances the overall schedule adjustments are posted monthly.

Notifying Subcontractors

It is critically important that these changes get communicated in as timely a fashion as possible, especially to subcontractors. When a subcontractor signs on to perform a portion of the work, he or she will create work plans and schedules based on the start date and finish date originally negotiated with the superintendent. Remember that subcontractors are performing work for a number of general contractors on a number of different jobs. They cannot drop everything they were working on just because you modified your schedule. The sooner the project manager or superintendent notifies them, the better. In this case, you don't want to wait until the overall schedule revisions are completed. You want to communicate specific time-line changes to your subcontractors using the more detailed short-interval schedules that I mentioned earlier in this chapter. These more detailed schedules are often done by hand and discussed with the individual subcontractor at an on-site meeting.

One of the common complaints lodged by subcontractors is that superintendents wait until the last minute to spring schedule changes on them. They then must hustle and scurry trying to adjust all of the schedules for their other jobs. They are forced to juggle their crews, causing significant inefficiencies and possibly disrupting the work flow on other projects. Getting such short notice is very frustrating and certainly not appreciated. Superintendents (and their companies) get a reputation for how they handle these schedule adjustments, and the subcontractors' pricing will often reflect their frustration with this handling. Companies that convey schedule changes promptly and do a good job keeping the subcontractor in the communication loop may actually receive lower subcontractor bids than those who have a reputation for last-minute adjustments.

As potent a management tool as the schedule is, a superintendent who fails to make proper use of it will never benefit from its value. Constant monitoring of the actual project performance relative to the planned performance helps the superintendent keep on top of the schedule changes. Once the actual performance data is inputted into the schedule, the updates can be made very quickly and revisions can be communicated to the subcontractors immediately. This allows the subcontractors to likewise adjust their schedules as the project moves along.

Terms to Know

backward pass	network diagrams
critical path	network logic
float	precedence diagramming
forward pass	short-interval schedules

Review Questions

1. What are the two most common types of schedules used in construction?

2. Name the two techniques used to create a network diagram.

3. What is another name for the activity-on-node (AON) network diagram?

4. What is a look-ahead schedule and how is it used?

5. What are the three stages of network diagram development?

6. Name the three different types of activities that are included in the typical schedule and give an example of each.

7. What is the critical path and why is it important from a project management standpoint?

8. What is float, or slack, in the schedule?

9. What are the three scheduling calculations that you must perform in order to determine the project duration and the critical path?

10. After you complete a forward and backward pass, how do you know which activities are on the critical path?

Chapter 10

Monitoring Project Performance

Once the construction contract is executed, it is the goal of the construction management team to complete the project for the contracted dollar amount and within the agreed time frame. This goal seems reasonable enough. After all, the superintendent and field crews can be counted on to do their jobs and we can assume that our estimates and schedules are accurate. All we have to do is get out there and get the job done, hoping that everything turns out all right.

If only it were that simple. Once the construction starts, the "keeping score" element of construction management (referenced way back in Chapter 2, "What Is Construction Management?") kicks in. Every purchase order, subcontract, material invoice, and employee time card must be monitored, tracked, and recorded to ensure that the project plays out according to plan and has a reasonable chance of meeting the project goals for time, cost, and quality. If any one of these goals appears to be headed in the wrong direction, the project manager and superintendent will work together to determine the best course of action to correct the situation.

In this chapter, you will learn how important it is to monitor and report accurate field information, and will see how this information is used to make management decisions that improve the overall chances of bringing the project in on time and within budget.

The Project Control Cycle

Construction is a dynamic process and no two projects are ever alike. Even if you have years of experience, every job presents a new set of circumstances and challenges no matter how good a job you do preparing during the pre-construction stage. The project manager and superintendent work together to come up with the best plan they can, trying to anticipate every obstruction and difficulty that might impede progress and jeopardize the successful completion of the project, but they still can't foresee every contingency.

Even with all of this expert planning, the project must be monitored from beginning to end to ensure that all of the targets for time, cost, and quality are met. The whole process must be properly managed through a project control system that utilizes the plans, specs, estimate, and schedule.

All of these documents taken together establish the road map for getting from the start of construction to the final completion of the project. Using this road map, the project manager and superintendent must maneuver all of the resources in the right direction, making adjustments as they go, to keep the project on track and on target. Project control requires continuous monitoring and evaluation of actual performance relative to the estimated performance for all aspects of the job that have an impact on cost, time, and quality.

The project control cycle begins with the project plan and ends with the final project debriefing and evaluation. There are seven fundamental steps to the process:

- Develop the project plan.
- Establish the project benchmarks.
- Monitor the project performance.
- Identify performance deviations.
- Evaluate corrective options.
- Make adjustments as needed.
- Document, report, and evaluate results.

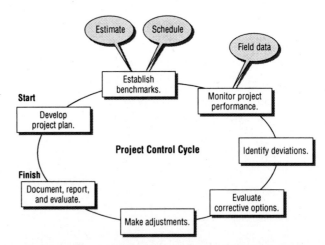

It is important to track every aspect of project performance all the way back to the planning stage. This is where every project begins and it is where every project should end—with a complete debriefing and evaluation of what worked and what didn't work. It is an excellent opportunity to capture lessons learned and to create some best practices for future implementation. Unfortunately, many construction teams fail to complete the last step in the cycle and never properly assess their project's overall performance. Everyone is usually anxious to move on to the next project, and it's very tough to get all of the parties together for even a couple of hours at the end of the job. It takes a great deal of discipline to consistently take advantage of this opportunity and learn from it. In my experience, I have found the project debriefing to be one of the most effective training mechanisms for every member of the team, from the project engineer to the project manager.

The Feedback Loop

At the heart of every project control system is information and a good reporting process. Successful construction management and project control depend on sound information, which comes from actual project performance data. This data originates in the field and is reported on a daily, weekly, and monthly basis. Some of the sources of information used to track job performance and feed back into the project control system are:

- Daily field reports
- Time cards
- Subcontractor billing statements
- Delivery tickets
- Material invoices
- Equipment time tickets
- Job logs

I cannot stress enough how important it is to get complete and accurate data from the field. This is a challenge, and I must say that it is often a weak link in the project control cycle. With all of the activity and commotion going on at the job site, it is hard to ask a superintendent to be meticulous about tracking and recording cost data and time card information. They usually have their hands full trying to manage all of the subcontractors, answering questions, scheduling inspections, and getting work ready for the next day. However, this information serves two critical functions:

- It is used to detect variances between the actual cost, time, and productivity performance and the planned estimate and schedule.
- It is used to develop the historical estimating databases and productivity factors used on future projects.

If this information is inaccurate or incomplete, it may mitigate the effectiveness of the project control system and feed faulty data into the estimating and scheduling references, tainting those procedures' reliability on future projects.

Factors Impacting Project Performance

Controlling project time and costs requires a heads-up kind of attitude. The ability to anticipate and ward off potential project disruptions is a basic characteristic of the successful construction manager. However, even when the project team applies all of the tools and techniques available to them, most projects will still be derailed somewhere along the way. Practically every job will experience time delays, cost overruns, or quality failures during the course of construction. As hard as we try to make a perfect plan, it is virtually impossible to predict and anticipate every possible occurrence that could cause a hiccup in our scheme. So hiccups are inevitable. Therefore, it is a good idea to know in advance where these glitches might come from.

There are a number of factors that can influence our job performance. Some of them are beyond our control, and some of them are a result of poor management or lack of foresight. I've listed some of these factors below and explain how they can influence project performance.

Weather conditions   Weather is probably the most common and most obvious reason for work slowdown resulting in cost overruns. Work proceeds much more slowly under adverse weather conditions, and such conditions can impact the quality of the work as well.

Quality of the workforce   As a general contractor who hires subcontractors, you don't really have any control over the subcontractor's workforce. Therefore you have to trust that your subcontractors will provide experienced workers on your job. This is why, in my opinion, all subcontractors should be pre-qualified. The risks associated with poor work quality are significant. If there is a problem, the poor quality will result in rework, and rework slows down job progress and can impact safety. The potential losses due to poor quality can put the entire project in a tailspin, and if this occurs, the project manager must take immediate steps to mitigate the situation.

Quality of the supervision   Obviously, if you don't have proper supervision on the job, there are going to be problems. Many issues have to be addressed every single day on the job, and everyone looks to the superintendent for direction and clarification regarding those issues. If you have an inexperienced superintendent who is not up to speed on the project, the type of work, or the systems in place to manage the project, you are going to have a disaster, plain and simple. As I've said before: this is why good superintendents are worth their weight in gold.

Incorrect sequencing of work   Unfortunately, there are times when pressure from an owner or from the main office can cause a superintendent to schedule work out of sequence and before it is ready, just to appease some unrealistic demand for action. But no one knows better than the superintendent and the field personnel how the work needs to be scheduled to keep things on track. Sometimes a work activity is initiated just to give the appearance of making progress when in reality these artificial starts just waste time and cause all kinds of havoc on the job. If this occurs too often, the inefficiencies will eventually show up and expose the real story.

Change orders   Change orders can be one of the most insidious factors influencing project performance. A little change here or there often seems like no big deal. Many contractors fail to ask for additional time when they process the cost of the change, thinking that they can wiggle the extra work into the existing schedule. Then all of a sudden, these seven or eight little change orders are causing the job to run two weeks behind, and then it is a *big* deal!

Overcrowded job site   One of the things that can actually hinder work productivity is having too many people on the job. I have heard more than one subcontractor complain about packing too many workers in tight quarters trying to get a job done. They end up getting in each other's way and tempers can flare. It becomes so counterproductive that it actually slows down the job instead of speeding it up as planned.

Defective materials   Discovering that the material or equipment that you were planning to install is defective is a real problem. It is certainly one that can be avoided with proper quality control. But in some cases, this defective material is not discovered until the workers are on the job ready to start the project. By this time, it is way too late. The time has already been wasted and it will take time to reorder the material and reschedule the crews to install it.

Inadequate tools and equipment   Having the right tools and equipment on a construction job may seem like a no-brainer. But again, when so much of the work of the contract is passed on to subcontractors, you don't always have control over even these simple aspects of the job. I can't tell you how many times I have seen work installed improperly because the craftsman didn't have the right piece of equipment or right tool that day, or how many times I have seen equipment operators go home early simply because they didn't have an extra linchpin or some other minor fitting for their $250,000 piece of equipment.

Whenever I interviewed new subcontractors, I would always try to meet them at their place of business or at a job site where I might get a glimpse of their people working, or at least get to see the subcontractor's pickup truck and equipment. It may seem silly, but I always thought that the way subcontractors kept their trucks (neat or messy) was a pretty good indication of how they did their work and took care of their tools and equipment. The subcontractors with the neat, clean trucks were usually the ones who produced the higher quality work—not always, but most of the time.

Late deliveries   Late deliveries are probably one of the most frustrating causes of schedule delays and cost growth in construction. Once again, the contractor has very little influence or control over the manufacturing or fabrication processes involved in the making of many of the products or equipment used on the project. However, the stakes can be very high for the project if items arrive late. That's why on projects with critical lead-time items, it is best to assign someone to do nothing but expedite deliveries and stay on top of the project buyout schedule.

No matter how well you had planned, estimated, and scheduled your job to go a certain direction, these are just a few of the things that can easily impact your project's outcome in a negative way. Some of them seem trivial and yet they are exactly the kinds of things that can get your cost, time, and quality off track in a hurry. As a construction manager, you must be forever vigilant and on the lookout for disruptions and inefficiencies that will derail your plans. You can never avoid all of the potential problems, but having some idea about how different factors can affect the job will give you a head start when trying to correct course after a problem does hit.

Real World Scenario

Sometimes Nice Guys Really *Do* Finish Last

In an effort to be amiable and cooperative, many contractors bypass the opportunity to add workdays to the schedule when processing a change order, especially if it is something minor. They carefully calculate the cost of the change but often do not fully consider the consequences to the schedule. However, change orders almost *always* cause an interruption in the workflow and impact productivity. Although one or two changes might be absorbed into the schedule, eventually these interruptions will show up as a problem. It is very difficult to backtrack after the extra work is already done and try to convince the architect and owner that you should have asked for additional time. It is in the best interest of the contractor to always make a request for additional time when processing a change order. Even if you aren't granted the extra time, documenting your request will help build your case when the 15th change comes around and you are now looking at a serious schedule issue.

Tracking Quality, Cost, and Time

By now, you are familiar with the three primary elements associated with managing the construction project: quality, cost, and time. These factors must be monitored throughout the duration of the job. Each of these elements has a corresponding tool that we use as a benchmark to track performance, as shown in Table 10.1.

Table 10.1   Management Elements and Tracking Tools

Management Element	Tracking Tool
Quality	Plans and Specifications
Cost	Estimate
Time	Schedule

Our goal as construction managers is to manage the project so that the performance of the project meets or exceeds our estimated or anticipated performance for each of these elements. And though we won't know if we have met all project goals until the job is complete, tracking the deviations between actual and planned performance throughout the project will help identify problem areas so adjustments can be made along the way to correct any significant discrepancies. Let's take a look at how each of these primary elements is tracked and monitored throughout the construction process.

Tracking Quality

The plans and specifications are the primary tool used to monitor project quality. The best way to track quality performance on a project is to prepare and implement a comprehensive quality plan. The project manager and superintendent usually team up to put this plan together and use it to monitor the project from start to finish. Depending on the project size, sometimes a special quality officer or quality engineer is assigned to the job to assist the superintendent in this task.

The fundamental purpose of the plan is to verify that all materials and workmanship comply with the requirements spelled out in the plans and specifications prepared by the designer. There are a number of administrative and physical checks used to track quality:

- Field observations
- Submittals
- Shop drawings
- Mock-ups
- Inspections
- Field tests

Because quality and safety contribute so greatly to project success, the control of these two elements is really classified as a separate construction management function. Therefore, the final chapter in this book (Chapter 11, "Managing Quality and Safety") is dedicated entirely to this topic. In this chapter, I will focus on the other two project controls—time and cost.

Tracking Project Cost

The original estimate used for bidding purposes is converted to a project budget and establishes the benchmark from which project costs are monitored and tracked. During this conversion process, which usually takes place right after the contract award, quoted prices are confirmed with purchase orders and subcontracts. Sometimes there are minor adjustments made in the budget due to price fluctuations between the time when the job was bid and when the work begins, but generally the budget contains the same work packages developed in the estimate.

cost control

A continuous monitoring process used to track the variances between actual performance and planned performance on a project, specifically concerning cost and time.

Each work package identifies the activities needed to complete a division or section of work. You'll remember from Chapter 6, "Estimating Project Costs," that these work packages and activities are usually identified by a CSI Master-format reference number. These reference numbers take on an even more important role when applied to project *cost control*.

Cost Control

cost code

A reference number used to track cost and schedule information on materials, labor, subcontracts, equipment, overhead, and fees throughout the project control process.

Once the budget is confirmed, each activity in the budget is assigned a *cost code*. Cost codes are used to track all items of work contributing to the overall project costs. That includes material, labor, equipment, subcontracts, and overhead. All job information regarding cost are tracked via these cost codes. Every item on a material invoice, every man-hour logged on a time card, and every subcontractor payment is assigned a cost code and recorded. These codes are used to compare actual job costs with the estimated job costs throughout the construction process.

These cost codes usually start with the original CSI reference number associated with the activity, and then for further detail another number is assigned that represents the type of cost. For example:

Activity	Code
Material	1
Self-performed labor	2
Subcontracted labor	3
Equipment	4
Job site overhead	5

So, if I were the job superintendent tracking building insulation cost on a project, I would assign the following cost codes to the invoices that came across my desk:

Item	Cost Code (CSI Number— Type of Cost)
Material invoice	07210-1
Subcontractor bill	07210-2
Equipment rental	07210-3

Larger contractors will also assign a year and job number to the cost code. For example, assuming that the above project were a large contractor's fourteenth job of this year, the material invoice might be coded as follows:

Year project started:	2004
Project no.:	14
CSI division:	07210
Type of cost:	1 (material)
Cost code:	0414 07210-1

Smaller contractors might simply identify each of the invoices by the client name along with the cost code.

Smith	07210-1

The point is to make the codes as user-friendly as possible while still providing the level of detail needed to properly analyze the project costs. Each invoice amount would be recorded according to the cost code assigned to it by the superintendent. Material costs, labor costs, and equipment costs could be tracked separately or you could combine them into a single work package total. Either way, you could compare the actual cost to do the building insulation with the budgeted amount and note any discrepancies.

All invoices and subcontractor billings are eventually transferred to the contractor's cost accounting department. The accounting department also tracks the project according to the cost codes and will submit reports identifying total material, labor, subcontract, equipment, and overhead costs incurred on the job. The project manager uses these and other reports to monitor the project performance from a big-picture perspective.

Spot Check the Cost Coding

It's not uncommon for a vendor to list more than one cost code item on a single invoice. For example, the same invoice could have materials that fall under three different divisions—let's say lumber (Division 6), mortar (Division 4), and rebar (Division 3). When this happens, it is important to make sure that someone is taking the time to separate the material costs according to their respective codes. Unfortunately, people get lax and they start lumping all of the material under one code. This of course taints the accuracy of the information, which results in faulty reporting. As a construction manager, I was always vigilant about doing random checks on job tickets just to make sure everything was being properly coded. It was part of my management systems quality assurance program.

Analyzing the Discrepancies

In many instances, merely knowing the aggregate cost of the item of work is not enough. This is especially true when you discover a significant discrepancy between actual costs and estimated costs. Further analysis is needed to figure out exactly what is causing the discrepancy.

For example, knowing that you have a cost overrun with building insulation might not be very useful if you don't know why. Even if there is nothing that you can do about the overrun, knowing what caused it will help better plan for the next job. (Remember, actual costs are what establish the estimating database and productivity rates in the first place. Very important information!)

In addition to analyzing the dollar amounts listed on job invoices and billings, it is often necessary to track the quantities purchased. For example, Table 10.2 illustrates a more detailed picture of what is going on regarding building insulation cost. Both the quantities and costs have been tracked and converted to unit costs so that an analysis can be made at a deeper level.

variance

The cost or time difference between the actual project performance and the planned project performance.

You'll notice that the building insulation work package is over budget by $1,564 (about a 14 percent overrun). With further analysis, you can see that the *variance* is not a result of either an increase in material unit cost, labor unit cost, or equipment unit cost. In fact, you can see that we were able to secure the labor at a better rate than we had estimated. If we hadn't been able to get a better buy on labor, we might be experiencing a much worse situation with a $2,242 loss. The problem appears to be the quantity of material needed—the overage is a little over 20 percent. This error in quantity has caused an overrun in material costs and equipment costs.

Table 10.2   Cost Analysis

Division 07210 Insulation	Estimated	Actual	Variance
Quantity	18,800 SF	22,600 SF	(3800 SF)
Material unit cost	$0.30/SF	$0.30/SF	—
Total material	$5,640	$6,780	($1,140)
Labor unit cost	$0.19/SF	$0.16/SF	$0.03/SF
Total labor	$3,572	$3,616	($44)
Equipment unit cost	$0.10/SF	$0.10/SF	—
Total equipment	$1,880	$2,260	($380)
Total	$11,092	$12,656	($1,564)

If the superintendent had looked only at the invoice amounts and compared those totals with the estimated totals, he might have blamed the problem on bad pricing of material and equipment. However, a more detailed analysis shows that the problem lies with the incorrect quantity amount. The superintendent can now investigate what is at the root of this error. There are four possible causes:

◆ Poor quantity takeoff (estimating problem)

◆ Poor quality plans (inaccurate dimensions)

◆ Excessive waste (poor quality control)

◆ Change order (new quantities not yet reflected in the estimate)

NOTE

Cost overruns resulting from doing extra work requested by the owner are not cost overruns at all. Remember, the extra work is performed as a change order to the contract and increases the contract price (and the schedule). It is best to track change orders as separate work items so they don't distort the costs (and time) associated with the original work.

It is important to understand that in making the comparison between actual and budgeted cost, the expectation is not for each individual component of the job to be within budget. Instead, the challenge is to manage the overall project cost within budget. In reality, it is very *unlikely* that each individual element of the job will come in exactly as estimated. Some work items will be over budget and some will be under budget. The hope is that in the end, the plusses and minuses will balance themselves out.

Table 10.2 (shown earlier) illustrates the types of variances that can be experienced when tracking job costs. Incorrect quantities may be the culprit causing the overrun (or surplus), as shown in our example. On the other hand, the estimated unit pricing for materials, labor, or equipment may be to blame. Whatever it is, it is the construction manager's job to find out and make a correction or adjustment along the way that will assist in getting the project back on track. The key is to have the information that you need to identify and assess the problem.

NOTE

You can see that there are many different angles from which to view project performance. Understanding how to organize and analyze the information that you have is a critical component of construction management. Computers have made this job much easier on everyone involved. Once the data is inputted, there are programs that can create just about any kind of report that you want. However, it is still very important to make sure that the information you are inputting is accurate. You know the saying—garbage in, garbage out!

Taking Corrective Action

Most cost overruns are not the result of bad material or subcontractor pricing or even quantity takeoff errors. After all, material prices are often locked in with a purchase order and vendors will usually honor their price quotes for 30 to 90 days. Likewise, subcontractor pricing is guaranteed through the subcontract. So material or subcontractor pricing variances are rare and are usually not the cause of budget overruns.

However, when overruns do occur, there are a few things that the superintendent or project manager can do to mitigate the impact on the budget:

Material price escalations   For the most part, small price fluctuations are non-events when it comes to cost control. As previously stated, the job of the construction manager is not to micromanage every single individual activity cost as much as it is to try to control the material costs within the various divisions of work. There will be wins and losses when it comes to individual activity material prices, but in the end, the goal is to meet the budget for the overall project.

However, there are occasions when material prices can drastically change between the time of the bid and the time you order the material for the job. Over the years, there have been periods when lumber, drywall, or some other product has seen extreme price fluctuations over relatively short periods of time. On smaller jobs, the contractor either absorbs the loss or negotiates with an understanding owner for some amicable compromise or shared exposure regarding the price increase. On larger jobs, these drastic price increases become quite troublesome.

For example, in the last year, steel prices have more than doubled in the United States. Multi-million-dollar projects had been bid and went under contract before the prices skyrocketed, and many of those projects are now negotiating *escalation clauses* into the contract. Steel is a primary building material, in some cases constituting a significant percentage of the project cost. No reasonable owner would try to hold a contractor to his or her original pricing of steel when the potential loss to the contractor could reach into the millions of dollars. There aren't many contractors who can suffer such catastrophic losses and still stay in business. And it certainly doesn't do the owner any good to let the contractor go and start the process from scratch. In these situations, the best deal is to negotiate a fair and equitable solution.

escalation clause
Usually negotiated into the construction contract when there is suspicion that some pricing component of the estimate is in a high state of flux. The clause allows for some fluctuation in the contract price based upon the current pricing of the suspected component.

Subcontract increases   Most subcontractors honor their price quotes once the subcontract is signed and the job has started, even if they experience minor price increases on their end of the deal. There is very little risk to the general contractor or to the project budget. The estimated price and the actual price are usually one and the same, unless of course, there are change orders.

Sometimes a subcontractor reneges on his or her price before the subcontract is executed. When this happens, the general contractor has three options: contact one of the other original bidders and try to negotiate a price that both parties can live with; rebid the section of work altogether; or go out and negotiate on the open market, trying to secure the original pricing or better.

The most difficult situation to remedy is when a subcontractor gets into financial trouble and goes out of business before the job is complete. When this happens, it puts the project in a real tailspin, especially if the subcontractor in trouble ends up being one of your primary subcontractors—such as steel or mechanical.

Often the bonding company will step in and provide another specialty contractor to complete the work, but you can imagine what this sort of disruption does to the schedule, and therefore the budget. The ramifications can be severe, and there may be no recovery from the damages. During a crisis like this, it is best for the owner, the contractor, and the architect to sit down and come up with a plan to mitigate the potential losses for everyone.

Quantity errors   As our previous example suggests, there are times when a simple quantity takeoff error throws a monkey wrench into our budget calculations. When this happens, it is best to find the error as soon as possible, preferably before you have committed to any purchase order or subcontract. If you find the error before committing to any pricing, you still have time to go out and negotiate your very best deal on the affected materials and labor in an effort to mitigate the obvious loss that you will suffer due to the inaccurate takeoff (presuming that the error results in a deficiency). Otherwise, the best that you can do is find other areas of work with opportunities to save budget dollars, offsetting the loss resulting from the quantity error.

Labor Risks

So if material and subcontractor pricing are not at the root of cost overruns, what is? Most budget problems originate from inaccurate labor estimates, particularly self-performed labor. The difficulty really lies with trying to accurately predict the work output of crews—in other words, in trying to guess what a given crew's productivity might be on any given day, under any given circumstances. Obviously this is not an easy prediction to make, but estimators, superintendents, and project managers do it every day, and sign contracts and plan multi-million-dollar jobs based on their guesses. (Now you understand why most work in construction is subcontracted to specialty contractors—far less risk, at least to the general contractor.)

Productivity is the most unpredictable element of project planning and project control. Productivity has a significant influence on both cost and time. The project estimate and the schedule are based upon certain productivity rates. There are so many things that can impact productivity that you are really just playing the odds when you plug a rate into your estimate. However, there are ways to increase those odds, and I will address productivity and its influence on both the budget and the schedule in the next section.

Tracking Project Time

Tracking project time is just as important as tracking project cost. Not only is the contractor obligated to complete the contract for a specified dollar amount, but he is also required to deliver the completed project within a specified time frame. Otherwise there may be some pretty serious consequences in the form of liquidated damages—or, at the very least, an extended schedule will cause a rise in overhead expenses, increasing the risk of financial loss on the project.

In the previous chapter, "Project Planning and Scheduling," you learned that overall project duration is calculated by figuring out how much time each individual work activity is going to take and by determining how that work will be sequenced. Once these two pieces of information are established, you can build the schedule. The schedule is the tool used to track progress throughout the construction process.

The schedule identifies the critical activities' start and finish dates, as well as the amount of flexibility that the superintendent has in scheduling activities with float. The critical path is, well, critical when it comes to managing the time to complete the project. If a single critical activity gets off track, the overall job duration will be extended and the planned completion date will shift.

Schedule Control

Schedule control requires a continuous monitoring of the activity durations identified in the schedule. The superintendent's job is to track the progress of each work item, trying to keep the job moving as efficiently as possible, and assessing the impact of any delay on the overall schedule.

If an activity does get off track, it is the superintendent's job to figure out what went wrong and then to take steps to get the project back on schedule as planned. There are numerous reasons why an activity may be delayed. It could be due to weather, a shortage of manpower, late deliveries, waiting for information, or countless other reasons. But most schedule glitches have to do with productivity.

NOTE

Schedule control is all about managing the durations associated with the individual work activities. Getting the subcontractors involved and creating specific work package short-interval schedules can really help this process.

Analyzing the Delays

As stated in the previous section, the greatest risk in planning and scheduling the work to be done on a project is in predicting workforce productivity. Productivity has to do with how much work can be produced by a fixed crew size in a certain unit of time. If you remember, back in Chapter 6, you learned that productivity rates are used in the estimate to calculate the unit costs for an activity. We then use that same productivity rate to come up with activity durations in our schedule. For example, if we stick with the building insulation scenario, it is estimated that:

- Two carpenters can install 2500 SF of wall insulation in an 8-hour day.
- If there is 22,600 SF of insulation to install on the job, it will take 9.04 days to complete the job.
- It would be logical to plug 9 days into our schedule for installation of the wall insulation.

However, what if the crew is unable to install 2500 square feet of insulation in an eight-hour day? Let's say that, for whatever reason, they are able to install only 1600 square feet of insulation per day. In this case, the job is going to take 14 days to finish instead of the planned 9 days. This becomes a real problem because a delay in the installation of the wall insulation will delay the installation of the drywall, which will also delay the interior trim work and painting. Obviously, this ripple effect is something that the superintendent needs to avoid if he wants to keep this project on course.

Taking Corrective Action

When one or more activities (especially critical ones) get seriously off track, the superintendent and project manager must decide what steps to take to mitigate the effects of the delayed schedule. They may choose to compress the schedule by accelerating certain activities within it. This process is called *crashing the schedule* and the superintendent can accomplish the objective by taking one of three actions (or if necessary, a combination of actions). He can:

crashing the schedule
To takes steps that accelerate activities in the schedule, resulting in an earlier completion date.

- Have the crew work overtime.
- Increase the size of the crew.
- Work two crew shifts per day.

Although crashing will accomplish getting the project back on schedule, there is a cost to achieving this goal. Crashing causes the direct costs (materials, labor, and equipment) of the activity to go up. The objective is to figure out the most efficient way to speed up the activity with the least amount of cost impact.

Using the previous example, let's presume that insulation is on the critical path for the project. The bottom line is that you don't have 14 days to install the insulation. The insulation work package must be completed in 9 days as planned or less, otherwise you jeopardize the project completion date. You must crash the schedule, and insulation is the work item to crash. Let's consider each of the choices listed above.

Scenario #1: Crew Works Overtime

Our first option would be to work our original crew overtime to complete the insulation work within the scheduled timeframe of 9 days.

- A production rate of 1600 SF per 8-hour day = 200 SF per crew hour.
- With a total quantity of insulation of 22,600 SF divided by 200 SF per hour = 113 crew hours needed to complete work.
- Must complete work in 9 days or less.
- 113 crew hours divided by 9 days = 12.5 crew hours per day to complete work in 9 days.
- 12.5 hours per day = 8 hours at regular pay and 4.5 hours at overtime pay for 9 days.
- Crew rate is $50 per hour for regular time.
- Overtime rate = 1.5 × $50 = $75 per crew hour.
- Total overtime = $75 × 4.5 hours per day × 9 days = $3,037.50.
- Total cost to crash the schedule using overtime = $3,037.50.

Things to consider: Can the crew maintain the 1600 SF per day production rate for all 12.5 hours per day for all 9 days? Will the crew be too tired to maintain the pace? Should part of the overtime be worked on Saturday? Will quality suffer?

Scenario #2: Size of Crew Increases

Our second option considers increasing the crew size to achieve the objective of completing the insulation work in 9 days or less.

- 1 crew working at a rate of $50 per hour × 8 hours (1 day) = $400.
- 22,600 SF divided by the productivity rate of the 1 crew (1600 SF per day) = 14 days × $400 per day = $5,600.
- We do not have 14 days to complete the work. We must complete the work in 9 days or less.
- Presuming that a second 2-person crew can install 1600 SF of insulation per day, the total productivity for 2 crews will be 3200 SF per day.

- 22,600 SF divided by 3200 SF per day = 7.06 days = 7 days.
- $50 per hour × 8 hours = $400 per day per crew × 2 crews = $800 per day × 7 days = $5,600 total.
- The cost to add the second crew is no more than the cost of letting the original crew work for 14 days. Both options will cost $5,600.
- However, working the one crew for 14 days is not an option. The cost to work the original crew for the allotted 9 days would cost 9 days × $400 per day = $3,600.
- The cost to work the two crews for 7 days less the cost to work the original crew for 9 days = $5,600 − $3,600 = $2,000.
- Crashing the schedule by increasing the crew size adds $2,000 more than the activity was planned to cost in the first place, but also reduces the overall schedule by 2 days.

Things to consider: Overcrowding of work area? Consistent quality? Decreasing the overall schedule by 2 days will decrease the overhead for the project by 2 days.

Scenario #3: Two Different Crew Shifts per Day

The third option assigns two crews to work different shifts in the same day. Although the second shift would be paid a shift differential wage, it would be less expensive than overtime.

- Original crew would have to work 14 days to install 22,600 SF of insulation at a production rate of 1600 SF per day.
- 5 days would have to be shaved off this duration to complete the insulation within the 9 days provided in the original schedule.
- Working the original crew for only 9 days (as planned) and adding a second shift (4:00 P.M.–12:00 midnight) of workers for the first 5 of those 9 days would accomplish the activity within the 9-day schedule, given the production rate of 1600 SF per day per crew.
- Keeping with the 9-day maximum schedule duration for insulation at a production rate of 1600 SF per day per crew, a second crew would have to work for 5 days.
- The first crew would work at $50 per crew hour × 8 hours = $400 per day.
- The second shift crew would be paid a shift differential wage of $60 per hour × 8 hours = $480 per day.
- First 5 days when both crews work 8-hour shifts = [$400 + $480] × 5 days = $4,400.
- Only the daytime crew works the next 4 days of the schedule = 4 × $400 = $1,600.
- Total cost for both crews = $4,400 + $1,600 = $6,000; less the cost of the original crew for 9 days as scheduled ($3,600) = $2,400 to crash the schedule.

Things to consider: Would night shift productivity be equal to daytime shift productivity? What about supervision at night? Must bring in temporary lighting and maybe heating, depending on the time of the year. Does the owner have any objections to working at night?

Three Scenarios Summary

Here is the final tally of the three scenarios:

◆ Scenario #1 costs $3,679 and meets original schedule requirements.

◆ Scenario #2 costs $2,000 and reduces original schedule by two days.

◆ Scenario #3 costs $2,400 and meets original schedule requirements.

Of these three scenarios, it appears that the least expensive way to crash the schedule is by doubling the crew size (Scenario 2). This effort would bring the activity back on schedule and cost only $2000. And because the work could be completed in seven days instead of the required nine days, the overall schedule would be shortened by two days. This would save on overhead expenses. The overhead savings would help offset a little bit of the cost to crash the schedule.

NOTE

Much more analysis takes place when professional construction managers contemplate crashing the schedule. Trying to fully detail that analysis process would go beyond the scope of this book. However, the example provided here demonstrates the principle behind crashing and some of the logic that goes into making the decision.

I hope you can begin to see the interrelationship between time and cost when it comes to project controls. Even though cost and schedule are independent management factors, when it comes to tracking project performance, they are interconnected. Let me give you a brief look at how construction managers consider both of these factors at the same time.

Assessing Overall Project Status

earned value analysis
A technique used in construction to determine the estimated value (earned value) of work completed to date on a project and comparing that to the actual work completed on the project.

Construction managers often use a technique called *earned value analysis* for determining the overall status of the project relative to both cost and schedule. We can use this technique to measure individual activity performance and total project performance.

The first step in the process is to determine what percentage of the work we have completed on the project. We can calculate this by literally measuring the quantity of work installed to date relative to the total quantity of work to install overall. For example, if we have a total of 3000 SF of floor tile to install and we have only installed 1500 SF so far, we are 50 percent complete with the work.

The next step determines the earned value of the completed tile work. To calculate earned value, we multiply the percentage of work completed times the budgeted dollars (budgeted in our estimate) or work hours (budgeted in our schedule) for that activity. So let's say the tile is budgeted to cost $21,000 and requires 261 man-hours to install. The calculation would look like this:

Earned value = % of work complete × budget for that work.

For cost: Earned value = 50% × $21,000 = $10,500.

For time: Earned value = 50% × 262 hours = 131 hours.

The work is 50% complete and has earned $10,500 and 131 hours.

The last step in the process is to determine the actual work hours or dollars spent to date on the project. Let's presume that we have actually worked 17 days (136 hours) and spent $11,300 so far to complete the tile work. There are two basic calculations that you can now perform to ascertain the cost and schedule variances to date:

Cost variance = Earned value − Actual dollars spent

Cost variance = $10,500 − $11,300 = (− $800)

Schedule variance = Earned work hours − Actual (budgeted) work hours

Schedule variance = 131 − 136 = (−5 hours)

In this example, the tile work is clearly over budget and taking more time than was planned. This example represents only one activity, but the same calculations could be done to evaluate overall cumulative project performance by adding up all of the project costs and all of the project man-hours and using the aggregate sums in the calculations. Obviously, if you were 50 percent complete with your project and you discovered that you were lagging in both cost and time, you would not be a happy camper. As a matter of fact, your job would be in pretty serious trouble.

This analysis should be performed at intervals that are appropriate to the job. The more complex the project, the more frequently these evaluations may be performed, but it all depends on the level of management detail desired by the project team.

Documenting Project Performance

The last stage in the project control cycle is the documentation stage. Throughout the entire project control process, information is being gathered and utilized to check status and make adjustments and changes to the project budget and the schedule as needed. Once these changes are made, they are communicated to all of the appropriate parties and the updated documents continue to be monitored, evaluated, and adjusted again and again until the project is complete.

Upon completion of the project, all of the actions that occurred relative to controlling the overall cost and schedule must be documented so that a historical record of the process can be archived for future reference. These historical records provide valuable information for the estimating and scheduling departments if they take advantage of these resources. However, I have found that this is sometimes an overlooked opportunity for process improvement.

Management Reports

forecasts
Periodic predictions stated in reports as to the final cost and schedule outcomes on a project while the work is still ongoing.

During the construction process, several formal reports are created that not only document project progress but also provide *forecasts* for the completion date and cost, and highlight any other risk factors or target dates that might significantly influence the project outcome. These reports are developed and issued to the project participants on a regular basis throughout the duration of the project. They may be distributed monthly, bimonthly, or quarterly. They are in addition to the numerous working reports used in the field by the superintendent and project manager to monitor the budget and schedule on a day-by-day basis.

It is certainly important that the superintendent and project manager be able to predict when the project will complete and what the budgetary results will be. But these reports also help inform senior management, owners, and designers of what to expect. These progress reports should address four fundamental project control questions:

- How is the project doing overall? Is it on target or off target?
- What sections of work appear to be most vulnerable?
- Is overall productivity improving or declining?
- What is the projected completion date and budget outcome?

These reports can be organized in any fashion that serves the project team. For example, some reports may reveal overall variances for a certain group of work packages—let's say sitework, concrete, and masonry. Others may be broken down into specific variances for labor, material, subcontracts, equipment, and overhead. And others may simply display overall job performance, forecasting completion costs and variances per division, similar to the one illustrated next.

Surprises are never a good thing in construction. The more informed your team is regarding the status of the project, the more likely that it can indeed be managed to a successful completion.

Rocky J. Construction
Project: Sedona Municipal Building
Project Manager: J.W. Jones
Superintendent: P.A. Weber

Cost Report

Report Date: June 15, 2004
Data Date: June 15, 2004
Start Date: March 14, 2004
Finish Date: March 30, 2005

WORK DIVISION	BUDGET	COMPLETE	ACTUAL TO DATE	THIS PERIOD	ESTIMATE TO COMPLETE	FORECAST	VARIANCE
Sitework	$97,900	90%	90,400	0	6,700	97,100	800
Concrete	$422,000	40%	168,800	50,000	204,300	423,100	(1100)
Masonry	$123,000	60%	70,200	2,300	48,500	121,000	2000
Steel	$39,800	30%	11,900	5,000	30,000	46,900	(7,100)
Wood	$41,300	0%	0	0	40,000	40,000	1,300
Therm/Moist	$96,000	0%	0	0	92,300	92,300	3,700
Doors/Window	$79,500	0%	0	0	79,500	79,500	0
Finishes	$279,000	0%	0	0	277,900	277,900	1,100
Specialties	$49,500	0%	0	0	51,000	51,000	(1,500)
Equipment	$4,300	0%	0	0	4,300	4,300	0
Furnishings	$9,800	0%	0	0	9,500	9,500	300
Special Construction	$32,400	10%	3,200	5,000	25,000	33,200	(800)
Conveying	$89,000	30%	28,000	0	58,500	86,500	2,500
Mechanical	$303,000	20%	61,000	0	240,000	301,000	2,000
Electrical	$184,500	20%	37,000	8,000	139,500	184,500	0
TOTALS	$1,851,000	25.42%	470,500	70,300	1,307,000	1,847,800	3,200
Job Overhead	$125,900	30%	37,800	2,500	85,000	125,300	600
TOTALS THIS REPORT	$1,976,900	25.71	508,300	72,800	1,392,000	1,973,100	3,800

Evaluating Project Performance

I started this chapter by expressing how important I think it is to debrief the over-all project performance when the job is all done. The purpose of this session is not simply to talk about whether the job made money or not, or was brought in on time. The purpose of this meeting is to share information about what worked and what didn't work all along the way. As I stated earlier, this debriefing can be one of the richest learning environments for everyone on the project team.

The value of the information that can come out of this type of evaluation meeting is tremendous. For example, the selection of a new subcontractor may have turned out to be a huge mistake and that information needs to be passed on to other superintendents and project managers. Or the team may want to report that this particular owner was one of the best that the company has ever worked for and the business development folks may want to instigate some public relations work with this client for future work. Or members of the project team may just want to share lessons learned about some construction technique or management strategy. Here are a few examples of topics that might get discussed at a project debriefing meeting:

- Target goals and achievement
- On-site field team performance
- Office support
- Owner issues
- Designer issues
- Building inspections
- Communication issues
- Quality control issues
- Subcontractor performance
- Vendor and supplier performance
- Unusual circumstances or conditions

The bottom line is this: The construction business is getting more and more competitive. It is the smart company that takes advantage of the learning opportunity available to them after each project. Setting aside a half day to debrief a project is a small investment to make for gaining construction management expertise, savvy, and know-how. Not only that, but it really contributes to a company's overall commitment to developing a quality management attitude up and down the ranks of the enterprise. You will learn a lot more about quality in the next chapter.

Terms to Know

cost code	escalation clauses
cost control	forecast
crashing the schedule	variance
earned value analysis	

Review Questions

1. What are the seven fundamental steps included in the project control cycle?

2. What are the two essentials of an effective project control system ?

3. Name three sources where you might gather field information needed to develop your project controls.

4. It is important to receive accurate and complete information from the construction job site. Name two specific construction management functions where this information is used.

5. What is a cost code and how is it used in project controls?

6. Name at least three factors that can impact project performance.

7. What is an escalation clause and how is it used in the construction contract?

8. What is the riskiest element of project planning and project control?

9. What does it mean to crash the schedule?

10. Regarding project controls, what does it mean to forecast in construction management?

Chapter 11

Managing Quality and Safety

In This Chapter

- Elements of a quality management plan
- How to define construction quality
- The difference between quality control and quality assurance
- Elements of a safety management plan
- About the economics associated with quality and safety

Quality is the third leg of the three-legged stool mentioned way back in Chapter 2, "What Is Construction Management?" You will recall that the three-legged stool represents the three primary elements of construction management: cost, time, and quality. You may also recall that safety makes up the foundation of that stool and that without it, the effectiveness of our management efforts is really in question.

Quality not only impacts aesthetics, appearance, and durability—it also impacts performance. And poor performance can lead to failures in everything from an improperly installed section of roof flashing resulting in a leak to the deflection of a structural steel beam resulting in a roof collapse. There is no question that failures due to poor quality cost dollars and time, but in some instances, poor quality can even cost lives or serious injury.

The characteristics of a good quality management plan and a good safety management plan are quite similar. Although each is defined by distinct concepts and specific mechanisms of control, which I will explain, it makes sense to administer quality and safety plans as one integrated management function. In this chapter, I present both of these very important components of construction management.

Attitude Is Everything

Good contractors stake their reputations on quality and safety. You can write all of the policies, procedures, and rules that you want, but the truth is, if the leadership of the company has not established a foundational attitude of superior workmanship and an immovable stance on safety, it will all be for naught. When it comes to quality and safety, attitude is everything. And this attitude must emanate from the highest levels of leadership and management down to every single worker and subcontractor in the field. Successful construction managers are well aware of what they must do to achieve quality results and maintain high safety performance. They must:

- Insist upon good quality plans and specifications whenever possible.
- Provide experienced and adequate supervision on all jobs.
- Provide thorough and adequate inspections.
- Make sure that all workers are qualified to do the job they are hired to do.
- Never accept inferior work.
- Above all else, instill an attitude toward high quality and safety throughout the company.

However, sometimes even these are not enough. Although the project manager and superintendent are accountable for developing and implementing the quality and safety plans on the job, they must have support and participation from the field: quality and safety are ultimately achieved at the labor force level. Employees and subcontractors alike must embrace the plans and be encouraged in and recognized for their efforts to produce high-quality work and a safe work environment. And when they are, it sends a loud message, not only to other workers on the job but also to the project owner and the public at large. This is the goal of the construction manager.

Developing the Quality Management Plan

High quality on the job site, or anyplace else, does not just happen automatically. There must be an intention about it. In other words, quality happens on purpose.

The construction manager must have a quality management plan in place long before the first shovel of dirt is turned on the job. Achieving high quality in construction requires a comprehensive, systematic approach that looks at every detail involved with moving the project from an idea on paper to the final product—a building, a bridge, or a highway.

If you think back to Chapter 2, you'll remember a number of characteristics that make construction unique. It is exactly these characteristics that make quality management such a great challenge. Let's take a quick look at a few of those characteristics once again just to refresh our memories and put this quality challenge in perspective.

- Unlike products produced in a factory, the construction project is built on-site, under uncontrolled climate conditions.
- Every project is built as a prototype.
- Every building site presents a unique set of conditions relative to topography, accessibility, and security.
- Many materials must be fabricated from scratch, so you can't depend on the consistency that comes from mass production.
- The workforce is primarily transient, with various specialty trades moving into and off of the site as needed.

Let's face it, even under the most stable of conditions, achieving consistent quality results is no easy task. In construction, quality becomes a huge undertaking and constitutes a large part of the construction management goal. In order to achieve success, we must consider the challenge from both a project perspective and a process perspective. But before we can do that, we must start with a clear understanding of the expectations for quality.

Defining Quality

In construction, quality is defined as meeting or exceeding the requirements established in the design documents. Fundamentally, the quality of the construction project is set through the plans and specifications provided by the architects and engineers. There are various levels of quality that can be specified for any given project. The design team works with the owner to determine exactly what their expectations for quality are. Budget is usually a factor that must be considered when setting the quality standard. Obviously there is a range of products and materials that can be selected for utilization in a new facility. Not every automobile is a Cadillac; some must be manufactured as Fords or Chevrolets to meet a particular market and budget need. The same is true in construction. Not all facilities will be constructed using Cadillac materials and standards. But that determination is made by the owner, not the contractor.

Back in Chapter 6 ("Estimating Project Costs"), you learned that there were several factors that would impact project cost. Quality was one of those factors. Just to give you an idea of how significantly quality can impact price, let's consider several different project types specified at various quality levels. R.S. Means (the cost manual publisher referenced in Chapter 6) provides an online *QuickCost Calculator* (www.rsmeans.com/calculator) for various building types in accordance with three distinct quality levels: low, medium, and high. Table 11.1 illustrates the range between the three quality levels. You can see that even with parking garage construction, the price range relative to quality can be considerable.

In construction, the job of the project team is to deliver whatever quality standard has been set for the facility by the design team.

Primary Objectives of the Plan

rework
A term used to describe defective construction work that must be redone or corrected.

Construction is not a perfect science and it would be impossible to produce a project without some defects, failures, or complaints. After all, you are working with imperfect materials and imperfect people. How could you expect otherwise? However, the goal of the construction manager is to produce a project with as few defects, failures, and complaints as possible. So how do you do that? Fundamentally, your plan must focus on three primary objectives. They are:

- Doing things right the first time
- Preventing things from going wrong
- Continually improving the process

callback
A request from an owner that a contractor return to the job site to correct or redo some item of work.

If your plan addresses these three objectives, then *rework*, *callbacks*, and corrective actions will be kept to a minimum and your job will have a much higher chance of success. Let's consider these objectives one at a time.

Doing Things Right the First Time

The first goal of the quality management plan is to get things done right the first time. Getting it right in construction doesn't always mean getting it perfect. For example, it is rare to find a concrete floor slab that is perfectly level. But it is commonly expected that a floor slab be level or flat within certain tolerances. For example, residential concrete slabs on grade are expected to be troweled smooth and flat to a tolerance of $1/4''$ in a $6'$ radius. This is not perfect, but it is a common standard of quality expected in the industry.

However, before we can focus on doing things right, the project team must first know what the quality standards are and the best way to achieve them. Workers can't do the job right the first time if they don't have the proper skills, the necessary level of experience, adequate supervision, and the tools and equipment needed to perform the task. In most cases, the superintendent is responsible for seeing to it that the workforce is prepared and motivated to complete the task at hand. This is just one more reason why superintendents are such a valuable asset to the company.

Preventing Things from Going Wrong

preparatory inspection
Inspections, sometimes called pre-inspections, that are designed to check progress and make sure that everything is ready for the next stage of construction.

We all know that hindsight is 20/20 but that won't cut it if your objective is to prevent things from going wrong in the first place. Meeting this objective requires a high sense of awareness, adequate preparations, and clear communications. In order to prevent things from going wrong, the team must stay one step ahead of the work in terms of oversight and supervision. A *preparatory inspection* is one

Table 11.1   Price Differences Based on Quality

Project Type	Square Footage	Low Quality	Medium Quality	High Quality	Difference High/Low
Apartment	70,000	$4,732,000	$5,605,000	$6,806,000	30%
High School	120,000	$6,999,000	$8,966,000	$11,345,000	38%
Warehouse	50,000	$1,520,000	$2,218,000	$3,091,000	51%
Parking Garage	90,000	$2,543,000	$3,737,000	$6,436,000	60%

of the best ways to avoid miscues and rework that can disrupt the schedule and negatively impact the budget. (Preparatory inspections will be discussed in detail later in this chapter.) Unfortunately, there are many projects whose pace is so fast and furious that the project team has all it can do to perform the required inspections, let alone these preparatory ones. So things do go wrong and they must be corrected, but the goal is to catch everything we can before it becomes an issue. And this job must be the responsibility of the entire project team, not just the superintendent, if we want to have any chance at all of achieving the objective.

Real World Scenario

What Is Right?

Usually the plans and specs dictate the expectations for quality and "what is right." However, I have found that many owners do not understand what the specifications actually say, even though they paid an architect to prepare the documents for them. On more than one occasion, I have had an owner come on to the job expressing concern for quality, only to find that we have indeed met the expectations spelled out in the plans and specs. Unfortunately, the expectations of the owner are not always reflected in the plans and specs and the end result is not what they had in mind. However, in my opinion, this is a communication and education problem between the architect and the owner more than it is a quality issue. Even so, it is the contractor who is usually left to deal with the owner's disappointment and frustration.

In my experience, I have found that an owner's expectations for quality are sometimes unrealistic and impractical. For example, anyone expecting perfectly matched wood grains on a set of oak cabinet doors has an unrealistic expectation that can never be met. Wood grains are random and that's just the way it is. And yet I have had clients ask for doors to be replaced (several times) for this very reason.

So the lesson here is to always make sure that everyone involved in the project—the owner, the architect, the contractor, and the craftsmen—all know what the quality expectation is so they can get it right the first time.

Continually Improving the Process

The third goal of the quality management plan is to continually improve the work processes and systems that support the work. The concept of continuous improvement is grounded in the work of Edward Deming, and is commonly known as *Total Quality Management (TQM)*. His theories suggest that no matter how good your product, process, or performance is, it can always and forever be enhanced. The key is to approach quality as a never-ending, incremental, continuous improvement process.

NOTE   Deming was a statistician by trade, and he defined high quality as meaning low variability. In other words, we have a quality expectation (or standard) and we have our performance relative to that expectation. The gap between the two variables equals our opportunity for improvement.

Tom Peters, the author of *In Search of Excellence*, once said that it was much easier to improve 100 things by 1 percent than it was to change one thing by 100 percent. When I was in business, I always tried to remember this concept and found that continuous improvement works best in baby steps versus giant leaps. Here are the steps that I used when implementing TQM in my firm and on the job:

1. Identify the problem.
2. Break the work down into its smallest pieces or steps.
3. Identify the weak link.
4. Determine the remedy.
5. Apply the remedy.
6. Measure the results.

The last step, measuring the results, is a critical one when it comes to TQM. It is important that you are able to document the improvements that you are making. From a management standpoint, "feeling" like you are making progress is not good enough. The only way that we can be sure that our remedies or corrections are working is to measure the results. Following is a simple technique for tracking improvement efforts.

Problem	Hairline cracks in drywall where wall and ceiling meet
Goal	Reduce number of customer callbacks to make drywall repairs

Remedy	Replace paper drywall tape with fiberglass flex tape
# of Callbacks Before Remedy (Jan to June)	47
# of Callbacks After Remedy (July to Dec)	9

In 1992, the Construction Industry Institute (CII) published *Guidelines for Implementing Total Quality Management in the Engineering and Construction Industry.* The manual is based on the results of a research study conducted earlier that showed that the implementation of TQM practices resulted in improved customer satisfaction, reduced cycle times, documented cost savings, and a more satisfied and productive workforce.

NOTE

The QA/QC Functions

The construction process can be complex and often chaotic. Given the number of products, players, and unique characteristics associated with construction, you can certainly understand how it might be very difficult to put together a comprehensive quality management plan. The task really requires a twofold approach.

We must consider quality first from a "project" perspective and then from a "process" perspective. The two approaches may be categorized as *quality control* at the project level and *quality assurance* at the process level. The industry often lumps the two concepts together, referring to the quality control function as the QA/QC function. However, each of the two concepts has a unique focus with distinct mechanisms and techniques for its management. Let's consider the differences.

quality control
A quality management approach that addresses quality at the project level and deals with conformance to the plans and specs through submittals, mock-ups, shop drawings, inspections, and testing.

Quality Assurance (QA)

Quality assurance takes a long-range view toward developing systems that produce high-quality work consistently over time. To be effective, a good quality assurance plan must influence every aspect of the company, from the management to the field. The concept implies that if the proper procedures, policies, and systems are institutionalized throughout the organization up front, the outcome at the project level will be much more reliable. Let's look at the ways some construction company practices can affect quality for better or worse.

quality assurance
A quality management approach that addresses quality at the process level and deals with policies and procedures associated with hiring, training, safety, subcontracting, and procurement.

Hiring practices   The quality of the hire will obviously affect the quality output on the job site. Finding people who have been trained properly in their respective trades is at the core of any quality assurance program.

When I was a construction employer, I discovered that an individual could learn the wrong way of doing things as easily as he or she could learn the right way. I was constantly on the lookout for people who were trained to do things the right way and had a good attitude to go along with it. Unfortunately, when workloads become very heavy, there is a tendency to hire just about anybody who knows anything about construction just to place bodies on the job. This is always a mistake and a sure bet that quality will suffer.

The construction industry is known for its high employee turnover, especially on the craft worker side. However, I found that setting high quality standards helped the company retain a high percentage of employees for longer periods of time. Most construction workers take great pride in their work and seek out job environments that promote high quality and safe practices.

Training programs   A commitment to quality requires a commitment to training. Quality assurance equates to a quality training program. Employees must be trained consistently in the technical skills and techniques needed to perform the work as well as in the policies, procedures, and methods of quality control to be implemented on the job site. Shortchanging the training component of your quality assurance program will result in inconsistent performance that will hurt the project in the long run. And once again, when the workload gets very busy, this commitment can sometimes lapse to the detriment of the whole company.

Safety   Safety must always be a part of the quality assurance plan. Establishing strict rules and regulations regarding safety procedures and practices is a must. These rules and regulations must apply to all aspects of the construction work: equipment use, material handling and storage, hazardous materials communications, substance abuse policies, accident prevention, and personal protective equipment requirements. This is one part of the overall quality assurance program that cannot be compromised no matter what the condition of the market or the pace of the project.

Subcontracting practices   You are well aware that the majority of the construction work on a project is performed by subcontractors. And subcontractors are often selected the same way that general contractors are selected—by low bid. Unfortunately, this methodology does not always result in the best quality. As a matter of fact, the old adage "You get what you pay for" often comes true when we award the contract to the subcontractor with the lowest price. However, if we are truly committed to high quality, it is crucial that we develop a subcontracting policy that will garner bids from the best craftspersons in the market. One way to do this is to prequalify subcontractors in advance of bidding. Prequalification can be accomplished by sending out questionnaires requesting information regarding past performance and client references. In my own practice, I would also interview subcontractors one on one before soliciting bids from them.

This helped me get a sense of their attitudes toward quality and safety as well as their actual skills and performance level. When bidding jobs, we always tried to work with subcontractors that were on our prequalified list. This practice would help ensure a quality workforce on the job.

Procurement methods I found very early on when running my company that one of the best things I could do to maintain high quality and high productivity on the job was to work with high-quality vendors. The practice of prequalification can also be applied to our procurement practices. There are hundreds—thousands—of materials and equipment that must be delivered to every project. We cannot afford to deal with companies that aren't able to meet our demands for quality and on-time delivery. Poor performance by our vendors can really sabotage our job and our commitment to quality. Implementing a vendor prequalification system as part of our quality assurance program is one way to increase the odds of receiving top-quality service when it comes to material and equipment procurement.

Employee incentives It is important for management to send clear messages about its commitment to quality. One of the best ways to do that is to create incentives and recognition awards as part of the quality assurance program. Recognizing and rewarding exceptional performance relative to quality (and safety) by individual employees, project teams, subcontractors, and vendors is one way to do just that. Rewards may or may not be monetary. Many contractors have found that public recognition with an award plaque, weekend getaways, fishing trips, and fancy dinners with spouses all work pretty well as incentives for high-quality performance. The point is that management must put its money where its mouth is and reward the good work and high quality that it demands.

Quality Control (QC)

Quality control addresses quality at the project level and is implemented on the job site. Quality control primarily deals with issues relating to conformance to the plans and specs. All of the materials, systems, and workmanship applied to the project must conform to the requirements set forth in the contract documents. Quality control is accomplished using a number of different mechanisms: submittals, mock-ups, shop drawings, inspections, and testing, which are all called for in the project manual.

Mandated Controls

The typical construction contract establishes a number of controls and procedures designed to ensure that the quality of the materials, equipment, and workmanship used on the job are as specified by the designer. Several of these requirements were introduced in Chapters 7 ("Contract Administration") and 8 ("Construction

Operations and Job Site Management"), but I want to go into a little more detail regarding exactly how we use them to control the quality of the project.

Submittals   In Chapter 7, you learned about submittals. The contractor is responsible for providing some form of documentation or sample to the architect to verify that all materials and equipment comply with the requirements set forth in the contract documents. This is the first step in the quality control process. The documentation usually consists of catalog specification sheets (often called cut sheets) or brochures that relay information regarding model number, size, configuration, color or finish, weight, and other specific data about the product. The architect is charged with approving or rejecting each submittal. Once the product is approved, the construction manager orders the material.

However, the quality control process does not end with the submittal approval. After the materials and equipment are ordered, each delivery arriving on the job site must be checked to ensure that it is correct and in accordance with the purchase order and the submittal. If the materials are not as specified and approved, they should not even be unloaded from the delivery truck. They should be rejected immediately and sent back to the supplier. The challenge is to make sure that every delivery gets inspected and checked as it arrives, and not days later—or worse yet, hours before we are ready to install the product. Finding out that a product is not as ordered this late in the game can really put a monkey wrench in the works, but considering how busy a job site can become, unfortunately, sometimes it does happen.

Mock-ups   Mock-ups (also referenced in Chapter 7) take the submittal concept one step further. Mock-ups require the contractor to build small models utilizing the specified materials. In a mock-up, specific nuances such as colors, shades, tones, patterns, and textures of an installation can be better observed and inspected. Although mock-ups are not practical for every installation, they are particularly useful when the expectation for quality cannot be easily conveyed in writing. For example, a catalog cut sheet can easily convey the color, style, and installation of a towel bar, or even the standard four-inch ceramic tile installed on the wall behind the towel bar. However, when it comes to a stained concrete patio, the actual look of a "sand drift" or "tawny brown" color cannot be easily conveyed in a brochure. The only way to confirm the quality expectation when it comes to the color and texture of the concrete would be to construct a small sample. The contract documents will specify when and where mock-ups are required; however, there are instances where it is definitely in the contractor's best interest to construct mock-ups for owner or architect approval even if the contract documents do not require them.

Shop drawings   You also learned in Chapter 7 that anything that has to be fabricated specifically for the project (roof trusses, steel girders, and so on) must first be approved via a shop drawing. These drawings indicate dimensions, materials, finishes, and details associated with their installation. They usually originate with the material supplier or the subcontractor, and eventually end up on the architect's desk for final approval. Once the drawing is approved, fabrication begins, and the product is eventually shipped to the job. The superintendent assigns a field engineer or a quality control person to verify that the product that arrives on the job site has been built in accordance with the shop drawing. If it has not, then it must be rejected and reordered. You are probably beginning to see how important it is to prequalify subcontractors and suppliers as part of your overall quality assurance plan. An error in the fabrication of a long lead (time) item can put the whole construction schedule in jeopardy.

Testing standards   There are a number of quality standards associated with the testing and manufacture of various products. The specifications spell out which testing standards must be met by the materials and equipment used on the project. The primary testing agency for construction in the United States is the American Society for Testing and Materials (ASTM). ASTM is one of the largest voluntary standards development organizations in the world for materials, products, systems, and services. Almost every division of the specifications makes some reference to an ASTM standard. Every product or procedure designated by an ASTM test number in the specifications must meet the standards set out by the agency. An example of a common ASTM standard as it appears in a set of specifications is shown below.

2.06 Concrete Mix

A. Mix Design: Select proportions for normal weight concrete in accordance with ACI 211.1. The laboratory used to prepare the mix design shall meet the requirements of ASTM 1077.

B. Ready Mix Concrete: Mix and deliver ready mix concrete, in accordance with ASTM C94.

C. Requirements: Provide concrete to comply with the following criteria:
1. Flexural strength (ASTM C78)
   a. Modulus of rupture at 28 days to be 650 psi minimum
   b. Modulus of rupture at 90 days to be 90 psi minimum
2. Compressive strength (ASTM C39): As determined by mix design for 7 and 28 days
3. Water/cement ratio: 0.45 maximum by weight
4. Cement content: 520 lbs./cubic yard minimum
5. Air entrainment (ASTM C231): 3–4%
6. Slump (ASTM C143): 3 inches maximum without plasticizer and 4 inches maximum with plasticizer

Another common testing agency often referenced in the specifications is Underwriters Laboratories Inc. (UL), an independent product-safety testing and certification organization. In 2002, seventeen billion products had the UL label attached to them. In most instances, the contractor doesn't really need to worry about whether a product is UL listed or not because almost all products manufactured in the United States carry the UL label. However, there is always a slight chance that a product could slip through the submittal process and not be checked. I learned my lesson years ago.

Real World Scenario

Always Check the Label

Several years ago when I was building a home for a client in Virginia, I left the selection of the zero clearance fireplace up to the owner. (A zero clearance fireplace consists of a metal firebox with a triple-walled stainless steel chimney instead of a masonry firebox and chimney and can be installed in close proximity to the wood framing.) The owner went down to the nearest fireplace store and picked out a popular brand of fireplace and we proceeded to install it in the house. We framed it in, installed the chimney, faced the firebox with a beautiful marble tile surround, and wired the automatic circulating blower fan attached to the firebox.

At the final inspection for owner occupancy, the building inspector informed me that the fireplace had to be removed because it did not meet code—the blower fan did not have a UL label on it. Instead, it had a Canadian testing agency label on it. Well, there was no way that the owner, or I, wanted to tear out the fireplace. We proceeded to research the Canadian testing agency and found that their standard met or exceeded the requirements of the UL label. However, the building inspector wouldn't budge and wouldn't allow the owner to move in. Finally, the city manager got involved and allowed the owner, who really wanted that particular fireplace and was perfectly satisfied with the quality, to write a letter holding the building department and me, the contractor, harmless for any damage or injury occurring as a result of using the fireplace. All of this effort took about four weeks to resolve and the owner was not allowed to move into his new home for that period of time. You can bet that from that point forward, I made sure we always checked the labeling of every device we installed.

Independent testing and inspections   There is another set of testing and inspection procedures often required by the contract that must be conducted in the field while the work is in progress. These inspections and tests are usually performed by an independent testing agency or engineering services firm. Some examples of common field tests are:

◆ Soil testing for compaction

- Concrete testing for slump and strength
- Structural steel testing of welds and bolt torque
- Asphalt testing for mix design and strength
- Aggregate testing for material composition

The test agencies will send specially trained personnel to the job site to perform the inspections or tests. Sometimes the test must be conducted in special laboratories off site, and samples are collected on-site to take back to the lab. After the results are obtained, test reports are submitted to the contractor and filed with the architect or owner. The products and installations that do not meet the test standards specified must be removed and redone. You can imagine how costly this can be if the deficiency shows up in something like a large concrete pour. Close coordination between construction operations and required testing is a must, and it is the superintendent's job to make sure that these tests happen in a timely fashion.

Building code inspections   Most people are familiar with the type of inspections related to the local building code authority. When we obtain a building permit, which is required for most construction projects, there is a schedule of inspections that must occur as the work progresses. The main purpose of these inspections is to make sure that the work conforms to the local building code. Originally there were three primary building codes, adopted by different areas of the United States, that set minimum quality standards for the various sections of work associated with construction.

- The Uniform Building Code was adopted by most of the western states.
- The National Building Code was used chiefly in the northeast and midwest.
- The Standard Building Code was used mainly in the south.

In 2000, the governing bodies of each of these different building codes developed a single comprehensive code called the International Building Code (IBC). Although not every state has adopted the new "I-Code," as it is sometimes called, about 44 states issue their building permits under the jurisdiction of this new code.

When a code violation is found, the building official issues either a Correction Notice or, in more serious instances, a Stop Work Notice to the contractor. Under the Correction Notice, the contractor may continue working but is ordered to make the correction within a reasonable time frame and call for a reinspection. However, when the deficiency is potentially life-threatening or requires immediate action, all work on the job must stop until the correction is made. The cost to shut down a project and restart operations is significant and must be absorbed by the contractor. Stop Work Notices are serious business and should always be avoided whenever possible.

Supervisory inspections   The contract specifically spells out the responsibility of the contractor to provide proper supervision of the work throughout the construction process. The superintendent is ultimately responsible for assuring the quality (and safety) of all self-performed work and subcontracted work. He or she is the one who sets the standards of performance on the job. Large projects may call for full-time quality-control inspectors or quality engineers. But on small to medium-sized jobs, the quality control tasks are often handled by an assistant superintendent or job foreman as directed by the superintendent. They often make use of quality inspection checklists similar to the one shown next.

ABC Construction
Peppermill, AZ

Job Name: Jefferson Natl. Bank
Location: 561 Piedmont Street
     Jefferson, AZ 90777

Contractor: Smith Excavating Service
Contact: Bob Smith
Phone: 555-714-3122

Quality Checklist – Backfill

X	Work complies with local, state, and national codes.
X	Foundation voids, cracks, or honeycombs patched and sealed watertight.
X	Wall ties in poured concrete foundation broken off and all tie holes filled with black plastic cement.
X	Seam between foundation and footing sealed watertight.
X	Basement foundation dampproofing completed according to quality standards.
X	Footing drains installed properly according to plans.
X	Debris and trash removed from trenches around foundation.
X	Utilities and plumbing connections approved and inspected, as required.
CR	Foundation properly braced.
HOLD	Backfill done in 8″ lifts and compacted as required.
HOLD	Fill dirt clean and free of rocks and debris.
HOLD	Backfill surface is at least 8″ down from the top of the foundation.

Superintendent's Signature: J.W. Jackson   Date: June 8, 2004

Correction Required (CR):
South elevation requires additional bracing. Do not backfill until all bracing is properly installed. Contacted Bob Smith on Tuesday, 6/8/04 at 3:30 p.m. Correction to be completed by Friday, 6/11/04. Bracing to be re-inspected before backfill begins on 6/14/04.

Although it is relatively easy to determine whether a model number, or color, or size conforms to the requirements of the contract, it is a little tougher to know what represents high quality when it comes to workmanship. Therefore, it is important that the quality control personnel be pretty familiar with standards associated with a number of trades. For example, he or she must be able to discern high-quality work from inferior work in plumbing as well as rough carpentry, in concrete as well as electrical, and in roofing as well as drywall. Obviously, there are some inspection tasks that must be handled by the more experienced members of the project team.

When work or materials are found to be inferior, they must be rejected outright. Each occurrence should be noted in an inspection report and all deficiencies should be tracked via a deficiency log. It is the quality control engineer's job to follow up on each deficiency until the item has been corrected to the satisfaction of the superintendent.

	**ABC Construction** Peppermill, AZ **Job Name:** Kramer Medical Lab **Superintendent:** JWJ **Job Number:** 22-04 **Quality Engineer:** CWP **Quality Deficiency Log**
No.	**Initial Inspection**	**Description**	**Location**	**Responsible Party**	**Contact**	**Date Corrected**	**Re-inspected**	**By**
1	6/08/04	Stair riser height is not per plans and spec.	West entrance	Baylor Bros. Concrete	Bob Smith	6/23/04	6/24/04 OK	CWP
2	6/08/04	Exterior light fixture has cracked globe.	West entrance	Carvel Lighting	Karen Jones	7/01/04	7/02/04 OK	CWP
3	6/17/04	Dent in metal toilet partition door–stall 3.	Men's room	Westside Specialties	Mike Davis	6/29/04	7/02/04 OK	CWP

Going the Extra Mile

Construction companies that enjoy good reputations for high quality usually go way beyond the mandated methods spelled out in the contract documents. Their quality assurance philosophy requires that they go the extra mile. They implement processes that help them achieve a level of quality beyond the minimum, resulting in less rework, fewer callbacks, and ultimately more repeat business Let's take a look at a few of these extra efforts.

Preparatory inspections   Preparatory inspections are usually conducted by personnel employed by the general contractor. These inspections are designed to check progress and make sure that everything is ready for the next stage of construction. A good example of a preparatory inspection is a pre-roofing inspection. There are a number of layers of materials that make up the typical roofing system. For a built-up roof, there is metal or wood decking, insulation, an underlayment of some kind, perimeter flashing, several layers of building felt, and gravel ballast. The superintendent may request a preparatory inspection at each step of the installation. For example, he or she may want to inspect the roof deck first, then the insulation, then the underlayment, and all the way down the line. This inspection process is very different from inspecting the installation only after the roof is 100 percent complete, and the chances of achieving superior results are much higher.

Not all contractors conduct preparatory inspections, but in my opinion, they should. If you remember the cost/influence curve from Chapter 2 ("What Is Construction Management?"), you know that it costs a lot less to correct an error or defect early in the work sequence than it does after the system is completed. This is the concept behind the preparatory inspection.

Zero-punch list   You learned about punch lists back in Chapter 5, "Project Stages." The concept behind a zero-punch list is to complete the final walk-through inspection with few or no punch items noted on the list. The methodology used for achieving a zero-punch list (or near-zero-punch list) is similar to the process used to conduct preparatory inspections. The idea is to inspect the work as it progresses, instead of waiting until it is completed, only to find that the quality is unacceptable. For example, let's assume that we have a 600 square foot area that is going to receive 6″ × 6″ ceramic tile. The contractor would first pre-inspect the area (preparatory inspection) to make sure that the subsurface is clean and free from defects. Then the contractor would request that the tile setter install only a small amount of work, say 100 square feet, and then call the superintendent for a pre-inspection. The superintendent would pre-inspect the small area of tile, noting any deficiencies or variations from the specified quality indicated in the specifications, such as the grout joint width. If there are any, the subcontractor would have to make the adjustments and corrections before proceeding with the work. This pre-inspection accomplishes two goals: first, the subcontractor is now well aware of the quality standard expected by the superintendent and therefore the end result should meet the expected quality; second, the cost to correct the deficiencies has been kept to a minimum.

field observation report (FOR)
A report used to track questionable quality and safety performance on the job site.

Field observation reports (FORs)   Even though we have a number of procedures set forth in the contract documents to ensure quality on the job, one of the most effective methods for managing quality, especially workmanship quality, is the *field observation report*. Many construction companies initiate a process by which every employee, subcontractor, and visiting vendor is encouraged to report any work item suspected of being installed incorrectly or failing to meet a quality or safety standard. Each of these observations is recorded on an FOR form and given to the quality engineer or person in charge of the task. The quality engineer notes each of these observations in an FOR log and follows through until the item in question is verified or corrected as needed. This is a little different from the standard deficiency report previously mentioned. The deficiency reports are a result of the formal supervisory inspection process; field observation reports are initiated by anyone at any level of the organization. In other words, a laborer who is cleaning up the job site might question the spacing on the anchor bolt layout on a concrete slab because something looks out of the ordinary. He or she would report that question to the quality engineer, who would be obligated to verify that the spacing is correct. And if the spacing was not correct, the quality engineer would be responsible for notifying the appropriate parties to get the problem fixed.

Safety as a Component of Quality

Much of the quality management plan focuses on compliance with the requirements of the plans and specs relative to materials and workmanship. Compliance with the quality requirements often equates to compliance with the safety requirements—at least up to a point. For example, construction specifications dictate quality, and most specifications call for electrical devices on the job to be UL certified. A UL label on a product certifies that the product is deemed to be safe. If the product meets the quality requirement in this case, it also meets the safety requirement. There are a number of instances where quality management and safety management overlap. However, there are some safety management issues that must be considered separately. Let's take a look at some of these issues and discuss the individual elements of a good safety management plan.

The Safety Manager Role

Project managers and superintendents are responsible for the overall safety of their workers on the job site and all of the equipment and materials that they must handle. They must set the standards for safety right up front and be forever diligent regarding adherence to the safety plan.

However, the day-to-day management of the safety plan is usually assigned to an individual project team member. Because there is such a close relationship between quality and safety, it is not uncommon for the project manager to assign one person to hold the position of both the quality engineer and the safety officer. It depends on the size of the job. Larger jobs may require an independent quality engineer and safety officer. On smaller jobs, the assistant superintendent often covers the responsibilities. But whether the functions are handled by one person, two persons, or someone in a dual role such as an assistant superintendent, it is very important that the individual(s) responsible for safety management take their job seriously. After all, the company's reputation and every worker's safety depend on their efforts.

The field observation report noted above can also be used to monitor and report any unsafe job conditions or work practices. Many quality control mechanisms double as safety control mechanisms.

NOTE

A Dangerous Business

Occupational Safety and Health Administration (OSHA)
The federal agency responsible for establishing safety standards for construction and all other industries in the United States. The agency also has the authority to enforce those standards through rigorous inspections at the job site and to issue citations to and assess fines against any contractor or subcontractor for violating these standards.

Construction is dangerous work and accounts for a little more than 20 percent of all occupational fatalities. Historically, the construction industry, above all others, has held the top spot for injuries and illnesses in the United States. (Recently, manufacturing has taken over this dubious distinction.) In 1970, the federal government established an agency specifically charged with developing safety standards for construction and all other industries in the United States. That agency is the *Occupational Safety and Health Administration (OSHA)*.

OSHA plays a big role in construction safety. They not only establish the safety standards for the construction industry but they also have the authority to enforce those standards through rigorous inspections at the job site. OSHA has the authority to issue citations to and assess fines against any contractor or subcontractor for violating these standards. A serious violation of an OSHA regulation can result in a fine of up to $7,000 per violation. A repeat violation can result in a fine as high as $70,000. These are serious penalties, the kind that can put a small builder or subcontractor out of business. And if the fines themselves don't put them out of business, the increased workers' compensation premiums will.

Repeat offenders aren't always easy to spot. Although owners often screen their general contractors' safety records through pre-qualification statements prior to bid, contractors generally do not have time to screen their subcontractors during the bidding process. (Remember the chaos on bid day mentioned in Chapter 3, "How We Get the Work"?). However, if a subcontractor has a history of multiple OSHA violations, word will get around and eventually the violator will more than likely be forced to close shop.

The consequences associated with unsafe practices and reckless behavior in construction are significant. It is important that superintendents and construction managers at all levels be rigorous and unrelenting when it comes to enforcing the safety policies of the company. However, the responsibility still boils down to the actions of the individual men and women on the job site. Every employee must be made aware of the safety policies and the consequences for failing to adhere to them. It takes only one employee to fail to tie off on a rebar cage or to leave their hard hat in their pickup truck for just a minute to risk the viability of a whole company and the livelihood of all of its employees, or even worse, someone's life.

NOTE   It is the superintendent's responsibility to see to it that every worker on the job site receives safety orientation and training on applicable OSHA standards and company safety requirements, and has enough experience to do his or her job safely.

Developing the Safety Management Plan

Obviously, it is in the contractor's best interest to do whatever he or she can to keep the workers and materials safe and the equipment in good working order. No construction project should start until a well-thought-out, written safety plan (often called a safety manual) is in place. The number one goal of the safety plan is to mitigate hazards and prevent accidents. Every worker on the job site should be encouraged to embrace a no-nonsense attitude toward safety and be trained rigorously in safe work habits and hazard awareness. According to the *NAHB-OSHA Jobsite Safety Handbook*, an effective safety management plan includes four primary components:

Management commitment   The job superintendent is responsible for setting the overall tone when it comes to safety on the job site. However, safety must be the number one priority for every level of management up and down the ladder. The most successful safety management plans include a clear statement of support and commitment by the company owner and include employee involvement in the structure and operation of the plan.

Job site analysis   Hazard awareness prevents accidents. An effective safety management plan includes procedures to analyze the job site and identify existing safety hazards and conditions that might become safety hazards. Every person who works on the job should be trained in hazard awareness and be given authority to report any item that may be of concern.

Hazard prevention and control   Obviously, if part of your plan is to discover hazards, another part of your plan must be to eliminate or mitigate those hazards. The safety management plan must establish procedures to correct or control present or potential hazards on the job site. This section of the plan focuses on specific safety issues. Four of the more common issues typically addressed in every safety management plan are:

- Personal protection
- Accident prevention
- Substance abuse
- Hazardous material communications

Each of these issues is discussed in greater detail in the next section of the chapter.

Safety and health training   The construction manager must be very persistent in seeing to it that every worker on the site has access to appropriate safety training. This is true for either self-performed work or subcontracted work. Training is an essential component of an effective safety management plan. The scope of the training depends on the size and complexity of the job as well as the characteristics of the potential hazards.

Personal Protection

Personal safety for the individual worker is a fundamental objective for any safety management plan. The superintendent must set strict rules regarding the requirements for personal protection equipment and furnish every worker with the equipment that is needed. If the work is being subcontracted, then the superintendent has to make sure that the subcontractor is providing this equipment for their own workers. Every person who comes on the job site must be made aware of the rules and be expected to follow them—even visitors. I visit a lot of job sites as a professor of construction management and I often take students with me. Every student is expected to show up on the site with hard shoes (no tennis shoes or sandals), a hard hat, long pants, and safety glasses, at a minimum. If anyone shows up without them, he or she is not allowed on-site, period. There are nine types of personal protection equipment:

Protection Equipment	Example
Body protection	Special suits or coveralls
Head protection	Hard hats
Respiratory protection	Respirators
Face protection	Face shields, masks
Eye protection	Safety glasses or goggles
Hearing protection	Ear plugs, ear protectors
Hand protection	Gloves
Foot protection	Steel-toed shoes or boots
Fall protection	Safety harnesses

Each type is designed to protect the individual against specific kinds of hazards. You don't have to wear all pieces of equipment for every job. Steel-toed shoes, hard hats, and safety glasses are pretty basic and are generally required to be worn at all times while on-site. But face protection, for example, is worn only for activities such as welding. This equipment is meant to protect individuals from accidents and injuries, and in some cases, even death. Once the contractor makes the personal protection equipment available, it is the individual worker's obligation to follow all rules and regulations pertaining to its use.

Accident Prevention

Accident prevention is the name of the game. This is what all of the safety equipment and tailgate training and awareness is about—and for good reason. In the

United States, 90 percent of all worksite fatalities are caused by accidents. The primary causes of job site accidents are:

Job Site Accident	Percentage of All Worksite Fatalities
Falls	33 percent
Being struck by materials, equipment, or other objects	22 percent
Being crushed or trapped	18 percent
Electrical shocks	17 percent

The project manager and superintendent (and the whole project team, for that matter) must do everything they can to mitigate hazards that may cause accidents or injuries to the workers and the general public alike. They must look at each item of work in advance and try to anticipate any hazards that might arise, and take steps to eliminate that potential. One of the tools that can be used to formalize this process is called a hazard mitigation plan. An example is shown below.

ABC Construction
Peppermill, AZ

Job Name: Kramer Medical Lab
Job Number: 22-04

Superintendent: JWJ
Quality Officer: TRD

Hazard Mitigation Plan

DIVISION OF WORK
MASONRY

Work Item	Potential Hazard	Mitigation Measures
Material delivery (mortar, sand, block)	Heavy traffic Heavy lifting injuries	(1) Traffic control officer to direct trucks – wear orange vest. (2) Wear back brace, steel-toed shoes, and gloves to unload materials.
Mixing mortar	Mortar mixing – turning drum Eye irritation from portland cement Skin irritation from portland cement Electrical shock	(1) No loose jewelry, chains, watches, or clothes. (2) No long hair. (3) Wear safety glasses. (4) Wear gloves. (5) Check electrical cord condition. (6) Check outlet for grounding.
Laying block	Eye and skin irritation from mortar Heavy lifting injuries Falls from scaffolding	(1) Wear safety glasses and gloves. (2) Wear back brace, steel-toed shoes, and gloves. (3) Inspect scaffolding and handrails.

Accidents are called accidents because no one saw the event coming. However, the truth is that most accidents can be anticipated and prevented. A good safety management plan is proactive—anticipating hazards, eliminating them, and preventing potential accidents before they occur.

Tailgate Safety Meetings

tailgate safety meeting
Weekly safety meetings held at the job site and usually conducted by the superintendent. Also called toolbox safety meetings.

One of the ways that the superintendent or safety officer reinforces safety as a high priority on the job site is by conducting weekly safety meetings with workers. Sometimes these meetings are referred to as *tailgate safety meetings* (or toolbox safety meetings) and they tend to be short and focused. The purpose of the meetings is to emphasize safe work habits, to remind everyone to keep a sharp eye out for any conditions that may pose a hazard, and to take any necessary corrective action immediately. There is a long list of tailgate safety topics available. Here are just a few:

- Keeping the job site clean
- Keeping stairways and ladders safe
- Making scaffolds and work platforms safe
- Working safely on roofs
- Ensuring excavation and trench safety
- Keeping tools safe
- Keeping vehicles safe
- Ensuring electrical safety

Keeping the job safe is the obligation of everyone on the work site. That's why it is so important to constantly engage the workforce in safety training and the implementation of the safety plan on a regular basis. The tailgate safety meetings are usually conducted by the superintendent, assistant superintendent, or job foreman on a weekly basis and usually only take a few minutes (10 to 20 minutes) to complete. The topics should relate to the type of work being performed at the time of the meeting. It is important that a record of each meeting be kept, noting the date and time, the attendees, and the topic discussed. Such a record is evidence that legitimate efforts have been made to communicate and encourage safe practices on a regular basis.

Substance Abuse

Construction is a dangerous enough business when people are on their toes and alert. However, any workers who might be under the influence of alcohol, illegal drugs, or even legal drugs pose an additional danger to themselves and others who might be working with or near them. Drug and alcohol abuse cannot be tolerated at any level in this industry. Reflexes and judgments must be quick and sharp in construction. People are using power tools and operating equipment on a daily basis, and these tools and equipment can do bodily harm in an instant.

Most construction companies have instituted a requirement for drug testing upon hiring. Some have also instituted random drug testing as an extra precaution. Of course, there is great debate in our society as to whether random testing should be allowed. Many argue that random drug testing is an invasion of privacy. However, in construction, the risks associated with personal safety and public safety are enormous, and effective measures must be taken to ensure that every person working on the site is drug and alcohol free.

When drug testing is employed in construction, whether as a condition of hire or as a preventive measure through random testing, the applicable labor unions must be made aware of the policy.

NOTE

Hazardous Materials Communication

There are numerous construction products that are constituted as compounds, solvents, adhesives, and liquids, and each of these is made up of various chemicals. By law, every worker on the job site has the right to information pertaining to each of the products that they may come into contact with while they do their jobs and any harmful effects that the products may cause. The contractor is obligated to communicate this information and make it readily available for viewing. Therefore, every Safety Management Plan must include a system for compiling and documenting pertinent chemical information on the various products used on the project. The official document used for this purpose is called a *Material Safety Data Sheet (MSDS)*.

An MSDS for most chemical products may be obtained from the manufacturer of the product. For example, Sherwin-Williams will provide an MSDS on any of their paint products upon request. It is the contractor's job to obtain all of these sheets and file them at the job site. This task is often given to a project engineer or the safety officer on the project. Some of the common products used in construction that require MSDS data are:

Material Safety Data Sheet (MSDS)
An information sheet documenting pertinent chemical information on various products used in construction.

- Gasoline and fuel oil
- Paints, shellacs, varnishes, turpentine, and mineral spirits
- Detergents, cleaning agents, degreasing agents, and janitorial supplies
- Wood preservatives
- Adhesives
- Acids

Each sheet contains information regarding chemical data and composition, fire and explosive hazard data, physical data such as appearance, odor, or evaporation rate, and handling and storage information. Although the compilation of this file may seem like a tedious job, it is one that cannot be overlooked by the construction manager. Failure to produce a complete MSDS file upon request by an OSHA inspector can result in a significant fine.

Economics of Quality and Safety

Poor quality and accidents cost the construction industry a lot of money. Rework, callbacks, inefficiencies, waste, and poor workmanship reportedly represent anywhere between 5 and 20 percent of the construction cost for any given project. These costs cut into profits and affect a contractor's ability to compete. Once a contractor gets a reputation for poor quality, it is very difficult to turn that perception around. Likewise, a reputation for high quality will bring work to the contractor without their even soliciting it.

Poor safety performance in construction is very costly as well. Accidents or serious safety violations result in delayed schedules or even job shutdowns. A delayed schedule means lost time, and lost time means increased overhead and lost profits. Labor costs are directly impacted by a construction firm's safety record. For example, when safety performance goes down, workers' compensation premiums go up. This factor alone can cause a project to go from being in the black (making a profit) to being in the red (losing money).

Poor quality and poor safety performance are serious issues that no construction firm can survive—at least not for very long. Is it any wonder that quality control, quality assurance, and job site safety are major components of the construction management function?

Bottom Line

Time and cost control are a constant pressure in construction, and the need for productivity cannot be denied. Still, we must always balance this pressure with good quality and safety management systems. High quality and safety standards are at the heart of successful construction management. Quality and safety impact everything else we are trying to do in construction management. Our estimates will end up being meaningless if our quality is poor and results in excessive rework and correction. Our budgets will go bust and our time-lines will be erroneous if we are unable to manage our quality and safety. Cost overruns and work delays will run rampant on a job where quality and safety are a low priority.

Fortunately, rework, accidents, and injury are all things that can be prevented. Given the complexity and unpredictability of the construction job site, it takes a tenacious effort. However, construction has seen marked improvements on both fronts in recent years, and as owners continue to make bold demands for higher quality, faster schedules, lower costs, and safe work environments, construction managers will continue to deliver the goods. The construction industry holds tremendous promise for improvement, growth, opportunity, and excellence, and I am certainly proud to be a part of it.

Terms to Know

callbacks	quality assurance
field observation report	quality control
Material Safety Data Sheet (MSDS)	rework
Occupational Safety and Health Administration (OSHA)	tailgate safety meetings
preparatory inspection	Total Quality Management (TQM)

Review Questions

1. What are the three fundamental objectives of a quality management plan?

2. What is the difference between quality control and quality assurance?

3. Name three quality control mechanisms typically mandated by the construction contract that are used to check for conformance to the plans and specifications.

4. Explain the concept behind a zero-punch list.

5. What is an FOR?

6. What is the name of the agency responsible for establishing safety standards and enforcing them through inspections conducted at construction job sites?

7. Identify the four primary components of an effective safety management plan.

8. What are the four primary causes of injuries in the construction industry?

9. Identify at least five items of personal protection equipment that might be utilized by workers on the job site.

10. What is an MSDS?

Appendix A

Answers to Review Questions

Chapter 1

1. What is the name of the stone carvings dating back to the pyramids that contained the first written regulations pertaining to construction, commonly referred to as the first known building code?

   Answer: The name of the stone carvings containing what is commonly referred to as the first known building code is the Code of Hammurabi.

2. By what specific measurement is construction used as an economic indicator for our nation's economy?

   Answer: The specific construction measurement used as an indicator regarding the health of our economy in the United States is housing starts.

3. What are the four primary sectors of the construction industry?

   Answer: The four primary sectors of the construction industry are residential, commercial, heavy civil, and industrial construction.

4. Which building sector makes up the largest portion of the construction industry?

   Answer: The residential construction sector makes up the largest portion of the construction industry.

5. What is the name of the organization credited with promoting construction management as a legitimate and unique area of study at four-year universities?

   Answer: The organization credited with promoting construction management as a legitimate and unique area of study is the Associated Schools of Construction (ASC).

6. What is the role of the owner on a construction project?

   Answer: The role of the owner on a construction project is to develop the program for the building, define the scope of the project, create the budget, and provide the funding for the project.

7. What is the name of the weekly magazine dedicated solely to the construction industry?

   Answer: Engineering News Record (ENR) is the weekly magazine dedicated to the construction industry.

8. Name three associations affiliated with the construction industry.

   Answer: There are many associations affiliated with the construction industry. Three of the best-known associations are the Associated General Contractors, the Associated Builders and Contractors, and the National Association of Home Builders.

9. What does LEED stand for and what is its purpose?

   Answer: LEED stands for Leadership in Energy and Environmental Design. It is a rating system that evaluates a building's environmental performance over its life cycle.

10. What two construction associations offer voluntary certification programs for construction managers?

    Answer: The two construction associations that offer voluntary certification programs for construction managers are the American Institute of Constructors and the Construction Management Association of America.

Chapter 2

1. Distinguish between construction management as a function and construction management as a project delivery method.

   Answer: The construction management function entails various tasks performed by the contractor such as estimating, scheduling, cost control, and contract administration in order to monitor, manage, and control the work of the contract for which the contractor is obligated. Construction management as a project delivery method is a contractual arrangement whereby the construction manager is hired by the owner to provide services to the owner, such as design review, overall scheduling, cost control, value engineering, constructability reviews, and construction coordination. Under CM project delivery, the construction manager may or may not be financially obligated to carry out the construction work itself.

2. Identify at least three characteristics that make the construction project unique from other industry sector projects.

   Answer: The construction project is unique in a variety of ways. Each construction project is built as a one-of-a-kind structure or facility. Every construction project is built on a different and unique building site. The building process takes place outside. Much of the work is performed by the human hand. The labor force is by and large made up of transient workers moving from job to job.

3. Name the four primary project values to be managed, monitored, and controlled.

   Answer: The four primary project values that need to be managed, monitored, and controlled on a construction project are time, cost, quality, and safety.

4. Why is scope definition so important in the construction process?

   Answer: Scope definition is important in the construction process because it describes the extent of the work that is to be performed by the contractor.

5. What is meant by the term project delivery?

   Answer: Project delivery is the overall structural or organizational framework used to put all the aspects of designing and building a construction project together.

6. Identify the three primary project delivery methods and discuss how they differ contractually.

   Answer: The three primary project delivery methods are design-bid-build, design-build, and construction management. With design-bid-build, the owner has separate contracts with the designer and the contractor.

With design-build, there is only one contract between the owner and the design-build entity for both the design and the construction. With construction management, the owner holds three contracts: one with the construction manager, one with the designer, and one with the contractor.

7. Explain how agency CM is different from at-risk CM.

Answer: The difference between agency CM and at-risk CM is in regard to who is responsible for performing the actual work of the contract. Under agency CM, the construction manager has no liability for the construction and acts only as an agent or advisor to the owner. With at-risk CM, the construction manager acts as an advisor to the owner during the design phase and is liable for the construction.

8. What is meant by the term fast tracking?

Answer: Fast tracking is a technique used to speed up the completion of a construction project by overlapping the design and construction processes.

9. Name the three basic ways in which a design-build entity may be configured.

Answer: The three basic ways in which a design-build entity may be configured are to have the contractor and the designer create an informal partnership for a project, or as a full-service design-build firm in which the designers and the contractors work for the same company, or to establish a legal joint venture between designer and contractor for a single project.

10. Identify the seven functions of construction management.

Answer: The seven functions of construction management are estimating the project, contract administration, managing job site and construction operations, planning and scheduling the project, controlling project performance, managing project quality, and managing project safety.

Chapter 3

1. Why is open bidding required on public projects?

Answer: Public projects require an open bidding procedure because taxpayer dollars are at stake and an open bid allows any contractor to submit, reducing the risk of fraud, favoritism, and undue influence and to reassure taxpayers that their tax dollars are being spent properly.

2. Name a tool used to reduce the number of bidders on a public project and increase the quality of the contractor pool.

Answer: The tool used to limit the number of contractors bidding on a public project is the requirement for a prequalification statement.

3. What is the purpose of a labor and materials payment bond?

Answer: A labor and materials payment bond is a guarantee, backed by a surety, that payment for the contractor's labor and materials used on the project will be made.

4. Identify the notice document that informs the public of upcoming construction projects funded with taxpayer dollars.

Answer: The notice document that is used to inform the public about upcoming construction projects is an Advertisement for Bids. These ads are typically published in newspapers and trade magazines.

5. Name the three selection methods used to buy construction services and identify the solicitation instrument used for each one.

    Answer: The three selection methods used to buy construction are low-bid selection, best-value selection, and qualifications-based selection. The solicitation instrument used for low-bid selection is the Invitation for Bids (or Advertisement for Bids). The solicitation instrument used for best-value selection is the Request for Proposals. The solicitation instrument used for qualifications-based selection is the Request for Qualifications.

6. Which procurement method is the most commonly used today and what is the selection criteria used to determine the winner?

    Answer: The most common procurement method used today is still design-bid-build. The selection criteria used to determine the winner when using design-bid-build is low price.

7. What is the name of the official document that the owner uses to notify the contractor to start construction?

    Answer: The document used to officially inform the contractor to proceed with the contract is called a notice to proceed.

8. Name the two primary selection criteria categories considered when using the best-value method.

    Answer: The two primary selection categories considered with the best-value procurement method are price (quantitative factors) and qualification factors such as design, management, or past performance.

9. Describe how the weighted criteria evaluation process works.

    Answer: Weighted criteria is a form of best-value selection in which maximum point values are preestablished for qualitative and price components, and award is based upon high total points earned by the proposers for both components.

10. List at least three factors that are commonly considered before deciding to bid on a construction job.

    Answer: There are many factors to consider when deciding whether to bid on a job or not. Some of these factors include location of the project, size of the job, who the architect or owner is, and the technical complexity of the project.

Chapter 4

1. What two major components make up the contract documents?

    Answer: The two major components that make up the contract documents are the drawings and the project manual.

2. When did architects first begin to use drawings to communicate their design intent?

    Answer: It was during the Renaissance when architects first started to use drawings instead of models to communicate design intent.

3. What does CADD stand for?

    Answer: CADD stands for computer-aided design and drafting.

4. There is a particular way in which the drawings are organized in a set of drawings. Identify the order of drawings in a typical set of plans.

    Answer: A typical set of drawings is ordered with the civil drawings first, then the architectural, then the structural, then the mechanical, and finally the electrical drawings.

5. What is the difference between a plan view and a section view in a set of drawings?

    Answer: A plan view represents a horizontal cut through the structure and a section view represents a vertical cut through the structure.

6. Name the four primary sections of a project manual.

    Answer: The four primary sections of a project manual are the bidding documents, the General Conditions, the Supplemental Conditions, and the technical specifications.

7. The CSI MasterFormat is broken down into how many divisions?

    Answer: There are 16 divisions to the MasterFormat.

8. Under which CSI division would you find building insulation?

    Answer: You would find building insulation under Division 7, Thermal and Moisture Protection.

9. Name the four basic types of construction contracts.

    Answer: The four basic types of construction contracts are the lump sum contract, cost-plus-fee contract, guaranteed maximum price (GMP) contract, and unit price contract.

10. Under a guaranteed maximum price contract, what happens if the actual cost is less than the guaranteed maximum contract price?

    Answer: If the actual cost of the project is less than the guaranteed maximum contract price, the owner benefits from 100 percent of the savings unless there is an arrangement to split the savings with the contractor.

Chapter 5

1. Name the four fundamental stages of the construction management process after the design stage.

    Answer: The four fundamental stages of the construction management process are pre-construction, procurement, construction, and post-construction.

2. What are the four distinct stages of the design process?

    Answer: The four distinct stages of design are programming and feasibility, schematic or conceptual design, design development, and contract documents.

3. How does the quality of the design drawings impact the quality of the construction?

    Answer: The construction contract calls for the contractor to build the project in accordance with the plans and the specs. If the plans, specs, or overall design is flawed or something is missing, then the contractor is obligated to perform as instructed or to bring the flaw or defect to the attention of the architect by processing a change order. Either way, the owner is left with paying the price for the error and is usually not happy.

4. In relation to construction, what is meant by the term due diligence?

   Answer: Due diligence is the process of identifying any problems associated with the project early on so that those problems can be factored into the decision making that occurs during the pre-construction stage.

5. What are the two procurement instruments used to buy out the construction job?

   Answer: The two procurement instruments used to buy out the construction job are subcontracts and purchase orders. Subcontracts are used to buy labor and purchase orders are used to buy materials and equipment.

6. Name at least three positions that make up the members of the on-site construction management team.

   Answer: Three positions that make up the on-site project team are superintendent, assistant superintendent, and field engineer.

7. What occurrence marks the official end of the project?

   Answer: The official end of the project occurs when the architect releases a Certificate of Substantial Completion.

8. What is the name of the tool used to keep track of and manage the completion of all of the loose ends, minor repairs, adjustments, and missing items at the end of the project?

   Answer: A punch list is used to manage all of the loose ends, minor repairs, adjustments, and missing items at the end of the project.

9. What is value engineering and what is its purpose?

   Answer: Value engineering is the process of analyzing the design, products, and materials associated with the project, to determine whether the proposed application, installation, or execution is the best approach or solution. The purpose of value engineering is to optimize resources to achieve the greatest value for the money being spent.

10. Why is it important to have a clear distinction between the project punchout and the warranty period?

    Answer: It is important to have a clear distinction between project punchout and warranty because the completion of punchout denotes substantial completion of the project. If work items continue to get added to the punch list, it will be very difficult to clearly mark the end of the project.

Chapter 6

1. What is a construction estimate?

   Answer: A construction estimate is a summary of probable quantities and costs of materials, labor, equipment, and subcontracts to complete a project, including taxes, overhead, and profit, based on the best available information at the time.

2. Name the four primary categories of costs in the construction estimate.

   Answer: The four primary categories of costs in the construction estimate are materials, labor, equipment, and subcontracts.

3. How are construction estimates typically organized?

    Answer: Typically, construction estimates are organized according to the 16-division outline of the CSI MasterFormat.

4. What type of estimate would we probably do if we were meeting with a client for the first time and they wanted to get a rough idea about their project cost?

    Answer: The type of estimate that would most likely be presented to a client who was seeking a rough idea of cost for a new project would be a rough order of magnitude (ROM) estimate.

5. Identify the four preparation steps taken to start the estimating process.

    Answer: The four preparation steps taken to start an estimate are to review the plans and specs, to develop a query list, to attend the pre-bid meeting, and to visit the site.

6. What are general conditions?

    Answer: General conditions are the same thing as indirect costs and represent the expenses incurred in order to deliver and manage the materials, labor, equipment, and subcontracts employed on any given job. Supervision, cleanup, temporary utilities, and security fencing are all examples of general conditions.

7. What unit of measure is typically employed for pricing general conditions?

    Answer: The unit of measure typically applied to general conditions is a unit of time such as hour, day, week, or month.

8. What is a scope sheet?

    Answer: A scope sheet identifies all of the items of work to be performed under a specific trade heading or work category such as masonry or siding.

9. Identify at least four characteristics exhibited in a quality estimate.

    Answer: There are many characteristics displayed in a quality estimate including correct quantities, accurate labor hours, correct pricing, accurate calculations, completeness, clear paper trail, proper overhead, and proper profit.

10. When will we know the true accuracy of our estimate?

    Answer: We will know the true accuracy of our estimate when the project is complete and all the costs and expenses have been added up.

Chapter 7

1. What is partnering?

    Answer: Partnering is a team-building technique to establish a set of common goals and objectives for the project and develop a mutually acceptable protocol for communication and conflict resolution through a formal agreement.

2. How does the contractor receive clarification from the architect regarding details of the design?

   Answer: The contractor receives clarification from the architect regarding details of the design by processing a formal request for information (RFI) in writing.

3. What is the purpose of a submittal?

   Answer: Submittals provide a means by which the architect and owner can confirm the intent of the design.

4. What is a shop drawing?

   Answer: A shop drawing is a special kind of submittal, usually required when a building material must be fabricated from scratch. The drawing includes details, dimensions, and the configuration of the item being fabricated.

5. What is the name of the document that establishes the template for measuring work progress as it relates to requests for payment?

   Answer: The name of the document that establishes the template for measuring work progress as it relates to requests for payment is a schedule of values.

6. What is the name of the document that formally and officially authorizes a payment to the contractor?

   Answer: The document that authorizes payment to the contractor is called an Application and Certificate for Payment.

7. What are liquidated damages?

   Answer: Liquidated damages are an amount of money that is assessed to the contractor for a failure to meet a specified completion date.

8. What is retainage?

   Answer: Retainage is a certain percentage of money owed to the contractor that is held back by the owner to encourage completion of the project.

9. Identify two instances when a change order might need to be initiated.

   Answer: A change order would be required to correct a detail of the design that contained an error or omitted information, or when an owner wants to add scope to the project.

10. Name three alternatives to traditional litigation for resolving construction contract disputes.

    Answer: Three alternatives to traditional litigation for resolving construction disputes are mediation, the minitrial, and arbitration.

Chapter 8

1. Identify at least three issues that the superintendent must be concerned with when trying to manage construction operations.

   Answer: Three issues that the superintendent must be concerned with when trying to manage construction operations are subcontractor coordination, material and equipment deliveries, and productivity.

2. When scheduling subcontractors for the job, there are three fundamental rules that you should try to follow. What are they?

    Answer: When scheduling subcontractors for the job, the three fundamental rules that you should try to follow are to resist bringing subcontractors onto the job until you are 100 percent ready for them; to make sure that once you bring them on the job, they have everything they need to proceed; and to pay all subcontractors promptly upon completion of their work.

3. What does it mean to order something on will-call?

    Answer: A will-call acts as a confirmation of an order that has been placed prior to the date it is actually due for delivery. The will-call generally occurs the afternoon before the scheduled delivery and confirms or denies that the delivery date is still a go.

4. Identify at least three factors that can negatively impact construction productivity.

    Answer: Factors that negatively impact construction productivity are crowded work spaces, poor coordination of work activities, poor supervision or lack of supervision, an inexperienced or poorly trained workforce, not having the proper tools and equipment, adverse weather conditions, confusing plans and specs, changes in the work plan, and inefficient job site layout.

5. Identify at least three environmental issues that might interfere with the project schedule and cause unexpected delays on the job.

    Answer: Environmental issues that can interfere with the construction schedule and cause unexpected delays on the job are soil erosion problems, encountering endangered species on site, having to protect vegetation on site, trying to protect and preserve wetlands during construction, and discovering historical or cultural artifacts while excavating.

6. What is a laydown area?

    Answer: A laydown area is a designated storage area within the construction site that is used for sorting out large orders such as the structural steel.

7. What types of information should be shown on a site logistics plan? Name at least four items.

    Answer: The types of things that should be shown on a site logistics plan are the location of the field office, the location of the temporary utilities, the location of the storage trailers, the location of the laydown area, the location of the portable toilets, the location of dumpsters, on-site parking areas, the security fencing, and the entrance and exit gates.

8. Why is it important for the job superintendent and the other members of the on-site team to keep project diaries?

    Answer: It is important to keep a project diary because there is so much information that must be communicated back and forth among the project participants, and there is a great opportunity for misunderstandings, confusion, and things falling through the cracks. The diaries help to keep straight all of the communications, conversations, and activities.

9. Why is it important to accurately report hours and cost codes on time cards?

    Answer: It is important to accurately record hours and cost codes on time cards because they provide the payroll clerk with all of the information needed to calculate wages and distribute paychecks. They also provide fundamental information needed to track and monitor productivity and labor expenditures.

10. Identify the way in which the construction industry has increased overall owner involvement in the construction process.

    Answer: The construction industry has increased overall owner involvement in the construction process through a variety of collaborative software programs that establish intranet sites. These programs allow the owner to take part in a variety of project communications and may have a web cam linked to them.

Chapter 9

1. What are the two most common types of schedules used in construction?

   Answer: The two most common types of schedules used in construction are the bar chart and the network diagram.

2. Name the two techniques used to create a network diagram.

   Answer: The two techniques used to create a network diagram are the activity-on-arrow method and the activity-on-node method.

3. What is another name for the activity-on-node (AON) network diagram?

   Answer: The activity-on-node network diagram is also called a precedence diagram.

4. What is a look-ahead schedule and how is it used?

   Answer: Look-ahead schedules are developed by superintendents and trade foremen to coordinate the work and activities over a relatively short period of time, usually two- to four-week intervals. They are often hand-drawn and are distributed to the specific trades involved.

5. What are the three stages of network diagram development?

   Answer: The three stages involved in developing a network diagram are the planning stage, the sequencing stage, and the scheduling stage.

6. Name the three different types of activities that are included in the typical schedule and give an example of each.

   Answer: The three different types of activities that are included in the typical schedule are production activities (for example, installing siding), procurement activities (for example, ordering windows), and administrative activities (for example, obtaining the building permit).

7. What is the critical path and why is it important from a project management standpoint?

   Answer: The critical path is the continuous chain of activities with the longest (combined) overall duration in the network diagram. The critical path is important from a management standpoint because the critical path determines the project duration and any delay in any activity along the critical path results in a delay in the overall project.

8. What is float, or slack, in the schedule?

   Answer: Float is the amount of time that an activity's start can be delayed before it impacts the project's planned completion.

9. What are the three scheduling calculations that you must perform in order to determine the project duration and the critical path?

   Answer: The three calculations that must be performed to determine the project duration and the critical path are the forward pass, the backward pass, and the float calculations.

10. After you complete a forward and backward pass, how do you know which activities are on the critical path?

    Answer: The activities that have no float will be the activities on the critical path.

Chapter 10

1. What are the seven fundamental steps included in the project control cycle?

   Answer: The seven fundamental steps included in the project control cycle are (1) develop the project plan, (2) establish the project benchmarks, (3) monitor the project performance, (4) identify performance deviations, (5) evaluate corrective options, (6) make adjustments as needed, and (7) document, report, and evaluate results.

2. What are the two essentials of an effective project control system ?

   Answer: The two essentials of an effective project control system are information and a good reporting system.

3. Name three sources where you might gather field information needed to develop your project controls.

   Answer: Three sources of field information needed to develop project controls are material invoices, time cards, and subcontractor billing statements.

4. It is important to receive accurate and complete information from the construction job site. Name two specific construction management functions where this information is used.

   Answer: Field information is used to detect variances between the actual and planned performance of a project regarding cost, time, and productivity. It is also used to develop the historical estimating databases and productivity factors used when creating the project estimate and schedule.

5. What is a cost code and how is it used in project controls?

   Answer: A cost code is a reference number assigned to each work activity identified in the project estimate and schedule. This code is often based on a CSI division number and another number identifying type of cost. Cost codes are used to track all items of work contributing to the overall project costs including materials, labor, equipment, subcontracts, and overhead. All job information regarding cost are tracked via these cost codes.

6. Name at least three factors that can impact project performance.

   Answer: There are numerous factors that can impact project performance; weather, quality of the workforce, inadequate tools and equipment, defective materials, and overcrowded job sites are just a few.

7. What is an escalation clause and how is it used in the construction contract?

   Answer: An escalation clause is a special clause, usually negotiated into the construction contract when there is suspicion that some pricing component of the estimate is in a high state of flux. The clause allows for adjustments to be made to the estimate based upon current pricing of the suspected component.

8. What is the riskiest element of project planning and project control?

   Answer: The riskiest element of project planning and project control is in estimating productivity.

9. What does it mean to crash the schedule?

   Answer: Crashing the schedule means to compress the overall schedule by accelerating certain activities within it so that they finish sooner, thereby shortening the overall schedule.

10. Regarding project controls, what does it mean to forecast in construction management?

    Answer: To forecast means to predict the final cost and schedule outcomes on a project while the work is still in progress. Construction managers forecast final cost and completion dates on a regular basis throughout the construction process.

Chapter 11

1. What are the three fundamental objectives of a quality management plan?

   Answer: The three fundamental objectives of a quality management plan are to do things right the first time, to prevent things from going wrong in the first place, and to continually improve the construction process.

2. What is the difference between quality control and quality assurance?

   Answer: Quality control addresses quality at the project level and deals with conformance to the plans and specs through submittals, mock-ups, shop drawings, inspections, and testing. Quality assurance addresses quality at the process level and deals with policies and procedures associated with hiring, training, safety, subcontracting, and procurement.

3. Name three quality control mechanisms typically mandated by the construction contract that are used to check for conformance to the plans and specifications.

   Answer: Three quality control mechanisms typically mandated by the construction contract that are used to check for conformance to the plans and specifications are submittals, mock-ups, and shop drawings.

4. Explain the concept behind a zero-punch list.

   Answer: The concept behind a zero-punch list is to complete the final walk-through inspection with few or no punch items noted on the list. The idea is to inspect and correct the work as it progresses, instead of waiting until it is completed, only to find that the quality is unacceptable.

5. What is an FOR?

   Answer: An FOR is a field observation report and involves a process in which employees, subcontractors, and visiting vendors are encouraged to report any work item suspected of being installed incorrectly or failing to meet a quality or safety standard. Each of these observations is logged by the quality engineer or person in charge of the task, and each item in question is verified or corrected as needed.

6. What is the name of the agency responsible for establishing safety standards and enforcing them through inspections conducted at construction job sites?

   Answer: The name of the agency responsible for establishing safety standards and enforcing them through inspections conducted at construction job sites is the Occupational Safety and Health Administration, commonly referred to as OSHA.

7. Identify the four primary components of an effective safety management plan.

    Answer: The four primary components of an effective safety management plan are management commitment, job site analysis, hazard prevention and control, and safety and health training.

8. What are the four primary causes of injuries in the construction industry?

    Answer: The four primary causes of injuries in the construction industry are falls, being struck by an object, being crushed or trapped, and electrical shocks.

9. Identify at least five items of personal protection equipment that might be utilized by workers on the job site.

    Answer: Personal protection equipment includes hard hats, safety glasses, steel-toed shoes or boots, face shields, ear plugs, special suits or coveralls, respirators, gloves, and safety harnesses.

10. What is an MSDS?

    Answer: An MSDS is a Material Safety Data Sheet. An MSDS must be obtained and maintained for every chemical product that is located on the job site.

Glossary

addendum   A change or addition to the contract documents issued after the documents have been released but before the bids are due.

add-ons   A term commonly used in construction estimating to describe the taxes, overhead, and profit added to the estimate after all other costs have been calculated.

Advertisement for Bids   A public notice, usually published in newspapers, trade magazines and journals, providing information regarding bidding procedures for public projects.

agency CM   A construction management project delivery option in which the construction manager acts in the owner's best interests at every stage of the project, from design through construction. The construction manager offers advice and project management services to the owner but is not financially responsible for the construction.

as-built drawings   Record drawings completed by the contractor and turned over to the owner at the end of the project identifying any changes or adjustments made to the conditions and dimensions of the work relative to the original plans and specifications.

at-risk CM   A project delivery option where the construction manager acts as a consultant to the owner in the development and design phases, but as the equivalent of a general contractor during the construction phase.

back charge   An amount of money charged against a subcontractor for work that the general contractor performed because the subcontractor failed to do so.

backward pass   A scheduling technique used to calculate an activity's late start and late finish.

base isolators   Large shock absorbers made of alternating layers of rubber and steel attached to a building's foundation to allow movement of the structure without causing damage.

best value   Any selection process in which proposals contain both price and qualitative components, and the award is based upon a combination of price and qualitative considerations.

callback   A request from an owner that a contractor return to the job site to correct or redo some item of work.

change order   Requests made by the owner to add or subtract features to the scope of the project resulting in changes to the contract.

claim   An issue that occurs during construction and remains unresolved after the job is complete.

closed bid   Used with private projects and is not open to the public. Bidding is by invitation only, via an Invitation for Bids, to a selected list of contractors.

cofferdam   A temporary watertight enclosure erected to prevent water from seeping into an area, allowing construction to take place in the water-free space.

commissioning   A process of testing and checking all equipment and systems within the facility at the end of a project to assure proper functioning and operation. May also include the training of owner personnel in the operation and maintenance of the equipment.

constructability reviews   A design review process in which experienced contractors and construction managers work with designers to ensure that the details of the design actually can be built in an efficient and cost-effective manner. The process entails review of materials, application, installation techniques, field execution, and building systems.

construction management   The planning, scheduling, evaluation, and controlling of construction tasks and activities to accomplish specific objectives outlined in the contract documents.

contract documents   The drawings, conditions, terms, and specifications setting forth the requirements for constructing the project.

cost code   A reference number used to track cost and schedule information on materials, labor, subcontracts, equipment, overhead, and fees throughout the project control process.

cost control   A continuous monitoring process used to track the variances between actual performance and planned performance on a project, specifically concerning cost and time.

crashing the schedule   To takes steps that accelerate activities in the schedule, resulting in an earlier completion date.

critical path   The longest path through a network diagram schedule and includes those activities that have zero days of float. The critical path determines the overall project duration.

curtain wall   An exterior cladding system that is supported entirely by the frame of the building, rather than being self-supporting or load-bearing.

design-bid-build   A project delivery method in which the owner holds two separate contracts for design and construction. This method is often referred to as the traditional project delivery method.

design-build   A project delivery method in which there is only one contract between the owner and a design-build entity. The design-builder is responsible for both the design and the construction of the project. This method is often referred to as single-source project delivery.

dry shacks   These facilities may be constructed on site or brought in as modular units equipped with tables and storage lockers. They provide a dry place for workers to eat their lunch and change their clothes. Union agreements often require that the contractor provide a dry shack on site.

earned value analysis   A technique used in construction to determine the estimated value (earned value) of work completed to date on a project and comparing that to the actual work completed on the project.

escalation clause   Usually negotiated into the construction contract when there is suspicion that some pricing component of the estimate is in a high state of flux. The clause allows for some fluctuation in the contract price based upon the current pricing of the suspected component.

fast tracking   A practice utilized to speed up a job by overlapping the design phase and the construction phase of a project. Often applied in design-build or construction management project delivery.

field observation report (FOR)   A report used to track questionable quality and safety performance on the job site. Employees, subcontractors, and visiting vendors are encouraged to report any work item suspected of being installed incorrectly or failing to meet a quality or safety standard. Each of these observations is logged by the quality engineer or person in charge of the task, and each item in question is verified or corrected as needed.

float   The amount of leeway available to start or complete an individual schedule activity before it affects the planned project completion.

forecasts   Periodic predictions stated in reports as to the final cost and schedule outcomes on a project while the work is still ongoing.

forward pass   A scheduling technique used to calculate an activity's early start and early finish. The forward pass must be completed before the project duration can be determined.

guaranteed maximum price (GMP) A contract methodology in which the contractor is reimbursed for actual costs of materials, labor, equipment, subcontracts, overhead, and profit up to a maximum fixed price amount. Any costs over the maximum price shall be borne by the contractor. Any savings below the maximum price will revert to the owner. This type of contract is often implemented when design is less than 100 percent complete.

infrastructure The basic roadways, bridges, tunnels, and utilities that support a community or society.

Invitation for Bids A notification sent to a selected list of contractors, furnishing information on the submission of bids on a private project.

laydown area A designated area on the building site where large orders can be stored and sorted in an organized manner so that the parts can be easily identified for use on the project.

lead time The amount of time it takes for a product or equipment to be delivered to the job site. Products that have a long delivery time are called long lead time items and require special planning considerations.

liquidated damages A daily amount of money paid by the contractor to the owner for each day that the project fails to meet the completion date specified in the contract. Not all contracts contain a liquidated damages clause.

Material Safety Data Sheet (MSDS) An information sheet documenting pertinent chemical information on various products used in construction.

mock-up Physical models or small samples constructed to allow the architect and owner to review the appearance and function of materials, colors, textures, and other aesthetic features before incorporating them into the actual project.

multiple prime A contracting methodology in which the owner bypasses the use of a general contractor and enters into multiple separate contracts with trade or specialty contractors for the various sections of the work associated with the project, such as concrete, framing, mechanical, and electrical work. Each of the specialty contractors involved becomes a prime contractor on the project.

network diagram A common type of construction schedule, also called the critical path method (CPM), that depicts a continuous chain of activities showing both activity durations and the relationship of the activities. There are two types of network diagrams: activity-on-arrow (AOA) and activity-on-node (AON).

network logic The order in which activities are sequenced in the network diagram relative to their interdependent relationships.

notice to proceed The owner authorizes the contractor to begin work on a project on a particular day or as soon as possible. This notice is linked to the duration of the project.

Occupational Safety and Health Administration (OSHA) The federal agency responsible for establishing safety standards for construction and all other industries in the United States. The agency also has the authority to enforce those standards through rigorous inspections at the job site and to issue citations to and assess fines against any contractor or subcontractor for violating these standards.

open bid A competitive bidding requirement for all public projects. An open bid is one that is advertised publicly and allows any qualified contractor to submit a bid on the project.

partnering A team-building technique, calling upon the parties to the construction contract to establish a common set of project goals and objectives and develop a mutually acceptable protocol for communication and conflict resolution through a formal agreement.

perspective drawing A three-dimensional drawing representing width, length, and height of a structure.

precedence diagram   A graphic presentation of a schedule depicting project activities on a node with an arrow that depicts the dependencies that exist between the activities.

preparatory inspection   Inspections, sometimes called pre-inspections, that are designed to check progress and make sure that everything is ready for the next stage of construction.

prequalification   The process in which an owner, based upon minimum financial, management, and other qualitative data, determines whether a construction firm is fundamentally qualified to compete for a certain project, or class of projects.

price proposal   The part of a design-build proposal that stipulates the price at which the design-builder will provide the design and construction services necessary to complete the project.

program   A written statement that identifies and describes an owner or end user's needs and requirements for a facility. Every design starts with a program.

project delivery   A comprehensive process by which a building, facility, or structure is designed and constructed.

punch list   The minor adjustments, repairs, and work items that must be done before substantial completion can be achieved. The list is prepared jointly by the owner, architect, and contractor. The architect confirms completion of each item on the list.

quality assurance   A quality management approach that addresses quality at the process level and deals with policies and procedures associated with hiring, training, safety, subcontracting, and procurement.

quality control   A quality management approach that addresses quality at the project level and deals with conformance to the plans and specs through submittals, mock-ups, shop drawings, inspections, and testing.

quantity surveyors   Individuals who are responsible for counting up and calculating all of the quantities of materials, labor, and equipment necessary to build a construction project.

query list   A list of questions and needed clarifications compiled by an estimator as he or she reviews the plans and specs during the estimating process.

request for information (RFI)   A written request for clarification regarding the details presented in the plans or specifications. The requests are usually made by subcontractors through the general contractor to the architect.

Request for Proposals (RFP)   A solicitation document, written by the owner, requesting pricing and a technical solution for design and/or construction services.

Request for Qualifications   A document issued by the owner prior to an RFP to solicit contractor or design-builder qualifications. The RFQ may be used by the owner to shortlist potential proposers, or it may be used by itself as the final competitive submittal employed in qualifications-based selection.

responsive bid (or proposal)   A bid or proposal package that meets all of the requirements of the solicitation instrument.

retainage   A certain percentage of money owed to the contractor for work progress that is held back by the owner to encourage completion of the project.

rework   A term used to describe defective construction work that must be redone or corrected.

schedule of values   A budget template established early on in the project against which progress payments are measured. The schedule summarizes the total project cost by the various divisions of work.

scope of work   The parameters defining the overall extent of work to be included in a construction contract. The project scope is commonly communicated through construction plans and written specifications.

scope sheet Similar to a work package, a scope sheet describes the items of work to be performed under a particular trade heading. Often accompanies a subcontractor's bid or a Request for Quotation.

self-performed work Construction work that is performed with the general contractor's own forces or labor. Work that is not subcontracted.

shop drawing A supplemental drawing to the plans and specifications that details fabrication methods, materials, and models of a product or installation associated with the project.

short-interval schedules Also called look-ahead schedules, they focus on a short period of time and a limited scope of work. They usually plan work for a two- to four-week time period.

shortlisting Narrowing the field of offerors through the selection of the most qualified proposers on the basis of qualifications.

site logistics plan A layout plan identifying the placement of all temporary facilities needed during the construction stage of the project, such as the office trailer, storage, security fencing, dumpsters, and portable toilets.

slip form Concrete forms that rise up the wall as construction progresses.

specifications The written instructions from an architect or engineer accompanying the project plans pertaining to the quality of materials and workmanship required for the project.

submittals Data, samples, details, colors, and product literature required by the terms of the contract to be presented to the architect by the contractor for approval prior to ordering and installation.

substantial completion The point at which all punch list work has been completed and the owner can occupy or take possession of the new facility.

tailgate safety meeting Weekly safety meetings held at the job site and usually conducted by the superintendent. Also called toolbox safety meetings.

takeoff A term commonly used in the construction industry to describe the process of measuring the plans to quantify materials, labor, and equipment.

technical proposal The part of a design-build proposal that contains the conceptual design for the project. May also include information regarding schedule, team makeup, and overall management plan for the project.

time and materials Another name for a cost-plus-fee contract. These are the two cost factors that are reimbursed under a cost-plus-fee contract. Time equates to the cost of the labor, and materials equates to the cost of the building products used in the construction.

Total Quality Management (TQM) A recognized quality control and quality assurance program based on continuous quality improvement practices.

transmittal A tracking document that serves as a cover notification to any communication, submittal, or shop drawing being transmitted among the project participants.

unforeseen conditions Unknown physical conditions at the site that were not anticipated by the owner or the contractor.

value engineering A process in which various alternative approaches are evaluated and considered regarding design, product selection, or building system in an effort to provide the most efficient, cost-effective solution possible relative to value in response to the desires of the owner.

variance The cost or time difference between the actual project performance and the planned project performance.

weighted criteria   An evaluation method used in best-value selection in which maximum point values are assessed for qualitative and price components of a proposal. Contract award is based upon the highest total points earned.

will-call   A will-call acts as a verbal confirmation of an order that has been placed prior to the date it is actually due for delivery. The will-call, generally made by the superintendent, occurs just before the scheduled delivery date.

work breakdown structure (WBS)   A tool used by estimators to organize the work of a contract in a hierarchical fashion.

work package   Detailed items of work bundled together under a particular trade. Also called a bid package.

working drawings   The final detailed drawings used for construction. Also called contract documents.

Index

Note to the Reader: Throughout this index, **boldfaced** page numbers indicate primary discussions of a topic. *Italicized* page numbers indicate illustrations.

T

U

Jump into Construction Management

Jump into Construction Management

Printed in the United States of America

ED-08-29-11